THE
NATIONAL CURRICULUM & THE TEACHERS' STANDARDS

2ND EDITION

Sara Miller McCune founded SAGE Publishing in 1965 to support the dissemination of usable knowledge and educate a global community. SAGE publishes more than 1000 journals and over 800 new books each year, spanning a wide range of subject areas. Our growing selection of library products includes archives, data, case studies and video. SAGE remains majority owned by our founder and after her lifetime will become owned by a charitable trust that secures the company's continued independence.

Los Angeles | London | New Delhi | Singapore | Washington DC | Melbourne

THE NATIONAL CURRICULUM & THE TEACHERS' STANDARDS

2ND EDITION

FOREWORD BY **DYLAN WILIAM**

Learning Matters
An imprint of SAGE Publications Ltd
1 Oliver's Yard
55 City Road
London EC1Y 1SP

SAGE Publications Inc.
2455 Teller Road
Thousand Oaks, California 91320

SAGE Publications India Pvt Ltd
B 1/I 1 Mohan Cooperative Industrial Area
Mathura Road
New Delhi 110 044

SAGE Publications Asia-Pacific Pte Ltd
3 Church Street
#10-04 Samsung Hub
Singapore 049483

Editor: Amy Thornton
Senior project editor: Chris Marke
Marketing manager: Lorna Patkai
Cover design: Wendy Scott
Typeset by: C&M Digitals (P) Ltd, Chennai, India
Printed and bound in the UK

Library of Congress Control Number: 2021936819

British Library Cataloguing in Publication Data

A catalogue record for this book is available from
the British Library

ISBN (pbk) 978-1-5297-7481-8

At SAGE we take sustainability seriously. Most of our products are printed in the UK using responsibly sourced papers
and boards. When we print overseas we ensure sustainable papers are used as measured by the PREPS grading
system. We undertake an annual audit to monitor our sustainability.

CONTENTS

ABOUT THIS BOOK

This book presents the Teachers' Standards and the National Curriculum for England for key stages 1–4. The National Curriculum is available online at:

https://www.gov.uk/government/collections/national-curriculum

This book brings together the Curriculum and the Teachers' Standards, two key statutory documents for those training and beginning to teach in England.

The text focuses on the need to provide children with a broad and balanced curriculum. In his foreword, Dylan Wiliam discusses how the curriculum was developed and goes back to explore its original aims. He looks at the current emphasis on the teaching of ALL curriculum subjects by OFSTED and asks some important questions about why this has not thus far been a focus in all schools.

For ease of reference, pages detailing the curriculum for key stages 3 are 4 are shaded.

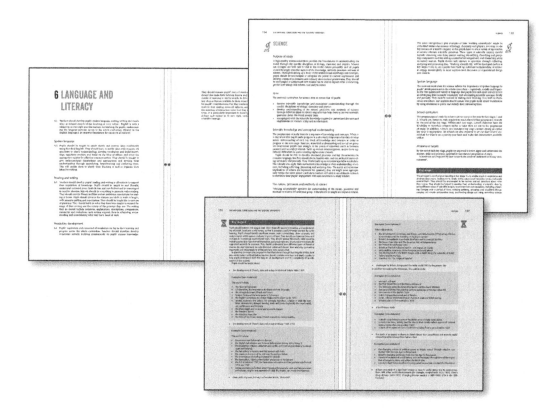

The book provides some detailed and focused indexes of the curriculum.

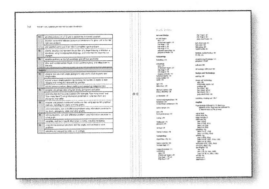 

FOREWORD BY DYLAN WILIAM

What should students be learning at school?

Dylan Wiliam

To many people in England, asking what students should be learning at school seems a silly question. The government has decided, and it's called the national curriculum. Even academies, which do not have to follow the national curriculum, tend to do so, so what students should be learning seems obvious.

However, even when a school is required to follow the national curriculum, this is not the end of the story, because there are several layers in it. The first, and the one that people usually think about when they hear the words 'national curriculum' are the documents published by the Department for Education about what students should be learning in each subject at various ages. This is the *intended* curriculum. However, a list of requirements about what students should be learning does not determine what actually happens in classrooms. The broad aims of a curriculum need to convert into things that teachers can actually use, such as schemes of work and textbooks. This is the *implemented* curriculum. But what really matters is the lived daily experience of students in school – the *achieved* curriculum – and this depends greatly on the teacher.

For example, with the same national curriculum, and even the same textbook and learning activities, the experiences of students in the classrooms of different teachers can be very diverse. One maths teacher might create the impression that there is only one correct way to solve a mathematics problem – the one given in the textbook – while another might ask students to explore whether the same problem could be solved in different ways. One science teacher might teach power, voltage, current and resistance as completely detached from students' daily lives while another might ask the students to calculate the resistance of a 60W domestic bulb, showing how what they are learning in science connects to their lives. Teachers create curriculum every day, through the choices they make about how to present material to their students, the types of knowledge they value, and how they manage to connect the things that students have to learn to the lives that students live. Indeed, my hunch is that one of the most important characteristics of more effective teachers is that they get their students to care about stuff they didn't care about when they came into the classroom.

What all of this means is that even if a school is required to follow the national curriculum, or some other scheme of work, every teacher still needs to give careful thought to the issue of the curriculum. This will include thinking about what students will learn, and it will also – because time is limited – require consideration of what they will *not* learn. Whose history gets prioritized, and whose history gets ignored (what Elliot Eisner called the 'null curriculum' (Eisner, 1979))? It will also include thinking about what is sometimes called the 'hidden curriculum' – the often unintended messages that students pick up through attending school.

In making these choices, it is important to bear in mind that a curriculum is just a means to an end. The curriculum is simply the way that we get the students to know the things that we want them to know. The problem is that in most societies there are many things that people want schools to teach students.

In a foreword of this length, there isn't space to do more than simply gloss over the major purposes that people have for education but it does seem that most of the goals that people have for education come under one of four broad categories.

One of the most important aims of education is to allow young people to take greater control of their own lives, perhaps best exemplified by the work of Paulo Freire and his 'Pedagogy of liberation' (Freire, 1986). The idea is that rather than simply training young people to fit into the existing systems, education is the means by which we help people deal critically and creatively with the world they experience, and also how to change that world. This is education as *personal empowerment*.

A second set of reasons for educating young people is, in Matthew Arnold's words, to pass on from one generation to the next 'the best that has been thought and known in the world' (Arnold, 1869) – education as *cultural transmission*.

In democratic societies, education has a third set of roles to fulfill, and that is to ensure citizens know enough about the issues on which they are asked to vote and are able to exercise their democratic rights responsibly. In other words, education is necessary as *preparation for democratic citizenship*.

Finally, education is increasingly important as a way of helping young people find fulfilling and satisfying employment. Education has always been important for employment, but as technology is used to a greater and greater extent in the world of work, higher levels of education are increasingly becoming not just desirable, but actually necessary. Education is also *preparation for work*.

The important point here is that education has to do all these things. We can't just pick the one or two that we favour. And many of these purposes conflict. What this means is that there will never be a perfect curriculum. There will inevitably be messy, uncomfortable compromises. What may be possible, however, is that by using a principled approach to thinking about the curriculum, we can try to ensure that the compromises we are making are ones we are happy with.

In the remainder of this foreword, I offer seven principles that can be used as 'tools for thinking' about curriculum. I do not claim that these are the only principles that are important–you may have others that you would like to add, or may think that some of these principles are not that important. However by applying these principles, I hope that you can see where you are making tradeoffs. No curriculum can satisfy all seven principles, but by making the tradeoffs explicit, I hope that they are planned, rather than just being a series of unintended consequences.

Balanced

Perhaps the most important feature of a curriculum is that it is balanced. English, maths and science are important, but they are not more important than art, or music, or dance, or drama, for at least three reasons. First, art, music, dance and drama are sources of personal fulfillment in adulthood in a way that maths and science rarely are. Second, these subjects, with their greater emphasis on creativity, are likely to be sources of employment in the future, because creativity is the one thing we know that machines can't do. Third, we are discovering that art, music, dance and drama make important contributions to a student's ability to read.

Recent research has shown that reading ability is not much more than decoding, and listening comprehension (this is sometimes called the 'simple view' of reading).

Once students can decode text, their understanding of it is primarily driven by their ability to construct a mental model of what is being described and what is crucial therefore is their background knowledge of what is being written about. Art, music, dance and drama are crucial sources of this background knowledge.

Rigorous

Any subject can be taught in a way that reflects the nature of the subject, or it can be taught in a way that trivializes the subject. Asking students in a history lesson to design costumes for historical characters may well keep them occupied, and they may even learn something about the characters for whom they are designing costumes. However, what they are doing is far removed from the discipline of history, because they are unlikely to be grappling with chronology, cause and effect, or reconciling conflicting accounts. An English teacher might discuss with a class what makes a good response to a poem the class has read, and try to incorporate the students' views into the marking scheme in a process that is sometimes called 'co-constructing'. But it is essential that the marking scheme reflects the nature of the discipline. The teacher has a duty of accountability to the discipline being taught.

This is particularly important in the development of what are sometimes called '21st century skills'. There seems to be relatively broad agreement that these include collaboration, communication, creativity, critical thinking and problem-solving, but too often these are regarded as generic skills, transferable from one subject to another, and they are not. We know that thinking critically in history is not the same as thinking critically in mathematics because no amount of teaching students to think critically in history has any impact on their ability to think critically in mathematics. If we want students to think critically in mathematics, then this has to be taught in mathematics. The 21st century skills are useful, but primarily as a checklist of the things that our teaching of that subject should include.

Vertically integrated

As well as being rigorous (i.e., reflecting accurately the nature of the subject), it is essential that there is clear progression in each subject. In other words, there needs to be a clear answer to the question, 'When someone gets better at this subject, what is it that gets better?' When clear lines of progression are identified, it becomes much easier to see what the 'big ideas' are in a subject, and which aspects of the curriculum are desirable, but do not provide foundations for learning. For example, while the phases of the moon is an interesting topic to study, little of what students learn in future years will depend on a thorough understanding of the phases of the moon. On the other hand, the knowledge that matter is made of small particles is a profound idea, and without a thorough understanding of this, students will struggle to make sense of what comes next. By being clear about progression in a subject, it is easier to see which aspects of the subject are essential for progress, and which are just desirable.

Coherent

Articulating the learning progressions in a subject forces us to think about the internal logic of each subject, but we also have to look across each student's whole experience to make sure that what they are learning is coherent. For example, science teachers tend to want maths teachers to teach equations and graphs before maths teachers want to teach it. Even when there is coordination between mathematics and science teachers in terms of the curriculum sequencing, if the science teacher is representing graphs using equations, such as $y = 3x + 2$ while the maths teacher is representing the same relationship as a function ($x \longrightarrow 3x + 2$) then students are likely to be confused, or, worse, see the two ways of representing graphs as unrelated.

The need for coherence is also clear from what we are learning about the nature of reading. As noted above, the research seems to suggest that once students have learned to read, then improving one's reading is mostly about acquiring the background knowledge that is needed to make sense of what one is reading. The more coherent the collection of curriculum experiences that a student receives, the more learning there will be.

Appropriate

It may seem obvious that a curriculum needs to be appropriate for each student, but this often turns out to be rather difficult to achieve, due to the range of achievement in a class, which is generally larger than most people assume. For example, in a mixed-ability class of 11-year-olds, there will be some students with an achievement level of a typical 6-year-old, and some who would outperform an average 16-year-old. While grouping students by ability is one solution to this, the available research evidence suggests that doing so tends to reduce average student achievement (by producing gains for the higher achievers and losses for the lower achievers, with the losses for lower achievers being greater than the gains for higher achievers, thus slightly lowering average achievement). Given such a range of achievement, making the curriculum equally appropriate for all students is clearly an all but impossible task, but teachers do need constantly to be looking for ways of making learning activities more appropriate for more students.

Focused

The national curriculum, like curricula all over the world, has too much stuff in it. Why this happens so consistently is obviously a matter of debate but one factor I think is important is that national curricula tend to be designed so as to make sure there is plenty to keep all students occupied. Because some students learn faster than others, this means that there is far too much in the curriculum for most students to learn at any depth. Of course, teachers could just teach the curriculum at the rate that is needed to ensure that everything is 'covered', but the result is generally a curriculum that William Schmidt described as 'a mile wide and an inch deep' (Schmidt *et al,* 1997). To maximise student learning, it is necessary, as noted above, to take some tough decisions about which aspects of the curriculum are essential, and which are desirable. If all students have mastered the essential elements, then they can move on to the desirable ones, but if they have not, then time is likely to be more fruitfully spent making sure that those aspects of the subject that are essential for future progress are well understood.

Relevant

Finally, the curriculum needs to be relevant to students. Some students are, for a variety of reasons, intrinsically motivated to learn certain things. For these students we should, of course, do all we can to sustain this intrinsic motivation. But the fact is that not enough students are intrinsically motivated to learn all the things that society has decided they need to learn, and that is why we need to make curriculum relevant. Of course, this is easier in some subjects than others, but effort expended in helping students understand why they need to be learning something (apart from passing tests and exams!) is rarely wasted.

Conclusion

By now it will be clear that it is impossible for a curriculum to satisfy all seven of these principles. However, by bearing the principles in mind, you will become more aware of the compromises you are making in designing effective learning experiences for your students. The principles may also suggest where you can make adjustments – for example by giving more attention to one principle and less to another – which will help you innovate in a more principled way rather than just 'trying something new'. The difference between a collection of topics to be studied and a well-designed curriculum is the same as between a pile of bricks and a house. The elements are important; how they are assembled is much more so.

References

Arnold, Matthew (1869). *Culture and Anarchy: An Essay in Political and Social Criticism.* Oxford: Project Gutenberg.

Eisner, E. (1979). *The Educational Imagination: On the Design and Evaluation of School* Programs. New York: Macmillan College Publishing.

Freire, Paulo (1986). *A Pedagogy for Liberation.* Connecticut: Praeger.

Schmidt, W. H., McKnight, C., and Raizen, S. (1997). *A Splintered Vision: An Investigation of U.S. Science and Mathematics Education.* Dordrecht: Kluwer.

SECTION 1

THE TEACHERS' STANDARDS

An introduction to the standards

The Teachers' Standards were introduced in September 2012. They replaced the existing (QTS) standards and the Code of Practice for Registered Teachers in England (from the General Teaching Council).

The Teachers' Standards are statutory and outline the minimum requirements for all teachers and trainee teachers' professional practice and conduct. Teachers and trainee teachers must demonstrate that they have met the Teachers' Standards.

School leaders use the Teachers' Standards to assess teachers' performance in schools. They do not detail a complete a list of the elements of good teaching. Instead, they provide a clear framework within which judgements on the quality of teaching can be made.

The Teachers' Standards are an important part of Initial Teacher Training. Trainees' ability to evidence their performance against the standards is essential and all trainee teachers make reference to the standards throughout their training.

Further guidance on the Teachers' Standards

The Learning Matters text *The Teachers' Standards in the Classroom* by Roy Blatchford provides full and detailed information on how and why the standards were developed. The text explores each of the eight standards and gives guidance on:

- How each standards relates to and impacts classroom practice
- How performance against each standard can be evidenced
- Some examples of good practice in classrooms

Also included are reflective questions to help beginning teachers to explore the impact of their teaching and detailed observations of good teaching and learning.

Teachers' Standards

Preamble

Teachers make the education of their pupils their first concern, and are accountable for achieving the highest possible standards in work and conduct. Teachers act with honesty and integrity; have strong subject knowledge, keep their knowledge and skills as teachers up to date and are self-critical; forge positive professional relationships; and work with parents in the best interests of their pupils.

Part One: Teaching

A teacher must:

1. **Set high expectations which inspire, motivate and challenge pupils**

   - establish a safe and stimulating environment for pupils, rooted in mutual respect
   - set goals that stretch and challenge pupils of all backgrounds, abilities and dispositions
   - demonstrate consistently the positive attitudes, values and behaviour which are expected of pupils.

2. **Promote good progress and outcomes by pupils**

   - be accountable for pupils' attainment, progress and outcomes
   - be aware of pupils' capabilities and their prior knowledge, and plan teaching to build on these
   - guide pupils to reflect on the progress they have made and their emerging needs
   - demonstrate knowledge and understanding of how pupils learn and how this impacts on teaching
   - encourage pupils to take a responsible and conscientious attitude to their own work and study.

3. **Demonstrate good subject and curriculum knowledge**

   - have a secure knowledge of the relevant subject(s) and curriculum areas, foster and maintain pupils' interest in the subject, and address misunderstandings
   - demonstrate a critical understanding of developments in the subject and curriculum areas, and promote the value of scholarship
   - demonstrate an understanding of and take responsibility for promoting high standards of literacy, articulacy and the correct use of Standard English, whatever the teacher's specialist subject
   - if teaching early reading, demonstrate a clear understanding of systematic synthetic phonics
   - if teaching early mathematics, demonstrate a clear understanding of appropriate teaching strategies.

4. **Plan and teach well-structured lessons**

   - impart knowledge and develop understanding through effective use of lesson time
   - promote a love of learning and children's intellectual curiosity

- set homework and plan other out-of-class activities to consolidate and extend the knowledge and understanding pupils have acquired
- reflect systematically on the effectiveness of lessons and approaches to teaching
- contribute to the design and provision of an engaging curriculum within the relevant subject area(s).

5. **Adapt teaching to respond to the strengths and needs of all pupils**

- know when and how to differentiate appropriately, using approaches which enable pupils to be taught effectively
- have a secure understanding of how a range of factors can inhibit pupils' ability to learn, and how best to overcome these
- demonstrate an awareness of the physical, social and intellectual development of children, and know how to adapt teaching to support pupils' education at different stages of development
- have a clear understanding of the needs of all pupils, including those with special educational needs; those of high ability; those with English as an additional language; those with disabilities; and be able to use and evaluate distinctive teaching approaches to engage and support them.

6. **Make accurate and productive use of assessment**

- know and understand how to assess the relevant subject and curriculum areas, including statutory assessment requirements
- make use of formative and summative assessment to secure pupils' progress
- use relevant data to monitor progress, set targets, and plan subsequent lessons
- give pupils regular feedback, both orally and through accurate marking, and encourage pupils to respond to the feedback.

7. **Manage behaviour effectively to ensure a good and safe learning environment**

- have clear rules and routines for behaviour in classrooms, and take responsibility for promoting good and courteous behaviour both in classrooms and around the school, in accordance with the school's behaviour policy
- have high expectations of behaviour, and establish a framework for discipline with a range of strategies, using praise, sanctions and rewards consistently and fairly
- manage classes effectively, using approaches which are appropriate to pupils' needs in order to involve and motivate them
- maintain good relationships with pupils, exercise appropriate authority, and act decisively when necessary.

8. **Fulfil wider professional responsibilities**

- make a positive contribution to the wider life and ethos of the school
- develop effective professional relationships with colleagues, knowing how and when to draw on advice and specialist support
- deploy support staff effectively
- take responsibility for improving teaching through appropriate professional development, responding to advice and feedback from colleagues
- communicate effectively with parents with regard to pupils' achievements and well-being.

Part Two: Personal and professional conduct

A teacher is expected to demonstrate consistently high standards of personal and professional conduct. The following statements define the behaviour and attitudes which set the required standard for conduct throughout a teacher's career.

- Teachers uphold public trust in the profession and maintain high standards of ethics and behaviour, within and outside school, by:
    - treating pupils with dignity, building relationships rooted in mutual respect, and at all times observing proper boundaries appropriate to a teacher's professional position
    - having regard for the need to safeguard pupils' well-being, in accordance with statutory provisions
    - showing tolerance of and respect for the rights of others
    - not undermining fundamental British values, including democracy, the rule of law, individual liberty and mutual respect, and tolerance of those with different faiths and beliefs
    - ensuring that personal beliefs are not expressed in ways which exploit pupils' vulnerability or might lead them to break the law.

- Teachers must have proper and professional regard for the ethos, policies and practices of the school in which they teach, and maintain high standards in their own attendance and punctuality.
- Teachers must have an understanding of, and always act within, the statutory frameworks which set out their professional duties and responsibilities.

SECTION 2

THE NATIONAL CURRICULUM IN ENGLAND

FRAMEWORK

December 2014

Contents

1 INTRODUCTION

1.1 This document sets out the framework for the national curriculum and includes:

- contextual information about both the overall school curriculum and the statutory national curriculum, including the statutory basis of the latter
- aims for the statutory national curriculum
- statements on inclusion, and on the development of pupils' competence in numeracy and mathematics, language and literacy across the school curriculum
- programmes of study for all the national curriculum subjects.

2 THE SCHOOL CURRICULUM IN ENGLAND

2.1 Every state-funded school must offer a curriculum which is balanced and broadly based and which:

- promotes the spiritual, moral, cultural, mental and physical development of pupils at the school and of society, and
- prepares pupils at the school for the opportunities, responsibilities and experiences of later life.

2.2 The school curriculum comprises all learning and other experiences that each school plans for its pupils. The national curriculum forms one part of the school curriculum.

2.3 All state schools are also required to make provision for a daily act of collective worship and must teach religious education to pupils at every key stage and sex and relationship education to pupils in secondary education.

2.4 Maintained schools in England are legally required to follow the statutory national curriculum which sets out in programmes of study, on the basis of key stages, subject content for those subjects that should be taught to all pupils. All schools must publish their school curriculum by subject and academic year online.

2.5 All schools should make provision for personal, social, health and economic education (PSHE), drawing on good practice. Schools are also free to include other subjects or topics of their choice in planning and designing their own programme of education.

3 THE NATIONAL CURRICULUM IN ENGLAND

Aims

3.1 The national curriculum provides pupils with an introduction to the essential knowledge that they need to be educated citizens. It introduces pupils to the best that has been thought and said; and helps engender an appreciation of human creativity and achievement.

3.2 The national curriculum is just one element in the education of every child. There is time and space in the school day and in each week, term and year to range beyond the national curriculum specifications. The national curriculum provides an outline of core knowledge around which teachers can develop exciting and stimulating lessons to promote the development of pupils' knowledge, understanding and skills as part of the wider school curriculum.

Structure

3.3 Pupils of compulsory school age in community and foundation schools, including community special schools and foundation special schools, and in voluntary aided and voluntary controlled schools, must follow the national curriculum. It is organised on the basis of four key stages and twelve subjects, classified in legal terms as 'core' and 'other foundation' subjects.

3.4 The Secretary of State for Education is required to publish programmes of study for each national curriculum subject, setting out the 'matters, skills and processes' to be taught at each key stage. Schools are free to choose how they organise their school day, as long as the content of the national curriculum programmes of study is taught to all pupils.

3.5 The structure of the national curriculum, in terms of which subjects are compulsory at each key stage, is set out in the table below:

	Key stage 1	Key stage 2	Key stage 3	Key stage 4
Age	5 – 7	7 – 11	11 – 14	14 – 16
Year groups	1 – 2	3 – 6	7 – 9	10 – 11
Core subjects				
English	✓	✓	✓	✓
Mathematics	✓	✓	✓	✓
Science	✓	✓	✓	✓
Foundation subjects				
Art and design	✓	✓	✓	
Citizenship			✓	✓
Computing	✓	✓	✓	✓
Design and technology	✓	✓	✓	
Languages	✓	✓	✓	
Geography	✓	✓	✓	
History	✓	✓	✓	
Music	✓	✓	✓	
Physical education	✓	✓	✓	✓

Figure 1   Structure of the national curriculum

3.6   All schools are also required to teach religious education at all key stages. Secondary schools must provide sex and relationship education.

	Key stage 1	Key stage 2	Key stage 3	Key stage 4
Age	5 – 7	7 – 11	11 – 14	14 – 16
Year groups	1 – 2	3 – 6	7 – 9	10 – 11
Religious education	✓	✓	✓	✓
Sex and relationship education			✓	✓

Figure 2   Statutory teaching of religious education and sex and relationship education

Key stage 4 entitlement areas

3.7   The arts (comprising art and design, music, dance, drama and media arts), design and technology, the humanities (comprising geography and history) and modern foreign language are not compulsory national curriculum subjects after the age of 14, but all pupils in maintained schools have a statutory entitlement to be able to study a subject in each of those four areas.

3.8   The statutory requirements in relation to the entitlement areas are:

- schools must provide access to a minimum of one course in each of the four entitlement areas
- schools must provide the opportunity for pupils to take a course in all four areas, should they wish to do so
- a course that meets the entitlement requirements must give pupils the opportunity to obtain an approved qualification.

4 INCLUSION

Setting suitable challenges

4.1 Teachers should set high expectations for every pupil. They should plan stretching work for pupils whose attainment is significantly above the expected standard. They have an even greater obligation to plan lessons for pupils who have low levels of prior attainment or come from disadvantaged backgrounds. Teachers should use appropriate assessment to set targets which are deliberately ambitious.

Responding to pupils' needs and overcoming potential barriers for individuals and groups of pupils

4.2 Teachers should take account of their duties under equal opportunities legislation that covers race, disability, sex, religion or belief, sexual orientation, pregnancy and maternity, and gender reassignment.

4.3 A wide range of pupils have special educational needs, many of whom also have disabilities. Lessons should be planned to ensure that there are no barriers to every pupil achieving. In many cases, such planning will mean that these pupils will be able to study the full national curriculum. The 0–25 Special Education and Disability Code of Practice includes statutory advice on approaches for identification and assessment which can support this. A minority of pupils will need access to specialist equipment and different approaches. The SEN and Disability Code of Practice is clear about what should be done to meet their needs.

4.4 With the right teaching, that recognises their individual needs, many disabled pupils may have little need for additional resources beyond the aids which they use as part of their daily life. Teachers must plan lessons so that these pupils can study every national curriculum subject. Potential areas of difficulty should be identified and addressed at the outset of work.

4.5 Teachers must also take account of the needs of pupils whose first language is not English. Monitoring of progress should take account of the pupil's age, length of time in this country, previous educational experience and ability in other languages.

4.6 The ability of pupils for whom English is an additional language to take part in the national curriculum may be in advance of their communication skills in English. Teachers should plan teaching opportunities to help pupils develop their English and should aim to provide the support pupils need to take part in all subjects.

5 NUMERACY AND MATHEMATICS

5.1 Teachers should use every relevant subject to develop pupils' mathematical fluency. Confidence in numeracy and other mathematical skills is a precondition of success across the national curriculum.

5.2 Teachers should develop pupils' numeracy and mathematical reasoning in all subjects so that they understand and appreciate the importance of mathematics. Pupils should be taught to apply arithmetic fluently to problems, understand and use measures, make estimates and sense check their work. Pupils should apply their geometric and algebraic understanding, and relate their understanding of probability to the notions of risk and uncertainty. They should also understand the cycle of collecting, presenting and analysing data. They should be taught to apply their mathematics to both routine and non-routine problems, including breaking down more complex problems into a series of simpler steps.

6 LANGUAGE AND LITERACY

6.1 Teachers should develop pupils' spoken language, reading, writing and vocabulary as integral aspects of the teaching of every subject. English is both a subject in its own right and the medium for teaching; for pupils, understanding the language provides access to the whole curriculum. Fluency in the English language is an essential foundation for success in all subjects.

Spoken language

6.2 Pupils should be taught to speak clearly and convey ideas confidently using Standard English. They should learn to justify ideas with reasons; ask questions to check understanding; develop vocabulary and build knowledge; negotiate; evaluate and build on the ideas of others; and select the appropriate register for effective communication. They should be taught to give well-structured descriptions and explanations and develop their understanding through speculating, hypothesising and exploring ideas. This will enable them to clarify their thinking as well as organise their ideas for writing.

Reading and writing

6.3 Teachers should develop pupils' reading and writing in all subjects to support their acquisition of knowledge. Pupils should be taught to read fluently, understand extended prose (both fiction and non-fiction) and be encouraged to read for pleasure. Schools should do everything to promote wider reading. They should provide library facilities and set ambitious expectations for reading at home. Pupils should develop the stamina and skills to write at length, with accurate spelling and punctuation. They should be taught the correct use of grammar. They should build on what they have been taught to expand the range of their writing and the variety of the grammar they use. The writing they do should include narratives, explanations, descriptions, comparisons, summaries and evaluations: such writing supports them in rehearsing, understanding and consolidating what they have heard or read.

Vocabulary development

6.4 Pupils' acquisition and command of vocabulary are key to their learning and progress across the whole curriculum. Teachers should therefore develop vocabulary actively, building systematically on pupils' current knowledge.

They should increase pupils' store of words in general; simultaneously, they should also make links between known and new vocabulary and discuss the shades of meaning in similar words. In this way, pupils expand the vocabulary choices that are available to them when they write. In addition, it is vital for pupils' comprehension that they understand the meanings of words they meet in their reading across all subjects, and older pupils should be taught the meaning of instruction verbs that they may meet in examination questions. It is particularly important to induct pupils into the language which defines each subject in its own right, such as accurate mathematical and scientific language.

7 PROGRAMMES OF STUDY AND ATTAINMENT TARGETS

7.1 The following pages set out the statutory programmes of study and attainment targets for all subjects. Schools are not required by law to teach the example content in [square brackets] or the content indicated as being 'non-statutory'.

ENGLISH

Purpose of study

English has a pre-eminent place in education and in society. A high-quality education in English will teach pupils to speak and write fluently so that they can communicate their ideas and emotions to others and through their reading and listening, others can communicate with them. Through reading in particular, pupils have a chance to develop culturally, emotionally, intellectually, socially and spiritually. Literature, especially, plays a key role in such development. Reading also enables pupils both to acquire knowledge and to build on what they already know. All the skills of language are essential to participating fully as a member of society; pupils, therefore, who do not learn to speak, read and write fluently and confidently are effectively disenfranchised.

Aims

The overarching aim for English in the national curriculum is to promote high standards of language and literacy by equipping pupils with a strong command of the spoken and written word, and to develop their love of literature through widespread reading for enjoyment. The national curriculum for English aims to ensure that all pupils:

- read easily, fluently and with good understanding
- develop the habit of reading widely and often, for both pleasure and information
- acquire a wide vocabulary, an understanding of grammar and knowledge of linguistic conventions for reading, writing and spoken language
- appreciate our rich and varied literary heritage
- write clearly, accurately and coherently, adapting their language and style in and for a range of contexts, purposes and audiences
- use discussion in order to learn; they should be able to elaborate and explain clearly their understanding and ideas
- are competent in the arts of speaking and listening, making formal presentations, demonstrating to others and participating in debate.

Spoken language

The national curriculum for English reflects the importance of spoken language in pupils' development across the whole curriculum – cognitively, socially and linguistically. Spoken language underpins the development of reading and writing. The quality and variety of language that pupils hear and speak are vital for developing their vocabulary and grammar and their understanding for reading and writing. Teachers should therefore ensure the continual development of pupils' confidence and competence in spoken language and listening skills. Pupils should develop a capacity to explain their understanding of books and other reading, and to prepare their ideas before they write. They must be assisted in making their thinking clear to themselves as well as to others and teachers should ensure that pupils build secure foundations by using discussion to probe and remedy their misconceptions. Pupils should also be taught to understand and use the conventions for discussion and debate.

All pupils should be enabled to participate in and gain knowledge, skills and understanding associated with the artistic practice of drama. Pupils should be able to adopt, create and sustain a range of roles, responding appropriately to others in role. They should have opportunities to improvise, devise and script drama for one another and a range of audiences, as well as to rehearse, refine, share and respond thoughtfully to drama and theatre performances.

Statutory requirements which underpin all aspects of spoken language across the six years of primary education form part of the national curriculum. These are reflected and contextualised within the reading and writing domains which follow.

Reading

The programmes of study for reading at key stages 1 and 2 consist of two dimensions:

- word reading
- comprehension (both listening and reading).

It is essential that teaching focuses on developing pupils' competence in both dimensions; different kinds of teaching are needed for each.

Skilled word reading involves both the speedy working out of the pronunciation of unfamiliar printed words (decoding) and the speedy recognition of familiar printed words. Underpinning both is the understanding that the letters on the page represent the sounds in spoken words. This is why phonics should be emphasised in the early teaching of reading to beginners (i.e. unskilled readers) when they start school.

Good comprehension draws from linguistic knowledge (in particular of vocabulary and grammar) and on knowledge of the world. Comprehension skills develop through pupils' experience of high-quality discussion with the teacher, as well as from reading and discussing a range of stories, poems and non-fiction. All pupils must be encouraged to read widely across both fiction and non-fiction to develop their knowledge of themselves and the world in which they live, to establish an appreciation and love of reading, and to gain knowledge across the curriculum. Reading widely and often increases pupils' vocabulary because they encounter words they would rarely hear or use in everyday speech. Reading also feeds pupils' imagination and opens up a treasure-house of wonder and joy for curious young minds.

It is essential that, by the end of their primary education, all pupils are able to read fluently, and with confidence, in any subject in their forthcoming secondary education.

Writing

The programmes of study for writing at key stages 1 and 2 are constructed similarly to those for reading:

- transcription (spelling and handwriting)
- composition (articulating ideas and structuring them in speech and writing).

It is essential that teaching develops pupils' competence in these two dimensions. In addition, pupils should be taught how to plan, revise and evaluate their writing.

These aspects of writing have been incorporated into the programmes of study for composition.

Writing down ideas fluently depends on effective transcription: that is, on spelling quickly and accurately through knowing the relationship between sounds and letters (phonics) and understanding the morphology (word structure) and orthography (spelling structure) of words. Effective composition involves forming, articulating and communicating ideas, and then organising them coherently for a reader. This requires clarity, awareness of the audience, purpose and context, and an increasingly wide knowledge of vocabulary and grammar. Writing also depends on fluent, legible and, eventually, speedy handwriting.

Spelling, vocabulary, grammar, punctuation and glossary

The two statutory appendices – on spelling and on vocabulary, grammar and punctuation – give an overview of the specific features that should be included in teaching the programmes of study.

Opportunities for teachers to enhance pupils' vocabulary arise naturally from their reading and writing. As vocabulary increases, teachers should show pupils how to understand the relationships between words, how to understand nuances in meaning, and how to develop their understanding of, and ability to use, figurative language. They should also teach pupils how to work out and clarify the meanings of unknown words and words with more than one meaning. References to developing pupils' vocabulary are also included within the appendices.

Pupils should be taught to control their speaking and writing consciously and to use Standard English. They should be taught to use the elements of spelling, grammar, punctuation and 'language about language' listed. This is not intended to constrain or restrict teachers' creativity, but simply to provide the structure on which they can construct exciting lessons. A non-statutory Glossary is provided for teachers.

Throughout the programmes of study, teachers should teach pupils the vocabulary they need to discuss their reading, writing and spoken language. It is important that pupils learn the correct grammatical terms in English and that these terms are integrated within teaching.

School curriculum

The programmes of study for English are set out year by year for key stage 1 and two-yearly for key stage 2. The single year blocks at key stage 1 reflect the rapid pace of development in word reading during these two years. Schools are, however, only required to teach the relevant programme of study by the end of the key stage. Within each key stage, schools therefore have the flexibility to introduce content earlier or later than set out in the programme of study. In addition, schools can introduce key stage content during an earlier key stage if appropriate. All schools are also required to set out their school curriculum for English on a year-by-year basis and make this information available online.

Attainment targets

By the end of each key stage, pupils are expected to know, apply and understand the matters, skills and processes specified in the relevant programme of study.

Schools are not required by law to teach the example content in [square brackets] or the content indicated as being 'non-statutory'.

Spoken language – years 1 to 6

Spoken language

Statutory requirements

Pupils should be taught to:

- listen and respond appropriately to adults and their peers
- ask relevant questions to extend their understanding and knowledge
- use relevant strategies to build their vocabulary
- articulate and justify answers, arguments and opinions
- give well-structured descriptions, explanations and narratives for different purposes, including for expressing feelings
- maintain attention and participate actively in collaborative conversations, staying on topic and initiating and responding to comments
- use spoken language to develop understanding through speculating, hypothesising, imagining and exploring ideas
- speak audibly and fluently with an increasing command of Standard English
- participate in discussions, presentations, performances, role-play, improvisations and debates
- gain, maintain and monitor the interest of the listener(s)
- consider and evaluate different viewpoints, attending to and building on the contributions of others
- select and use appropriate registers for effective communication.

Notes and guidance (non-statutory)

These statements apply to all years. The content should be taught at a level appropriate to the age of the pupils. Pupils should build on the oral language skills that have been taught in preceding years.

Pupils should be taught to develop their competence in spoken language and listening to enhance the effectiveness with which they are able to communicate across a range of contexts and to a range of audiences. They should therefore have opportunities to work in groups of different sizes – in pairs, small groups, large groups and as a whole class. Pupils should understand how to take turns and when and how to participate constructively in conversations and debates.

Attention should also be paid to increasing pupils' vocabulary, ranging from describing their immediate world and feelings to developing a broader, deeper and richer vocabulary to discuss abstract concepts and a wider range of topics, and to enhancing their knowledge about language as a whole.

Pupils should receive constructive feedback on their spoken language and listening, not only to improve their knowledge and skills but also to establish secure foundations for effective spoken language in their studies at primary school, helping them to achieve in secondary education and beyond.

Key stage 1 – year 1

During year 1, teachers should build on work from the Early Years Foundation Stage, making sure that pupils can sound and blend unfamiliar printed words quickly and accurately using the phonic knowledge and skills that they have already learnt. Teachers should also ensure that pupils continue to learn new grapheme-phoneme correspondences (GPCs) and revise and consolidate those learnt earlier. The understanding that the letter(s) on the page represent the sounds in spoken words should underpin pupils' reading and spelling of all words. This includes common words containing unusual GPCs. The term 'common exception words' is used throughout the programmes of study for such words.

Alongside this knowledge of GPCs, pupils need to develop the skill of blending the sounds into words for reading and establish the habit of applying this skill whenever they encounter new words. This will be supported by practice in reading books consistent with their developing phonic knowledge and skill and their knowledge of common exception words. At the same time they will need to hear, share and discuss a wide range of high-quality books to develop a love of reading and broaden their vocabulary.

Pupils should be helped to read words without overt sounding and blending after a few encounters. Those who are slow to develop this skill should have extra practice.

Pupils' writing during year 1 will generally develop at a slower pace than their reading. This is because they need to encode the sounds they hear in words (spelling skills), develop the physical skill needed for handwriting, and learn how to organise their ideas in writing.

Pupils entering year 1 who have not yet met the early learning goals for literacy should continue to follow their school's curriculum for the Early Years Foundation Stage to develop their word reading, spelling and language skills. However, these pupils should follow the year 1 programme of study in terms of the books they listen to and discuss, so that they develop their vocabulary and understanding of grammar, as well as their knowledge more generally across the curriculum. If they are still struggling to decode and spell, they need to be taught to do this urgently through a rigorous and systematic phonics programme so that they catch up rapidly.

Teachers should ensure that their teaching develops pupils' oral vocabulary as well as their ability to understand and use a variety of grammatical structures, giving particular support to pupils whose oral language skills are insufficiently developed.

Year 1 programme of study

Reading – word reading

Statutory requirements

Pupils should be taught to:

- apply phonic knowledge and skills as the route to decode words
- respond speedily with the correct sound to graphemes (letters or groups of letters) for all 40+ phonemes, including, where applicable, alternative sounds for graphemes
- read accurately by blending sounds in unfamiliar words containing GPCs that have been taught
- read common exception words, noting unusual correspondences between spelling and sound and where these occur in the word
- read words containing taught GPCs and –s, –es, –ing, –ed, –er and –est endings
- read other words of more than one syllable that contain taught GPCs

(Continued)

(Continued)

- read words with contractions [for example, I'm, I'll, we'll], and understand that the apostrophe represents the omitted letter(s)
- read aloud accurately books that are consistent with their developing phonic knowledge and that do not require them to use other strategies to work out words
- re-read these books to build up their fluency and confidence in word reading.

Notes and guidance (non-statutory)

Pupils should revise and consolidate the GPCs and the common exception words taught in Reception. As soon as they can read words comprising the year 1 GPCs accurately and speedily, they should move on to the year 2 programme of study for word reading.

The number, order and choice of exception words taught will vary according to the phonics programme being used. Ensuring that pupils are aware of the GPCs they contain, however unusual these are, supports spelling later.

Young readers encounter words that they have not seen before much more frequently than experienced readers do, and they may not know the meaning of some of these. Practice at reading such words by sounding and blending can provide opportunities not only for pupils to develop confidence in their decoding skills, but also for teachers to explain the meaning and thus develop pupils' vocabulary.

Pupils should be taught how to read words with suffixes by being helped to build on the root words that they can read already. Pupils' reading and re-reading of books that are closely matched to their developing phonic knowledge and knowledge of common exception words supports their fluency, as well as increasing their confidence in their reading skills. Fluent word reading greatly assists comprehension, especially when pupils come to read longer books.

Reading – comprehension

Statutory requirements

Pupils should be taught to:

- develop pleasure in reading, motivation to read, vocabulary and understanding by:
  - listening to and discussing a wide range of poems, stories and non-fiction at a level beyond that at which they can read independently
  - being encouraged to link what they read or hear read to their own experiences
  - becoming very familiar with key stories, fairy stories and traditional tales, retelling them and considering their particular characteristics
  - recognising and joining in with predictable phrases
  - learning to appreciate rhymes and poems, and to recite some by heart
  - discussing word meanings, linking new meanings to those already known

- understand both the books they can already read accurately and fluently and those they listen to by:
  - drawing on what they already know or on background information and vocabulary provided by the teacher
  - checking that the text makes sense to them as they read and correcting inaccurate reading

- o   discussing the significance of the title and events
- o   making inferences on the basis of what is being said and done
- o   predicting what might happen on the basis of what has been read so far

- participate in discussion about what is read to them, taking turns and listening to what others say
- explain clearly their understanding of what is read to them.

Notes and guidance (non-statutory)

Pupils should have extensive experience of listening to, sharing and discussing a wide range of high-quality books with the teacher, other adults and each other to engender a love of reading at the same time as they are reading independently.

Pupils' vocabulary should be developed when they listen to books read aloud and when they discuss what they have heard. Such vocabulary can also feed into their writing. Knowing the meaning of more words increases pupils' chances of understanding when they read by themselves. The meaning of some new words should be introduced to pupils before they start to read on their own, so that these unknown words do not hold up their comprehension.

However, once pupils have already decoded words successfully, the meaning of those that are new to them can be discussed with them, so contributing to developing their early skills of inference. By listening frequently to stories, poems and non-fiction that they cannot yet read for themselves, pupils begin to understand how written language can be structured in order, for example, to build surprise in narratives or to present facts in non-fiction. Listening to and discussing information books and other non-fiction establishes the foundations for their learning in other subjects. Pupils should be shown some of the processes for finding out information.

Through listening, pupils also start to learn how language sounds and increase their vocabulary and awareness of grammatical structures. In due course, they will be able to draw on such grammar in their own writing.

Rules for effective discussions should be agreed with and demonstrated for pupils. They should help to develop and evaluate them, with the expectation that everyone takes part. Pupils should be helped to consider the opinions of others.

Role-play can help pupils to identify with and explore characters and to try out the language they have listened to.

Writing – transcription

Statutory requirements

Spelling (see English Appendix 1)

Pupils should be taught to:

- spell:

   - o   words containing each of the 40+ phonemes already taught
   - o   common exception words
   - o   the days of the week

(Continued)

(Continued)

- name the letters of the alphabet:

  ○ naming the letters of the alphabet in order
  ○ using letter names to distinguish between alternative spellings of the same sound

- add prefixes and suffixes:

  ○ using the spelling rule for adding –s or –es as the plural marker for nouns and the third person singular marker for verbs
  ○ using the prefix un–
  ○ using –ing, –ed, –er and –est where no change is needed in the spelling of root words [for example, helping, helped, helper, eating, quicker, quickest]

- apply simple spelling rules and guidance, as listed in English Appendix 1
- write from memory simple sentences dictated by the teacher that include words using the GPCs and common exception words taught so far.

Notes and guidance (non-statutory)

Reading should be taught alongside spelling, so that pupils understand that they can read back words they have spelt.

Pupils should be shown how to segment spoken words into individual phonemes and then how to represent the phonemes by the appropriate grapheme(s). It is important to recognise that phoneme-grapheme correspondences (which underpin spelling) are more variable than grapheme-phoneme correspondences (which underpin reading). For this reason, pupils need to do much more word-specific rehearsal for spelling than for reading.

At this stage pupils will be spelling some words in a phonically plausible way, even if sometimes incorrectly. Misspellings of words that pupils have been taught to spell should be corrected; other misspelt words should be used to teach pupils about alternative ways of representing those sounds.

Writing simple dictated sentences that include words taught so far gives pupils opportunities to apply and practise their spelling.

Statutory requirements

Handwriting

Pupils should be taught to:

- sit correctly at a table, holding a pencil comfortably and correctly
- begin to form lower-case letters in the correct direction, starting and finishing in the right place
- form capital letters
- form digits 0–9
- understand which letters belong to which handwriting 'families' (i.e. letters that are formed in similar ways) and to practise these.

Writing – composition

Statutory requirements

Pupils should be taught to:

- write sentences by:

  - saying out loud what they are going to write about
  - composing a sentence orally before writing it
  - sequencing sentences to form short narratives
  - re-reading what they have written to check that it makes sense

- discuss what they have written with the teacher or other pupils
- read aloud their writing clearly enough to be heard by their peers and the teacher.

Notes and guidance (non-statutory)

At the beginning of year 1, not all pupils will have the spelling and handwriting skills they need to write down everything that they can compose out loud.

Pupils should understand, through demonstration, the skills and processes essential to writing: that is, thinking aloud as they collect ideas, drafting, and re-reading to check their meaning is clear.

Writing – vocabulary, grammar and punctuation

Statutory requirements

Pupils should be taught to:

- develop their understanding of the concepts set out in English Appendix 2 by:

  - leaving spaces between words
  - joining words and joining clauses using and
  - beginning to punctuate sentences using a capital letter and a full stop, question mark or exclamation mark

(Continued)

> *(Continued)*
>
> - o   using a capital letter for names of people, places, the days of the week, and the personal pronoun 'I'
> - o   learning the grammar for year 1 in English Appendix 2
> - •   use the grammatical terminology in English Appendix 2 in discussing their writing.

Notes and guidance (non-statutory)

Pupils should be taught to recognise sentence boundaries in spoken sentences and to use the vocabulary listed in English Appendix 2 ('Terminology for pupils') when their writing is discussed.

Pupils should begin to use some of the distinctive features of Standard English in their writing. 'Standard English' is defined in the Glossary.

Key stage 1 – year 2

By the beginning of year 2, pupils should be able to read all common graphemes. They should be able to read unfamiliar words containing these graphemes, accurately and without undue hesitation, by sounding them out in books that are matched closely to each pupil's level of word reading knowledge. They should also be able to read many common words containing GPCs taught so far [for example, shout, hand, stop, or dream], without needing to blend the sounds out loud first. Pupils' reading of common exception words [for example, you, could, many, or people], should be secure. Pupils will increase their fluency by being able to read these words easily and automatically. Finally, pupils should be able to retell some familiar stories that have been read to and discussed with them or that they have acted out during year 1.

During year 2, teachers should continue to focus on establishing pupils' accurate and speedy word reading skills. They should also make sure that pupils listen to and discuss a wide range of stories, poems, plays and information books; this should include whole books. The sooner that pupils can read well and do so frequently, the sooner they will be able to increase their vocabulary, comprehension and their knowledge across the wider curriculum.

In writing, pupils at the beginning of year 2 should be able to compose individual sentences orally and then write them down. They should be able to spell correctly many of the words covered in year 1 (see English Appendix 1). They should also be able to make phonically plausible attempts to spell words they have not yet learnt. Finally, they should be able to form individual letters correctly, so establishing good handwriting habits from the beginning.

It is important to recognise that pupils begin to meet extra challenges in terms of spelling during year 2. Increasingly, they should learn that there is not always an obvious connection between the way a word is said and the way it is spelt. Variations include different ways of spelling the same sound, the use of so-called silent letters and groups of letters in some words and, sometimes, spelling that has become separated from the way that words are now pronounced, such as the 'le' ending in table. Pupils' motor skills also need to be sufficiently advanced for them to write down ideas that they may be able to compose orally. In addition, writing is intrinsically harder than reading: pupils are likely to be able to read and understand more complex writing (in terms of its vocabulary and structure) than they are capable of producing themselves.

For pupils who do not have the phonic knowledge and skills they need for year 2, teachers should use the year 1 programmes of study for word reading and spelling so that pupils' word reading skills catch up. However, teachers should use the year 2 programme of study for comprehension so that these pupils hear and talk about new books, poems, other writing, and vocabulary with the rest of the class.

Year 2 programme of study

Reading – word reading

Statutory requirements

Pupils should be taught to:

- continue to apply phonic knowledge and skills as the route to decode words until automatic decoding has become embedded and reading is fluent
- read accurately by blending the sounds in words that contain the graphemes taught so far, especially recognising alternative sounds for graphemes
- read accurately words of two or more syllables that contain the same graphemes as above
- read words containing common suffixes
- read further common exception words, noting unusual correspondences between spelling and sound and where these occur in the word
- read most words quickly and accurately, without overt sounding and blending, when they have been frequently encountered
- read aloud books closely matched to their improving phonic knowledge, sounding out unfamiliar words accurately, automatically and without undue hesitation
- re-read these books to build up their fluency and confidence in word reading.

Notes and guidance (non-statutory)

Pupils should revise and consolidate the GPCs and the common exception words taught in year 1. The exception words taught will vary slightly, depending on the phonics programme being used. As soon as pupils can read words comprising the year 2 GPCs accurately and speedily, they should move on to the years 3 and 4 programme of study for word reading.

When pupils are taught how to read longer words, they should be shown syllable boundaries and how to read each syllable separately before they combine them to read the word.

Pupils should be taught how to read suffixes by building on the root words that they have already learnt. The whole suffix should be taught as well as the letters that make it up.

Pupils who are still at the early stages of learning to read should have ample practice in reading books that are closely matched to their developing phonic knowledge and knowledge of common exception words. As soon as the decoding of most regular words and common exception words is embedded fully, the range of books that pupils can read independently will expand rapidly. Pupils should have opportunities to exercise choice in selecting books and be taught how to do so.

Reading – comprehension

Statutory requirements

Pupils should be taught to:

- develop pleasure in reading, motivation to read, vocabulary and understanding by:
    - listening to, discussing and expressing views about a wide range of contemporary and classic poetry, stories and non-fiction at a level beyond that at which they can read independently
    - discussing the sequence of events in books and how items of information are related
    - becoming increasingly familiar with and retelling a wider range of stories, fairy stories and traditional tales
    - being introduced to non-fiction books that are structured in different ways
    - recognising simple recurring literary language in stories and poetry
    - discussing and clarifying the meanings of words, linking new meanings to known vocabulary
    - discussing their favourite words and phrases
    - continuing to build up a repertoire of poems learnt by heart, appreciating these and reciting some, with appropriate intonation to make the meaning clear

- understand both the books that they can already read accurately and fluently and those that they listen to by:
    - drawing on what they already know or on background information and vocabulary provided by the teacher
    - checking that the text makes sense to them as they read and correcting inaccurate reading
    - making inferences on the basis of what is being said and done
    - answering and asking questions
    - predicting what might happen on the basis of what has been read so far

- participate in discussion about books, poems and other works that are read to them and those that they can read for themselves, taking turns and listening to what others say
- explain and discuss their understanding of books, poems and other material, both those that they listen to and those that they read for themselves.

Notes and guidance (non-statutory)

Pupils should be encouraged to read all the words in a sentence and to do this accurately, so that their understanding of what they read is not hindered by imprecise decoding (for example, by reading 'place' instead of 'palace').

Pupils should monitor what they read, checking that the word they have decoded fits in with what else they have read and makes sense in the context of what they already know about the topic.

The meaning of new words should be explained to pupils within the context of what they are reading, and they should be encouraged to use morphology (such as prefixes) to work out unknown words.

Pupils should learn about cause and effect in both narrative and non-fiction (for example, what has prompted a character's behaviour in a story; why certain dates are commemorated annually). 'Thinking aloud' when reading to pupils may help them to understand what skilled readers do.

Deliberate steps should be taken to increase pupils' vocabulary and their awareness of grammar so that they continue to understand the differences between spoken and written language.

Discussion should be demonstrated to pupils. They should be guided to participate in it and they should be helped to consider the opinions of others. They should receive feedback on their discussions.

Role-play and other drama techniques can help pupils to identify with and explore characters. In these ways, they extend their understanding of what they read and have opportunities to try out the language they have listened to.

Writing – transcription

Statutory requirements

Spelling (see English Appendix 1)

Pupils should be taught to:

- spell by:
  - o segmenting spoken words into phonemes and representing these by graphemes, spelling many correctly
  - o learning new ways of spelling phonemes for which one or more spellings are already known, and learn some words with each spelling, including a few common homophones
  - o learning to spell common exception words
  - o learning to spell more words with contracted forms
  - o learning the possessive apostrophe (singular) [for example, the girl's book]
  - o distinguishing between homophones and near-homophones

- add suffixes to spell longer words, including –ment, –ness, –ful, –less, –ly
- apply spelling rules and guidance, as listed in English Appendix 1
- write from memory simple sentences dictated by the teacher that include words using the GPCs, common exception words and punctuation taught so far.

Notes and guidance (non-statutory)

In year 2, pupils move towards more word-specific knowledge of spelling, including homophones. The process of spelling should be emphasised: that is, that spelling involves segmenting spoken words into phonemes and then representing all the phonemes by graphemes in the right order. Pupils should do this both for single-syllable and multi-syllabic words.

(Continued)

(Continued)

At this stage children's spelling should be phonically plausible, even if not always correct. Misspellings of words that pupils have been taught to spell should be corrected; other misspelt words can be used as an opportunity to teach pupils about alternative ways of representing those sounds.

Pupils should be encouraged to apply their knowledge of suffixes from their word reading to their spelling. They should also draw from and apply their growing knowledge of word and spelling structure, as well as their knowledge of root words.

Statutory requirements

Handwriting

Pupils should be taught to:

- form lower-case letters of the correct size relative to one another
- start using some of the diagonal and horizontal strokes needed to join letters and understand which letters, when adjacent to one another, are best left unjoined
- write capital letters and digits of the correct size, orientation and relationship to one another and to lower case letters
- use spacing between words that reflects the size of the letters.

Notes and guidance (non-statutory)

Pupils should revise and practise correct letter formation frequently. They should be taught to write with a joined style as soon as they can form letters securely with the correct orientation.

Writing – composition

Statutory requirements

Pupils should be taught to:

- develop positive attitudes towards and stamina for writing by:
  - writing narratives about personal experiences and those of others (real and fictional)
  - writing about real events
  - writing poetry
  - writing for different purposes
- consider what they are going to write before beginning by:
  - planning or saying out loud what they are going to write about
  - writing down ideas and/or key words, including new vocabulary
  - encapsulating what they want to say, sentence by sentence

- make simple additions, revisions and corrections to their own writing by:
    - evaluating their writing with the teacher and other pupils
    - re-reading to check that their writing makes sense and that verbs to indicate time are used correctly and consistently, including verbs in the continuous form
    - proof-reading to check for errors in spelling, grammar and punctuation [for example, ends of sentences punctuated correctly]
- read aloud what they have written with appropriate intonation to make the meaning clear.

Notes and guidance (non-statutory)

Reading and listening to whole books, not simply extracts, helps pupils to increase their vocabulary and grammatical knowledge, including their knowledge of the vocabulary and grammar of Standard English. These activities also help them to understand how different types of writing, including narratives, are structured. All these can be drawn on for their writing.

Pupils should understand, through being shown these, the skills and processes essential to writing: that is, thinking aloud as they collect ideas, drafting, and re-reading to check their meaning is clear.

Drama and role-play can contribute to the quality of pupils' writing by providing opportunities for pupils to develop and order their ideas through playing roles and improvising scenes in various settings.

Pupils might draw on and use new vocabulary from their reading, their discussions about it (one to one and as a whole class) and from their wider experiences.

Writing – vocabulary, grammar and punctuation

Statutory requirements

Pupils should be taught to:

- develop their understanding of the concepts set out in English Appendix 2 by:
    - learning how to use both familiar and new punctuation correctly (see English Appendix 2), including full stops, capital letters, exclamation marks, question marks, commas for lists and apostrophes for contracted forms and the possessive (singular)
- learn how to use:
    - sentences with different forms: statement, question, exclamation, command
    - expanded noun phrases to describe and specify [for example, the blue butterfly]
    - the present and past tenses correctly and consistently including the progressive form

(Continued)

> *(Continued)*
>
> - ○ subordination (using when, if, that, or because) and co-ordination (using or, and, or but)
> - ○ the grammar for year 2 in English Appendix 2
> - ○ some features of written Standard English
>
> - • use and understand the grammatical terminology in English Appendix 2 in discussing their writing.

Notes and guidance (non-statutory)

The terms for discussing language should be embedded for pupils in the course of discussing their writing with them. Their attention should be drawn to the technical terms they need to learn.

Lower key stage 2 – years 3 and 4

By the beginning of year 3, pupils should be able to read books written at an age-appropriate interest level. They should be able to read them accurately and at a speed that is sufficient for them to focus on understanding what they read rather than on decoding individual words. They should be able to decode most new words outside their spoken vocabulary, making a good approximation to the word's pronunciation. As their decoding skills become increasingly secure, teaching should be directed more towards developing their vocabulary and the breadth and depth of their reading, making sure that they become independent, fluent and enthusiastic readers who read widely and frequently. They should be developing their understanding and enjoyment of stories, poetry, plays and non-fiction, and learning to read silently. They should also be developing their knowledge and skills in reading non-fiction about a wide range of subjects. They should be learning to justify their views about what they have read: with support at the start of year 3 and increasingly independently by the end of year 4.

Pupils should be able to write down their ideas with a reasonable degree of accuracy and with good sentence punctuation. Teachers should therefore be consolidating pupils' writing skills, their vocabulary, their grasp of sentence structure and their knowledge of linguistic terminology. Teaching them to develop as writers involves teaching them to enhance the effectiveness of what they write as well as increasing their competence. Teachers should make sure that pupils build on what they have learnt, particularly in terms of the range of their writing and the more varied grammar, vocabulary and narrative structures from which they can draw to express their ideas. Pupils should be beginning to understand how writing can be different from speech. Joined handwriting should be the norm; pupils should be able to use it fast enough to keep pace with what they want to say.

Pupils' spelling of common words should be correct, including common exception words and other words that they have learnt (see English Appendix 1). Pupils should spell words as accurately as possible using their phonic knowledge and other knowledge of spelling, such as morphology and etymology.

Most pupils will not need further direct teaching of word reading skills: they are able to decode unfamiliar words accurately, and need very few repeated experiences of this before the word is stored in such a way that they can read it without overt sound-blending. They should demonstrate understanding of figurative language, distinguish shades of meaning among related words and use age-appropriate, academic vocabulary.

As in key stage 1, however, pupils who are still struggling to decode need to be taught to do this urgently through a rigorous and systematic phonics programme so that they catch up rapidly with their peers. If they cannot decode independently and fluently, they will find it increasingly difficult to understand what they read and to write down what they want to say. As far as possible, however, these pupils should follow the year 3 and 4 programme of study in terms of listening to new books, hearing and learning new vocabulary and grammatical structures, and discussing these.

Specific requirements for pupils to discuss what they are learning and to develop their wider skills in spoken language form part of this programme of study. In years 3 and 4, pupils should become more familiar with and confident in using language in a greater variety of situations, for a variety of audiences and purposes, including through drama, formal presentations and debate.

Years 3 and 4 programme of study

Reading – word reading

Statutory requirements

Pupils should be taught to:

- apply their growing knowledge of root words, prefixes and suffixes (etymology and morphology) as listed in English Appendix 1, both to read aloud and to understand the meaning of new words they meet
- read further exception words, noting the unusual correspondences between spelling and sound, and where these occur in the word.

Notes and guidance (non-statutory)

At this stage, teaching comprehension should be taking precedence over teaching word reading directly. Any focus on word reading should support the development of vocabulary.

When pupils are taught to read longer words, they should be supported to test out different pronunciations. They will attempt to match what they decode to words they may have already heard but may not have seen in print [for example, in reading 'technical', the pronunciation /tɛtʃnɪkəl/ ('tetchnical') might not sound familiar, but /tɛknɪkəl/ ('teknical') should].

Reading – comprehension

Statutory requirements

Pupils should be taught to:

- develop positive attitudes to reading and understanding of what they read by:
  o listening to and discussing a wide range of fiction, poetry, plays, non-fiction and reference books or textbooks
  o reading books that are structured in different ways and reading for a range of purposes

(Continued)

(Continued)

- o   using dictionaries to check the meaning of words that they have read
- o   increasing their familiarity with a wide range of books, including fairy stories, myths and legends, and retelling some of these orally
- o   identifying themes and conventions in a wide range of books
- o   preparing poems and play scripts to read aloud and to perform, showing understanding through intonation, tone, volume and action
- o   discussing words and phrases that capture the reader's interest and imagination
- o   recognising some different forms of poetry [for example, free verse, narrative poetry]

- •   understand what they read, in books they can read independently, by:

  - o   checking that the text makes sense to them, discussing their understanding and explaining the meaning of words in context
  - o   asking questions to improve their understanding of a text
  - o   drawing inferences such as inferring characters' feelings, thoughts and motives from their actions, and justifying inferences with evidence
  - o   predicting what might happen from details stated and implied
  - o   identifying main ideas drawn from more than one paragraph and summarising these
  - o   identifying how language, structure, and presentation contribute to meaning

- •   retrieve and record information from non-fiction
- •   participate in discussion about both books that are read to them and those they can read for themselves, taking turns and listening to what others say.

Notes and guidance (non-statutory)

The focus should continue to be on pupils' comprehension as a primary element in reading. The knowledge and skills that pupils need in order to comprehend are very similar at different ages. This is why the programmes of study for comprehension in years 3 and 4 and years 5 and 6 are similar: the complexity of the writing increases the level of challenge.

Pupils should be taught to recognise themes in what they read, such as the triumph of good over evil or the use of magical devices in fairy stories and folk tales.

They should also learn the conventions of different types of writing (for example, the greeting in letters, a diary written in the first person or the use of presentational devices such as numbering and headings in instructions).

Pupils should be taught to use the skills they have learnt earlier and continue to apply these skills to read for different reasons, including for pleasure, or to find out information and the meaning of new words.

Pupils should continue to have opportunities to listen frequently to stories, poems, non-fiction and other writing, including whole books and not just extracts, so that they build on what was taught previously. In this way, they also meet books and authors that they might not choose themselves. Pupils should also have opportunities to exercise choice in selecting books and be taught how to do so, with teachers making use of any library services and expertise to support this.

Reading, re-reading, and rehearsing poems and plays for presentation and performance give pupils opportunities to discuss language, including vocabulary, extending their interest in the meaning and origin of words. Pupils should be encouraged to use drama approaches to understand how to perform plays and poems to support their understanding of the meaning. These activities also provide them with an incentive to find out what expression is required, so feeding into comprehension.

In using non-fiction, pupils should know what information they need to look for before they begin and be clear about the task. They should be shown how to use contents pages and indexes to locate information.

Pupils should have guidance about the kinds of explanations and questions that are expected from them. They should help to develop, agree on, and evaluate rules for effective discussion. The expectation should be that all pupils take part.

Writing – transcription

Statutory requirements

Spelling (see English Appendix 1)

Pupils should be taught to:

- use further prefixes and suffixes and understand how to add them (English Appendix 1)
- spell further homophones
- spell words that are often misspelt (English Appendix 1)
- place the possessive apostrophe accurately in words with regular plurals [for example, girls', boys'] and in words with irregular plurals [for example, children's]
- use the first two or three letters of a word to check its spelling in a dictionary
- write from memory simple sentences, dictated by the teacher, that include words and punctuation taught so far.

Notes and guidance (non-statutory)

Pupils should learn to spell new words correctly and have plenty of practice in spelling them.

As in years 1 and 2, pupils should continue to be supported in understanding and applying the concepts of word structure (see English Appendix 2).

Pupils need sufficient knowledge of spelling in order to use dictionaries efficiently.

Statutory requirements

Handwriting

Pupils should be taught to:

- use the diagonal and horizontal strokes that are needed to join letters and understand which letters, when adjacent to one another, are best left unjoined
- increase the legibility, consistency and quality of their handwriting [for example, by ensuring that the downstrokes of letters are parallel and equidistant; that lines of writing are spaced sufficiently so that the ascenders and descenders of letters do not touch].

Writing – composition

Statutory requirements

Pupils should be taught to:

- plan their writing by:
  - discussing writing similar to that which they are planning to write in order to understand and learn from its structure, vocabulary and grammar
  - discussing and recording ideas
- draft and write by:
  - composing and rehearsing sentences orally (including dialogue), progressively building a varied and rich vocabulary and an increasing range of sentence structures (English Appendix 2)
  - organising paragraphs around a theme
  - in narratives, creating settings, characters and plot
  - in non-narrative material, using simple organisational devices [for example, headings and sub-headings]
- evaluate and edit by:
  - assessing the effectiveness of their own and others' writing and suggesting improvements
  - proposing changes to grammar and vocabulary to improve consistency, including the accurate use of pronouns in sentences
- proof-read for spelling and punctuation errors
- read aloud their own writing, to a group or the whole class, using appropriate intonation and controlling the tone and volume so that the meaning is clear.

Writing – vocabulary, grammar and punctuation

Statutory requirements

Pupils should be taught to:

- develop their understanding of the concepts set out in English Appendix 2 by:

  o extending the range of sentences with more than one clause by using a wider range of conjunctions, including when, if, because, although
  o using the present perfect form of verbs in contrast to the past tense
  o choosing nouns or pronouns appropriately for clarity and cohesion and to avoid repetition
  o using conjunctions, adverbs and prepositions to express time and cause
  o using fronted adverbials
  o learning the grammar for years 3 and 4 in English Appendix 2

- indicate grammatical and other features by:

  o using commas after fronted adverbials
  o indicating possession by using the possessive apostrophe with plural nouns
  o using and punctuating direct speech

- use and understand the grammatical terminology in English Appendix 2 accurately and appropriately when discussing their writing and reading.

Notes and guidance (non-statutory)

Grammar should be taught explicitly: pupils should be taught the terminology and concepts set out in English Appendix 2, and be able to apply them correctly to examples of real language, such as their own writing or books that they have read.

At this stage, pupils should start to learn about some of the differences between Standard English and non-Standard English and begin to apply what they have learnt [for example, in writing dialogue for characters].

Upper key stage 2 – years 5 and 6

By the beginning of year 5, pupils should be able to read aloud a wider range of poetry and books written at an age-appropriate interest level with accuracy and at a reasonable speaking pace. They should be able to read most words effortlessly and to work out how to pronounce unfamiliar written words with increasing automaticity. If the pronunciation sounds unfamiliar, they should ask for help in determining both the meaning of the word and how to pronounce it correctly.

They should be able to prepare readings, with appropriate intonation to show their understanding, and should be able to summarise and present a familiar story in their own words. They should be reading widely and frequently, outside as well as in school, for pleasure and information. They should be able to read silently, with good understanding, inferring the meanings of unfamiliar words, and then discuss what they have read.

Pupils should be able to write down their ideas quickly. Their grammar and punctuation should be broadly accurate. Pupils' spelling of most words taught so far should be accurate and they should be able to spell words that they have not yet been taught by using what they have learnt about how spelling works in English.

During years 5 and 6, teachers should continue to emphasise pupils' enjoyment and understanding of language, especially vocabulary, to support their reading and writing. Pupils' knowledge of language, gained from stories, plays, poetry, non-fiction and textbooks, will support their increasing fluency as readers, their facility as writers, and their comprehension. As in years 3 and 4, pupils should be taught to enhance the effectiveness of their writing as well as their competence.

It is essential that pupils whose decoding skills are poor are taught through a rigorous and systematic phonics programme so that they catch up rapidly with their peers in terms of their decoding and spelling. However, as far as possible, these pupils should follow the upper key stage 2 programme of study in terms of listening to books and other writing that they have not come across before, hearing and learning new vocabulary and grammatical structures, and having a chance to talk about all of these.

By the end of year 6, pupils' reading and writing should be sufficiently fluent and effortless for them to manage the general demands of the curriculum in year 7, across all subjects and not just in English, but there will continue to be a need for pupils to learn subject-specific vocabulary. They should be able to reflect their understanding of the audience for and purpose of their writing by selecting appropriate vocabulary and grammar. Teachers should prepare pupils for secondary education by ensuring that they can consciously control sentence structure in their writing and understand why sentences are constructed as they are. Pupils should understand nuances in vocabulary choice and age-appropriate, academic vocabulary. This involves consolidation, practice and discussion of language.

Specific requirements for pupils to discuss what they are learning and to develop their wider skills in spoken language form part of this programme of study. In years 5 and 6, pupils' confidence, enjoyment and mastery of language should be extended through public speaking, performance and debate.

Years 5 and 6 programme of study

Reading – word reading

Statutory requirements

Pupils should be taught to:

- apply their growing knowledge of root words, prefixes and suffixes (morphology and etymology), as listed in English Appendix 1, both to read aloud and to understand the meaning of new words that they meet.

Notes and guidance (non-statutory)

At this stage, there should be no need for further direct teaching of word reading skills for almost all pupils. If pupils are struggling or failing in this, the reasons for this should be investigated. It is imperative that pupils are taught to read during their last two years at primary school if they enter year 5 not being able to do so.

Pupils should be encouraged to work out any unfamiliar word. They should focus on all the letters in a word so that they do not, for example, read 'invitation' for 'imitation' simply because they might be more familiar with the first word.

Accurate reading of individual words, which might be key to the meaning of a sentence or paragraph, improves comprehension.

When teachers are reading with or to pupils, attention should be paid to new vocabulary – both a word's meaning(s) and its correct pronunciation.

Reading – comprehension

Statutory requirements

Pupils should be taught to:

- maintain positive attitudes to reading and understanding of what they read by:
  - o continuing to read and discuss an increasingly wide range of fiction, poetry, plays, non-fiction and reference books or textbooks
  - o reading books that are structured in different ways and reading for a range of purposes
  - o increasing their familiarity with a wide range of books, including myths, legends and traditional stories, modern fiction, fiction from our literary heritage, and books from other cultures and traditions
  - o recommending books that they have read to their peers, giving reasons for their choices
  - o identifying and discussing themes and conventions in and across a wide range of writing
  - o making comparisons within and across books
  - o learning a wider range of poetry by heart
  - o preparing poems and plays to read aloud and to perform, showing understanding through intonation, tone and volume so that the meaning is clear to an audience
- understand what they read by:
  - o checking that the book makes sense to them, discussing their understanding and exploring the meaning of words in context
  - o asking questions to improve their understanding
  - o drawing inferences such as inferring characters' feelings, thoughts and motives from their actions, and justifying inferences with evidence
  - o predicting what might happen from details stated and implied
  - o summarising the main ideas drawn from more than one paragraph, identifying key details that support the main ideas
  - o identifying how language, structure and presentation contribute to meaning
- discuss and evaluate how authors use language, including figurative language, considering the impact on the reader
- distinguish between statements of fact and opinion
- retrieve, record and present information from non-fiction
- participate in discussions about books that are read to them and those they can read for themselves, building on their own and others' ideas and challenging views courteously
- explain and discuss their understanding of what they have read, including through formal presentations and debates, maintaining a focus on the topic and using notes where necessary
- provide reasoned justifications for their views.

Notes and guidance (non-statutory)

Even though pupils can now read independently, reading aloud to them should include whole books so that they meet books and authors that they might not choose to read themselves.

The knowledge and skills that pupils need in order to comprehend are very similar at different ages. Pupils should continue to apply what they have already learnt to more complex writing.

Pupils should be taught to recognise themes in what they read, such as loss or heroism. They should have opportunities to compare characters, consider different accounts of the same event and discuss viewpoints (both of authors and of fictional characters), within a text and across more than one text.

They should continue to learn the conventions of different types of writing, such as the use of the first person in writing diaries and autobiographies.

Pupils should be taught the technical and other terms needed for discussing what they hear and read, such as metaphor, simile, analogy, imagery, style and effect.

In using reference books, pupils need to know what information they need to look for before they begin and need to understand the task. They should be shown how to use contents pages and indexes to locate information.

The skills of information retrieval that are taught should be applied, for example, in reading history, geography and science textbooks, and in contexts where pupils are genuinely motivated to find out information, for example, reading information leaflets before a gallery or museum visit or reading a theatre programme or review. Teachers should consider making use of any library services and expertise to support this.

Pupils should have guidance about and feedback on the quality of their explanations and contributions to discussions.

Pupils should be shown how to compare characters, settings, themes and other aspects of what they read.

Writing – transcription

Statutory requirements

Spelling (see English Appendix 1)

Pupils should be taught to:

- use further prefixes and suffixes and understand the guidance for adding them
- spell some words with 'silent' letters [for example, knight, psalm, solemn]
- continue to distinguish between homophones and other words which are often confused
- use knowledge of morphology and etymology in spelling and understand that the spelling of some words needs to be learnt specifically, as listed in English Appendix 1
- use dictionaries to check the spelling and meaning of words
- use the first three or four letters of a word to check spelling, meaning or both of these in a dictionary
- use a thesaurus.

Notes and guidance (non-statutory)

As in earlier years, pupils should continue to be taught to understand and apply the concepts of word structure so that they can draw on their knowledge of morphology and etymology to spell correctly.

Statutory requirements

Writing – handwriting and presentation

Pupils should be taught to:

- write legibly, fluently and with increasing speed by:
  - o choosing which shape of a letter to use when given choices and deciding whether or not to join specific letters
  - o choosing the writing implement that is best suited for a task.

Notes and guidance (non-statutory)

Pupils should continue to practise handwriting and be encouraged to increase the speed of it, so that problems with forming letters do not get in the way of their writing down what they want to say. They should be clear about what standard of handwriting is appropriate for a particular task, for example, quick notes or a final handwritten version. They should also be taught to use an unjoined style, for example, for labelling a diagram or data, writing an email address, or for algebra and capital letters, for example, for filling in a form.

Writing – composition

Statutory requirements

Pupils should be taught to:

- plan their writing by:
  - o identifying the audience for and purpose of the writing, selecting the appropriate form and using other similar writing as models for their own
  - o noting and developing initial ideas, drawing on reading and research where necessary
  - o in writing narratives, considering how authors have developed characters and settings in what pupils have read, listened to or seen performed

(Continued)

(Continued)

- draft and write by:

    o selecting appropriate grammar and vocabulary, understanding how such choices can change and enhance meaning
    o in narratives, describing settings, characters and atmosphere and integrating dialogue to convey character and advance the action
    o précising longer passages
    o using a wide range of devices to build cohesion within and across paragraphs
    o using further organisational and presentational devices to structure text and to guide the reader [for example, headings, bullet points, underlining]

- evaluate and edit by:

    o assessing the effectiveness of their own and others' writing
    o proposing changes to vocabulary, grammar and punctuation to enhance effects and clarify meaning
    o ensuring the consistent and correct use of tense throughout a piece of writing
    o ensuring correct subject and verb agreement when using singular and plural, distinguishing between the language of speech and writing and choosing the appropriate register

- proof-read for spelling and punctuation errors
- perform their own compositions, using appropriate intonation, volume, and movement so that meaning is clear.

Notes and guidance (non-statutory)

Pupils should understand, through being shown, the skills and processes essential for writing: that is, thinking aloud to generate ideas, drafting, and re-reading to check that the meaning is clear.

Writing – vocabulary, grammar and punctuation

Statutory requirements

Pupils should be taught to:

- develop their understanding of the concepts set out in English Appendix 2 by:

    o recognising vocabulary and structures that are appropriate for formal speech and writing, including subjunctive forms
    o using passive verbs to affect the presentation of information in a sentence
    o using the perfect form of verbs to mark relationships of time and cause
    o using expanded noun phrases to convey complicated information concisely
    o using modal verbs or adverbs to indicate degrees of possibility
    o using relative clauses beginning with who, which, where, when, whose, that or with an implied (i.e. omitted) relative pronoun
    o learning the grammar for years 5 and 6 in English Appendix 2

- indicate grammatical and other features by:
  - using commas to clarify meaning or avoid ambiguity in writing
  - using hyphens to avoid ambiguity
  - using brackets, dashes or commas to indicate parenthesis
  - using semi-colons, colons or dashes to mark boundaries between independent clauses
  - using a colon to introduce a list
  - punctuating bullet points consistently

- use and understand the grammatical terminology in English Appendix 2 accurately and appropriately in discussing their writing and reading.

Notes and guidance (non-statutory)

Pupils should continue to add to their knowledge of linguistic terms, including those to describe grammar, so that they can discuss their writing and reading.

English Appendix 1: Spelling

Most people read words more accurately than they spell them. The younger pupils are, the truer this is.

By the end of year 1, pupils should be able to read a large number of different words containing the GPCs that they have learnt, whether or not they have seen these words before. Spelling, however, is a very different matter. Once pupils have learnt more than one way of spelling particular sounds, choosing the right letter or letters depends on their either having made a conscious effort to learn the words or having absorbed them less consciously through their reading. Younger pupils have not had enough time to learn or absorb the accurate spelling of all the words that they may want to write.

This appendix provides examples of words embodying each pattern which is taught. Many of the words listed as 'example words' for years 1 and 2, including almost all those listed as 'exception words', are used frequently in pupils' writing, and therefore it is worth pupils learning the correct spelling. The 'exception words' contain GPCs which have not yet been taught as widely applicable, but this may be because they are applicable in very few age-appropriate words rather than because they are rare in English words in general.

The word lists for years 3 and 4 and years 5 and 6 are statutory. The lists are a mixture of words pupils frequently use in their writing and those which they often misspell. Some of the listed words may be thought of as quite challenging, but the 100 words in each list can easily be taught within the four years of key stage 2 alongside other words that teachers consider appropriate.

The rules and guidance are intended to support the teaching of spelling. Phonic knowledge should continue to underpin spelling after key stage 1; teachers should still draw pupils' attention to GPCs that do and do not fit in with what has been taught so far. Increasingly, however, pupils also need to understand the role of morphology and etymology. Although particular GPCs in root words simply have to be learnt, teachers can help pupils to understand relationships between meaning and spelling where these are relevant. For example, understanding the relationship between *medical* and *medicine* may help pupils to spell the /s/ sound in *medicine* with the letter 'c'. Pupils can also be helped to spell words with prefixes and suffixes correctly if they understand some general principles for adding them. Teachers should be familiar with what pupils have been taught about spelling in earlier years, such as which rules pupils have been taught for adding prefixes and suffixes.

In this spelling appendix, the left-hand column is statutory; the middle and right-hand columns are non-statutory guidance.

The International Phonetic Alphabet (IPA) is used to represent sounds (phonemes). A table showing the IPA is provided in this document.

Spelling – work for year 1

Revision of reception work

Statutory requirements

The boundary between revision of work covered in Reception and the introduction of new work may vary according to the programme used, but basic revision should include:

- all letters of the alphabet and the sounds which they most commonly represent
- consonant digraphs which have been taught and the sounds which they represent
- vowel digraphs which have been taught and the sounds which they represent
- the process of segmenting spoken words into sounds before choosing graphemes to represent the sounds
- words with adjacent consonants
- guidance and rules which have been taught

Statutory requirements	Rules and guidance (non-statutory)	Example words (non-statutory)
The sounds /f/, /l/, /s/, /z/ and /k/ spelt ff, ll, ss, zz and ck	The /f/, /l/, /s/, /z/ and /k/ sounds are usually spelt as **ff**, **ll**, **ss**, **zz** and **ck** if they come straight after a single vowel letter in short words. **Exceptions**: if, pal, us, bus, yes.	off, well, miss, buzz, back
The /ŋ/ sound spelt n before k		bank, think, honk, sunk
Division of words into syllables	Each syllable is like a 'beat' in the spoken word. Words of more than one syllable often have an unstressed syllable in which the vowel sound is unclear.	pocket, rabbit, carrot, thunder, sunset
-tch	The /tʃ/ sound is usually spelt as **tch** if it comes straight after a single vowel letter. **Exceptions**: rich, which, much, such.	catch, fetch, kitchen, notch, hutch
The /v/ sound at the end of words	English words hardly ever end with the letter **v**, so if a word ends with a /v/ sound, the letter **e** usually needs to be added after the 'v'.	have, live, give

Adding s and es to words (plural of nouns and the third person singular of verbs)	If the ending sounds like /s/ or /z/, it is spelt as **-s**. If the ending sounds like /ɪz/ and forms an extra syllable or 'beat' in the word, it is spelt as **-es**.	cats, dogs, spends, rocks, thanks, catches
Adding the endings –ing, –ed and –er to verbs where no change is needed to the root word	**–ing** and **–er** always add an extra syllable to the word and **–ed** sometimes does. The past tense of some verbs may sound as if it ends in /ɪd/ (extra syllable), /d/ or /t/ (no extra syllable), but all these endings are spelt **–ed**. If the verb ends in two consonant letters (the same or different), the ending is simply added on.	hunting, hunted, hunter, buzzing, buzzed, buzzer, jumping, jumped, jumper
Adding –er and –est to adjectives where no change is needed to the root word	As with verbs (see above), if the adjective ends in two consonant letters (the same or different), the ending is simply added on.	grander, grandest, fresher, freshest, quicker, quickest

Vowel digraphs and trigraphs

Some may already be known, depending on the programmes used in Reception, but some will be new.

Vowel digraphs and trigraphs	Rules and guidance (non-statutory)	Example words (non-statutory)
ai, oi	The digraphs ai and oi are virtually never used at the end of English words.	rain, wait, train, paid, afraid oil, join, coin, point, soil
ay, oy	**ay** and **oy** are used for those sounds at the end of words and at the end of syllables.	day, play, say, way, stay boy, toy, enjoy, annoy
a–e		made, came, same, take, safe
e–e		these, theme, complete
i–e		five, ride, like, time, side
o–e		home, those, woke, hope, hole
u–e	Both the /uː/ and /juː/ ('oo' and 'yoo') sounds can be spelt as **u–e**.	June, rule, rude, use, tube, tune
ar		car, start, park, arm, garden
ee		see, tree, green, meet, week
ea (/iː/)		sea, dream, meat, each, read (present tense)

Vowel digraphs and trigraphs	Rules and guidance (non-statutory)	Example words (non-statutory)
ea (/ɛ/)		head, bread, meant, instead, read (past tense)
er (/ɜ:/)		(stressed sound): her, term, verb, person
er (/ə/)		(unstressed *schwa* sound): better, under, summer, winter, sister
ir		girl, bird, shirt, first, third
ur		turn, hurt, church, burst, Thursday
oo (/u:/)	Very few words end with the letters **oo**, although the few that do are often words that primary children in year 1 will encounter, for example, *zoo*	food, pool, moon, zoo, soon
oo (/ʊ/)		book, took, foot, wood, good
oa	The digraph **oa** is very rare at the end of an English word.	boat, coat, road, coach, goal
oe		toe, goes
ou	The only common English word ending in **ou** is *you*.	out, about, mouth, around, sound
ow (/aʊ/) ow (/əʊ/) ue ew	Both the /u:/ and /ju:/ ('oo' and 'yoo') sounds can be spelt as **u–e**, **ue** and **ew**. If words end in the /oo/ sound, **ue** and **ew** are more common spellings than **oo**.	now, how, brown, down, town own, blow, snow, grow, show blue, clue, true, rescue, Tuesday new, few, grew, flew, drew, threw
ie (/aɪ/)		lie, tie, pie, cried, tried, dried
ie (/i:/)		chief, field, thief
igh		high, night, light, bright, right
or		for, short, born, horse, morning
ore		more, score, before, wore, shore
aw		saw, draw, yawn, crawl
au		author, August, dinosaur, astronaut

air		air, fair, pair, hair, chair
ear		dear, hear, beard, near, year
ear (/ɛə/)		bear, pear, wear
are (/ɛə/)		bare, dare, care, share, scared

Statutory requirements	Rules and guidance (non-statutory)	Example words (non-statutory)
Words ending –y (/i:/ or /ɪ/)		very, happy, funny, party, family
New consonant spellings ph and wh	The /f/ sound is not usually spelt as **ph** in short everyday words (e.g. *fat*, *fill*, *fun*).	dolphin, alphabet, phonics, elephant when, where, which, wheel, while
Using k for the /k/ sound	The /k/ sound is spelt as **k** rather than as **c** before **e, i** and **y**.	Kent, sketch, kit, skin, frisky
Adding the prefix –un	The prefix **un–** is added to the beginning of a word without any change to the spelling of the root word.	unhappy, undo, unload, unfair, unlock
Compound words	Compound words are two words joined together. Each part of the longer word is spelt as it would be if it were on its own.	football, playground, farmyard, bedroom, blackberry
Common exception words	Pupils' attention should be drawn to the grapheme-phoneme correspondences that do and do not fit in with what has been taught so far.	the, a, do, to, today, of, said, says, are, were, was, is, his, has, I, you, your, they, be, he, me, she, we, no, go, so, by, my, here, there, where, love, come, some, one, once, ask, friend, school, put, push, pull, full, house, our – and/or others, according to the programme used

Spelling – work for year 2

Revision of work from year 1

As words with new GPCs are introduced, many previously-taught GPCs can be revised at the same time as these words will usually contain them.

New work for year 2

Statutory requirements	Rules and guidance (non-statutory)	Example words (non-statutory)
The /dʒ/ sound spelt as ge and dge at the end of words, and sometimes spelt as g elsewhere in words before e, i and y	The letter j is never used for the /dʒ/ sound at the end of English words.	
	At the end of a word, the /dʒ/ sound is spelt –**dge** straight after the /æ/, /ɛ/, /ɪ/, /ɒ/, /ʌ/ and /ʊ/ sounds (sometimes called 'short' vowels).	badge, edge, bridge, dodge, fudge
	After all other sounds, whether vowels or consonants, the /dʒ/ sound is spelt as –**ge** at the end of a word.	age, huge, change, charge, bulge, village
	In other positions in words, the /dʒ/ sound is often (but not always) spelt as g before e, i, and y. The /dʒ/ sound is always spelt as j before a, o and u.	gem, giant, magic, giraffe, energy, jacket, jar, jog, join, adjust
The /s/ sound spelt c before e, i and y		race, ice, cell, city, fancy
The /n/ sound spelt kn and (less often) gn at the beginning of words	The 'k' and 'g' at the beginning of these words was sounded hundreds of years ago.	knock, know, knee, gnat, gnaw
The /r/ sound spelt wr at the beginning of words	This spelling probably also reflects an old pronunciation.	write, written, wrote, wrong, wrap
The /l/ or /əl/ sound spelt –le at the end of words	The –**le** spelling is the most common spelling for this sound at the end of words.	table, apple, bottle, little, middle
The /l/ or /əl/ sound spelt –el at the end of words	The –**el** spelling is much less common than –**le**. The –**el** spelling is used after **m, n, r, s, v, w** and more often than not after **s**.	camel, tunnel, squirrel, travel, towel, tinsel
The /l/ or /əl/ sound spelt –al at the end of words	Not many nouns end in –**al**, but many adjectives do.	metal, pedal, capital, hospital, animal
Words ending –il	There are not many of these words.	pencil, fossil, nostril
The /aɪ/ sound spelt –y at the end of words	This is by far the most common spelling for this sound at the end of words.	cry, fly, dry, try, reply, July

Adding –es to nouns and verbs ending in –y	The **y** is changed to **i** before **–es** is added.	flies, tries, replies, copies, babies, carries
Adding –ed, –ing, –er and –est to a root word ending in –y with a consonant before it	The **y** is changed to **i** before **–ed**, **–er** and **–est** are added, but not before **– ing** as this would result in **ii**. The only ordinary words with **ii** are *skiing* and *taxiing*.	copied, copier, happier, happiest, cried, replied ...**but** copying, crying, replying
Adding the endings – ing, –ed, –er, –est and –y to words ending in –e with a consonant before it	The **–e** at the end of the root word is dropped before **–ing**, **–ed**, **–er**, **–est**, **–y** or any other suffix beginning with a vowel letter is added. **Exception:** *being*.	hiking, hiked, hiker, nicer, nicest, shiny
Adding –ing, –ed, –er, –est and –y to words of one syllable ending in a single consonant letter after a single vowel letter	The last consonant letter of the root word is doubled to keep the /æ/, /ɛ/, /ɪ/, /ɒ/ and /ʌ/ sound (i.e. to keep the vowel 'short'). **Exception:** The letter 'x' is never doubled: *mixing, mixed, boxer, sixes.*	patting, patted, humming, hummed, dropping, dropped, sadder, saddest, fatter, fattest, runner, runny
The /ɔ:/ sound spelt a before l and ll	The /ɔ:/ sound ('or') is usually spelt as **a** before **l** and **ll**.	all, ball, call, walk, talk, always
The /ʌ/ sound spelt o		other, mother, brother, nothing, Monday
The /i:/ sound spelt –ey	The plural of these words is formed by the addition of **–s** (*donkeys, monkeys*, etc.).	key, donkey, monkey, chimney, valley
The /ɒ/ sound spelt a after w and qu	**a** is the most common spelling for the /ɒ/ ('h<u>o</u>t') sound after **w** and **qu**.	want, watch, wander, quantity, squash
The /ɜ:/ sound spelt or after w	There are not many of these words.	word, work, worm, world, worth
The /ɔ:/ sound spelt ar after w	There are not many of these words.	war, warm, towards
The /ʒ/ sound spelt s		television, treasure, usual
The suffixes –ment, –ness, –ful , –less and –ly	If a suffix starts with a consonant letter, it is added straight on to most root words without any change to the last letter of those words. **Exceptions:** (1) *argument* (2) root words ending in –y with a consonant before it but only if the root word has more than one syllable.	enjoyment, sadness, careful, playful, hopeless, plainness (plain + ness), badly merriment, happiness, plentiful, penniless, happily

Statutory requirements	Rules and guidance (non-statutory)	Example words (non-statutory)
Contractions	In contractions, the apostrophe shows where a letter or letters would be if the words were written in full (e.g. *can't – cannot*). *It's* means *it is* (e.g. *It's* raining) or sometimes *it has* (e.g. *It's* been raining), but *it's* is never used for the possessive.	can't, didn't, hasn't, couldn't, it's, I'll
The possessive apostrophe (singular nouns)		Megan's, Ravi's, the girl's, the child's, the man's
Words ending in –tion		station, fiction, motion, national, section
Homophones and near-homophones	It is important to know the difference in meaning between homophones.	there/their/they're, here/hear, quite/quiet, see/sea, bare/bear, one/won, sun/son, to/too/two, be/bee, blue/blew, night/knight
Common exception words	Some words are exceptions in some accents but not in others – e.g. *past, last, fast, path* and *bath* are not exceptions in accents where the **a** in these words is pronounced /æ/, as in *cat*. *Great, break* and *steak* are the only common words where the /eɪ/ sound is spelt **ea**.	door, floor, poor, because, find, kind, mind, behind, child, children*, wild, climb, most, only, both, old, cold, gold, hold, told, every, everybody, even, great, break, steak, pretty, beautiful, after, fast, last, past, father, class, grass, pass, plant, path, bath, hour, move, prove, improve, sure, sugar, eye, could, should, would, who, whole, any, many, clothes, busy, people, water, again, half, money, Mr, Mrs, parents, Christmas – and/or others according to programme used. **Note:** 'children' is not an exception to what has been taught so far but is included because of its relationship with 'child'.

Spelling – work for years 3 and 4

Revision of work from years 1 and 2

Pay special attention to the rules for adding suffixes.

New work for years 3 and 4

Statutory requirements	Rules and guidance (non-statutory)	Example words (non-statutory)
Adding suffixes beginning with vowel letters to words of more than one syllable	If the last syllable of a word is stressed and ends with one consonant letter which has just one vowel letter before it, the final consonant letter is doubled before any ending beginning with a vowel letter is added. The consonant letter is not doubled if the syllable is unstressed.	forgetting, forgotten, beginning, beginner, prefer, preferred gardening, gardener, limiting, limited, limitation
The /ɪ/ sound spelt y elsewhere than at the end of words	These words should be learnt as needed.	myth, gym, Egypt, pyramid, mystery
The /ʌ/ sound spelt ou	These words should be learnt as needed.	young, touch, double, trouble, country
More prefixes	Most prefixes are added to the beginning of root words without any changes in spelling, but see **in–** below. Like **un–**, the prefixes **dis–** and **mis–** have negative meanings. The prefix **in–** can mean both 'not' and 'in'/'into'. In the words given here it means 'not'.	**dis–**: disappoint, disagree, disobey **mis–**: misbehave, mislead, misspell (mis + spell) **in–**: inactive, incorrect
	Before a root word starting with **l**, **in–** becomes **il**.	illegal, illegible
	Before a root word starting with **m** or **p**, **in–** becomes **im–**.	immature, immortal, impossible, impatient, imperfect
	Before a root word starting with **r**, **in–** becomes **ir–**.	irregular, irrelevant, irresponsible
	re– means 'again' or 'back'.	**re–**: redo, refresh, return, reappear, redecorate

Statutory requirements	Rules and guidance (non-statutory)	Example words (non-statutory)
	sub– means 'under'.	**sub–:** subdivide, subheading, submarine, submerge
	inter– means 'between' or 'among'.	**inter–:** interact, intercity, international, interrelated (inter + related)
	super– means 'above'.	**super–:** supermarket, superman, superstar
	anti– means 'against'.	**anti–:** antiseptic, anti-clockwise, antisocial
	auto– means 'self' or 'own'.	**auto–:** autobiography, autograph
The suffix –ation	The suffix –**ation** is added to verbs to form nouns. The rules already learnt still apply.	information, adoration, sensation, preparation, admiration
The suffix –ly	The suffix –**ly** is added to an adjective to form an adverb. The rules already learnt still apply. The suffix –**ly** starts with a consonant letter, so it is added straight on to most root words.	sadly, completely, usually (usual + ly), finally (final + ly), comically (comical + ly)
	Exceptions: (1) If the root word ends in –y with a consonant letter before it, the **y** is changed to **i**, but only if the root word has more than one syllable.	happily, angrily
	(2) If the root word ends with –**le**, the –**le** is changed to –**ly**.	gently, simply, humbly, nobly
	(3) If the root word ends with –**ic**, –**ally** is added rather than just –**ly**, except in the word *publicly*.	basically, frantically, dramatically
	(4) The words *truly, duly, wholly*.	
Words with endings sounding like /ʒə/ or /tʃə/	The ending sounding like /ʒə/ is always spelt –**sure**. The ending sounding like /tʃə/ is often spelt –**ture**, but check that the word is not a root word ending in **(t)ch** with an **er** ending – e.g. *teacher, catcher, richer, stretcher*.	measure, treasure, pleasure, enclosure creature, furniture, picture, nature, adventure
Endings which sound like /ʒən/	If the ending sounds like /ʒən/, it is spelt as –**sion**.	division, invasion, confusion, decision, collision, television

The suffix –ous	Sometimes the root word is obvious and the usual rules apply for adding suffixes beginning with vowel letters.	poisonous, dangerous, mountainous, famous, various
	Sometimes there is no obvious root word.	tremendous, enormous, jealous
	–our is changed to **–or** before **–ous** is added.	humorous, glamorous, vigorous
	A final 'e' of the root word must be kept if the /dʒ/ sound of 'g' is to be kept.	courageous, outrageous
	If there is an /iː/ sound before the **–ous** ending, it is usually spelt as **i**, but a few words have **e**.	serious, obvious, curious hideous, spontaneous, courteous
Endings which sound like /ʃən/, spelt –tion, –sion, –ssion, –cian	Strictly speaking, the suffixes are **–ion** and **–ian**. Clues about whether to put **t**, **s**, **ss** or **c** before these suffixes often come from the last letter or letters of the root word.	
	–tion is the most common spelling. It is used if the root word ends in **t** or **te**.	invention, injection, action, hesitation, completion
	–ssion is used if the root word ends in **ss** or **–mit.**	expression, discussion, confession, permission, admission
	–sion is used if the root word ends in **d** or **se.** **Exceptions:** *attend – attention, intend – intention.*	expansion, extension, comprehension, tension
	–cian is used if the root word ends in **c** or **cs.**	musician, electrician, magician, politician, mathematician
Words with the /k/ sound spelt ch (Greek in origin)		scheme, chorus, chemist, echo, character
Words with the /ʃ/ sound spelt ch (mostly French in origin)		chef, chalet, machine, brochure
Words ending with the /g/ sound spelt –gue and the /k/ sound spelt –que (French in origin)		league, tongue, antique, unique

Statutory requirements	Rules and guidance (non-statutory)	Example words (non-statutory)
Words with the /s/ sound spelt sc (Latin in origin)	In the Latin words from which these words come, the Romans probably pronounced the **c** and the **k** as two sounds rather than one –/s//k/.	science, scene, discipline, fascinate, crescent
Words with the /eɪ/ sound spelt ei, eigh, or ey		vein, weigh, eight, neighbour, they, obey
Possessive apostrophe with plural words	The apostrophe is placed after the plural form of the word; –**s** is not added if the plural already ends in –**s**, but *is* added if the plural does not end in –**s** (i.e. is an irregular plural – e.g. *children's*).	girls', boys', babies', children's, men's, mice's (**Note:** singular proper nouns ending in an *s* use the 's suffix e.g. Cyprus's population)
Homophones and near-homophones		accept/except, affect/effect, ball/bawl, berry/bury, brake/break, fair/fare, grate/great, groan/grown, here/hear, heel/heal/he'll, knot/not, mail/male, main/mane, meat/meet, medal/meddle, missed/mist, peace/piece, plain/plane, rain/rein/reign, scene/seen, weather/whether, whose/who's

Word list – years 3 and 4

accident(ally)	certain	experiment	important
actual(ly)	circle	extreme	increase
address	complete	famous	interest
answer	consider	favourite	island
appear	continue	February	knowledge
arrive	decide	forward(s)	learn
believe	describe	fruit	length
bicycle	different	grammar	library
breath	difficult	group	material
breathe	disappear	guard	medicine
build	early	guide	mention
busy/business	earth	heard	minute
calendar	eight/eighth	heart	natural
caught	enough	height	naughty
centre	exercise	history	notice
century	experience	imagine	occasion(ally)

often	possible	regular	suppose
opposite	potatoes	reign	surprise
ordinary	pressure	remember	therefore
particular	probably	sentence	though/although
peculiar	promise	separate	thought
perhaps	purpose	special	through
popular	quarter	straight	various
position	question	strange	weight
possess(ion)	recent	strength	woman/women

Notes and guidance (non-statutory)

Teachers should continue to emphasise to pupils the relationships between sounds and letters, even when the relationships are unusual. Once root words are learnt in this way, longer words can be spelt correctly, if the rules and guidance for adding prefixes and suffixes are also known.
Examples:

- *business*: once busy is learnt, with due attention to the unusual spelling of the /i/ sound as 'u', business can then be spelt as **busy** + **ness**, with the **y** of **busy** changed to **i** according to the rule.
- *disappear*: the root word *appear* contains sounds which can be spelt in more than one way so it needs to be learnt, but the prefix **dis**– is then simply added to **appear**.

Understanding the relationships between words can also help with spelling. *Examples:*

- *bicycle* is *cycle* (from the Greek for *wheel*) with **bi**– (meaning 'two') before it.
- *medicine* is related to *medical* so the /s/ sound is spelt as **c**.
- *opposite* is related to *oppose*, so the schwa sound in *opposite* is spelt as **o**.

Spelling – years 5 and 6

Revise work done in previous years

New work for years 5 and 6

Statutory requirements	Rules and guidance (non-statutory)	Example words (non-statutory)
Endings which sound like /ʃəs/ spelt –cious or –tious	Not many common words end like this. If the root word ends in –**ce**, the /ʃ/ sound is usually spelt as **c** – e.g. *vice – vicious, grace – gracious, space –spacious, malice – malicious.* **Exception:** *anxious.*	vicious, precious, conscious, delicious, malicious, suspicious ambitious, cautious, fictitious, infectious, nutritious

Statutory requirements	Rules and guidance (non-statutory)	Example words (non-statutory)
Endings which sound like /ʃəl/	**–cial** is common after a vowel letter and **–tial** after a consonant letter, but there are some exceptions. **Exceptions:** initial, financial, commercial, provincial (the spelling of the last three is clearly related to *finance, commerce* and *province*).	official, special, artificial, partial, confidential, essential
Words ending in –ant, –ance/–ancy, –ent, –ence/–ency	Use **–ant** and **–ance/–ancy** if there is a related word with a /æ/ or /eɪ/ sound in the right position; **–ation** endings are often a clue.	observant, observance, (observation), expectant (expectation), hesitant, hesitancy (hesitation), tolerant, tolerance (toleration), substance (substantial)
	Use **–ent** and **–ence/–ency** after soft **c** (/s/ sound), soft **g** (/dʒ/ sound) and **qu**, or if there is a related word with a clear /ɛ/ sound in the right position.	innocent, innocence, decent, decency, frequent, frequency, confident, confidence (confidential)
	There are many words, however, where the above guidance does not help. These words just have to be learnt.	assistant, assistance, obedient, obedience, independent, independence
Words ending in –able and –ible Words ending in –ably and –ibly	The **–able/–ably** endings are far more common than the **–ible/–ibly** endings. As with **–ant** and **–ance/–ancy**, the **–able** ending is used if there is a related word ending in **–ation**.	adorable/adorably (adoration), applicable/ applicably (application), considerable/considerably (consideration), tolerable/ tolerably (toleration)
	If the **–able** ending is added to a word ending in **–ce** or **–ge**, the **e** after the **c** or **g** must be kept as those letters would otherwise have their 'hard' sounds (as in *cap* and *gap*) before the **a** of the **–able** ending.	changeable, noticeable, forcible, legible
	The **–able** ending is usually but not always used if a complete root word can be heard before it, even if there is no related word ending in **–ation**. The first five examples opposite are obvious; in *reliable*, the complete word *rely* is heard, but the **y** changes to **i** in accordance with the rule.	dependable, comfortable, understandable, reasonable, enjoyable, reliable
	The **–ible** ending is common if a complete root word can't be heard before it but it also sometimes occurs when a complete word *can* be heard (e.g. *sensible*).	possible/possibly, horrible/ horribly, terrible/terribly, visible/visibly, incredible/ incredibly, sensible/ sensibly

Adding suffixes beginning with vowel letters to words ending in –fer	The **r** is doubled if the **–fer** is still stressed when the ending is added. The **r** is not doubled if the **–fer** is no longer stressed.	referring, referred, referral, preferring, preferred, transferring, transferred reference, referee, preference, transference
Use of the hyphen	Hyphens can be used to join a prefix to a root word, especially if the prefix ends in a vowel letter and the root word also begins with one.	co-ordinate, re-enter, co-operate, co-own
Words with the /i:/ sound spelt ei after c	The '**i** before **e** except after **c**' rule applies to words where the sound spelt by **ei** is /i:/. **Exceptions:** *protein, caffeine, seize* (and *either* and *neither* if pronounced with an initial /i:/ sound).	deceive, conceive, receive, perceive, ceiling
Words containing the letter-string ough	**ough** is one of the trickiest spellings in English – it can be used to spell a number of different sounds.	ought, bought, thought, nought, brought, fought rough, tough, enough cough though, although, dough through thorough, borough plough, bough
Words with 'silent' letters (i.e. letters whose presence cannot be predicted from the pronunciation of the word)	Some letters which are no longer sounded used to be sounded hundreds of years ago: e.g. in *knight*, there was a /k/ sound before the /n/, and the **gh** used to represent the sound that 'ch' now represents in the Scottish word *loch*.	doubt, island, lamb, solemn, thistle, knight
Homophones and other words that are often confused	In the pairs of words opposite, nouns end **–ce** and verbs end **–se**. *Advice* and *advise* provide a useful clue as the word *advise* (verb) is pronounced with a /z/ sound – which could not be spelt **c**. More examples: aisle: a gangway between seats (in a church, train, plane). isle: an island. aloud: out loud. allowed: permitted. affect: usually a verb (e.g. *The weather may affect our plans*).	advice/advise device/devise licence/license practice/practise prophecy/prophesy farther: further father: a male parent guessed: past tense of the verb *guess* guest: visitor heard: past tense of the verb *hear*

Statutory requirements	Rules and guidance (non-statutory)	Example words (non-statutory)
Homophones and other words that are often confused (continued)	effect: usually a noun (e.g. *It may have an effect on our plans*). If a verb, it means 'bring about' (e.g. *He will effect changes in the running of the business*). altar: a table-like piece of furniture in a church. alter: to change. ascent: the act of ascending (going up). assent: to agree/agreement (verb and noun). bridal: to do with a bride at a wedding. bridle: reins etc. for controlling a horse. cereal: made from grain (e.g. breakfast cereal). serial: adjective from the noun *series* – a succession of things one after the other. compliment: to make nice remarks about someone (verb) or the remark that is made (noun). complement: related to the word *complete* – to make something complete or more complete (e.g. *her scarf complemented her outfit*). descent: the act of descending (going down). dissent: to disagree/disagreement (verb and noun). desert: as a noun – a barren place (stress on first syllable); as a verb – to abandon (stress on second syllable) dessert: (stress on second syllable) a sweet course after the main course of a meal. draft: noun – a first attempt at writing something; verb – to make the first attempt; also, to draw in someone (e.g. *to draft in extra help*) draught: a current of air.	herd: a group of animals led: past tense of the verb *lead* lead: present tense of that verb, or else the metal which is very heavy (*as heavy as lead*) morning: before noon mourning: grieving for someone who has died past: noun or adjective referring to a previous time (e.g. *In the past*) or preposition or adverb showing place (e.g. *he walked past me*) passed: past tense of the verb 'pass' (e.g. *I passed him in the road*) precede: go in front of or before proceed: go on principal: adjective – most important (e.g. *principal ballerina*) noun – important person (e.g. *principal of a college*) principle: basic truth or belief profit: money that is made in selling things prophet: someone who foretells the future stationary: not moving stationery: paper, envelopes etc. steal: take something that does not belong to you steel: metal wary: cautious weary: tired who's: contraction of *who is* or *who has* whose: belonging to someone (e.g. *Whose jacket is that?*)

Word list – years 5 and 6

accommodate	correspond	identity	queue
accompany	criticise (critic + ise)	immediate(ly)	recognise
according	curiosity	individual	recommend
achieve	definite	interfere	relevant
aggressive	desperate	interrupt	restaurant
amateur	determined	language	rhyme
ancient	develop	leisure	rhythm
apparent	dictionary	lightning	sacrifice
appreciate	disastrous	marvellous	secretary
attached	embarrass	mischievous	shoulder
available	environment	muscle	signature
average	equip (–ped, –ment)	necessary	sincere(ly)
awkward	especially	neighbour	soldier
bargain	exaggerate	nuisance	stomach
bruise	excellent	occupy	sufficient
category	existence	occur	suggest
cemetery	explanation	opportunity	symbol
committee	familiar	parliament	system
communicate	foreign	persuade	temperature
community	forty	physical	thorough
competition	frequently	prejudice	twelfth
conscience*	government	privilege	variety
conscious*	guarantee	profession	vegetable
controversy	harass	programme	vehicle
convenience	hindrance	pronunciation	yacht

Notes and guidance (non-statutory)

Teachers should continue to emphasise to pupils the relationships between sounds and letters, even when the relationships are unusual. Once root words are learnt in this way, longer words can be spelt correctly if the rules and guidance for adding prefixes and suffixes are also known. Many of the words in the list above can be used for practice in adding suffixes.

Understanding the history of words and relationships between them can also help with spelling.

Examples:

- *Conscience* and *conscious* are related to *science*: *conscience* is simply *science* with the prefix *con-* added. These words come from the Latin word *scio* meaning *I know*.
- The word *desperate*, meaning 'without hope', is often pronounced in English as *desp'rate*, but the *–sper-* part comes from the Latin *spero*, meaning 'I hope', in which the **e** was clearly sounded.
- *Familiar* is related to *family*, so the /ə/ sound in the first syllable of *familiar* is spelt as **a**.

International Phonetic Alphabet (non-statutory)

The table below shows each symbol of the International Phonetic Alphabet (IPA) and provides examples of the associated grapheme(s). The table is not a comprehensive alphabetic code chart; it is intended simply as guidance for teachers in understanding the IPA symbols used in the spelling appendix (English Appendix 1). The pronunciations in the table are, by convention, based on Received Pronunciation and could be significantly different in other accents.

Consonants	
/b/	bad
/d/	dog
/ð/	this
/dʒ/	gem, jug
/f/	if, puff, photo
/g/	gum
/h/	how
/j/	yes
/k/	cat, check, key, school
/l/	leg, hill
/m/	man
/n/	man
/ŋ/	sing
/θ/	both
/p/	pet
/r/	red
/s/	sit, miss, cell
/ʃ/	she, chef
/t/	tea
/tʃ/	check
/v/	vet
/w/	wet, when
/z/	zip, hens, buzz
/ʒ/	pleasure

Vowels	
/ɑ:/	father, arm
/ɒ/	hot
/æ/	cat
/aɪ/	mind, fine, pie, high
/aʊ/	out, cow
/ɛ/	hen, head
/eɪ/	say, came, bait
/ɛə/	air
/əʊ/	cold, boat, cone, blow
/ɪ/	hit
/ɪə/	beer
/i:/	she, bead, see, scheme, chief
/ɔ:/	launch, raw, born
/ɔɪ/	coin, boy
/ʊ/	book
/ʊə/	tour
/u:/	room, you, blue, brute
/ʌ/	cup
/3:/	fern, turn, girl
/ə/	farmer

English Appendix 2: Vocabulary, grammar and punctuation

The grammar of our first language is learnt naturally and implicitly through interactions with other speakers and from reading. Explicit knowledge of grammar is, however, very important, as it gives us more conscious control and choice in our language. Building this knowledge is best achieved through a focus on grammar within the teaching of reading, writing and speaking. Once pupils are familiar with a grammatical concept [for example 'modal verb'], they should be encouraged to apply and explore this concept in the grammar of their own speech and writing and to note where it is used by others. Young pupils, in particular, use more complex language in speech than in writing, and teachers should build on this, aiming for a smooth transition to sophisticated writing.

The table below focuses on Standard English and should be read in conjunction with the programmes of study as it sets out the statutory requirements. The table shows when concepts should be introduced first, not necessarily when they should be completely understood. It is very important, therefore, that the content in earlier years be revisited in subsequent years to consolidate knowledge and build on pupils' understanding. Teachers should also go beyond the content set out here if they feel it is appropriate.

The grammatical terms that pupils should learn are labelled as 'terminology for pupils'. They should learn to recognise and use the terminology through discussion and practice. All terms in **bold** should be understood with the meanings set out in the Glossary.

Vocabulary, grammar and punctuation – Years 1 to 6

Year 1: Detail of content to be introduced (statutory requirement)	
Word	Regular **plural noun suffixes** –s or –es [for example, *dog, dogs; wish, wishes*], including the effects of these suffixes on the meaning of the noun **Suffixes** that can be added to **verbs** where no change is needed in the spelling of root words (e.g. *helping, helped, helper*) How the **prefix** *un–* changes the meaning of **verbs** and **adjectives** [negation, for example, *unkind*, or *undoing: untie the boat*]
Sentence	How **words** can combine to make **sentences** Joining **words** and joining **clauses** using *and*
Text	Sequencing **sentences** to form short narratives
Punctuation	Separation of **words** with spaces Introduction to capital letters, full stops, question marks and exclamation marks to demarcate **sentences** Capital letters for names and for the personal **pronoun** *I*
Terminology for pupils	letter, capital letter word, singular, plural sentence punctuation, full stop, question mark, exclamation mark

Year 2: Detail of content to be introduced (statutory requirement)	
Word	Formation of **nouns** using **suffixes** such as *–ness, –er* and by compounding [for example, *whiteboard, superman*] Formation of **adjectives** using **suffixes** such as *–ful, –less* (A fuller list of **suffixes** can be found on page 53 in the year 2 spelling section in English Appendix 1) Use of the **suffixes** *–er, –est* in **adjectives** and the use of *–ly* in Standard English to turn adjectives into **adverbs**

Year 2: Detail of content to be introduced (statutory requirement)	
Sentence	**Subordination** (using *when, if, that, because*) and **co-ordination** (using *or, and, but*)
	Expanded **noun phrases** for description and specification [for example, *the blue butterfly, plain flour, the man in the moon*]
	How the grammatical patterns in a sentence indicate its function as a statement, question, exclamation or command
Text	Correct choice and consistent use of **present tense** and **past tense** throughout writing
	Use of the **progressive** form of **verbs** in the **present** and **past tense** to mark actions in progress [for example, *she is drumming, he was shouting*]
Punctuation	Use of capital letters, full stops, question marks and exclamation marks to demarcate **sentences**
	Commas to separate items in a list
	Apostrophes to mark where letters are missing in spelling and to mark singular possession in nouns [for example, *the girl's name*]
Terminology for pupils	noun, noun phrase
	statement, question, exclamation, command
	compound, suffix
	adjective, adverb, verb
	tense (past, present)
	apostrophe, comma

Year 3: Detail of content to be introduced (statutory requirement)	
Word	Formation of **nouns** using a range of **prefixes** [for example *super–, anti–, auto–*]
	Use of the **forms** *a* or *an* according to whether the next **word** begins with a **consonant** or a **vowel** [for example, *a rock, an open box*]
	Word families based on common **words**, showing how words are related in form and meaning [for example, *solve, solution, solver, dissolve, insoluble*]
Sentence	Expressing time, place and cause using **conjunctions** [for example, *when, before, after, while, so, because*], **adverbs** [for example, *then, next, soon, therefore*], or **prepositions** [for example, *before, after, during, in, because of*]
Text	Introduction to paragraphs as a way to group related material
	Headings and sub-headings to aid presentation
	Use of the **present perfect** form of **verbs** instead of the simple past [for example, *He has gone out to play* contrasted with *He went out to play*]
Punctuation	Introduction to inverted commas to **punctuate** direct speech
Terminology for pupils	preposition, conjunction
	word family, prefix
	clause, subordinate clause
	direct speech
	consonant, consonant letter vowel, vowel letter
	inverted commas (or 'speech marks')

Year 4: Detail of content to be introduced (statutory requirement)	
Word	The grammatical difference between **plural** and **possessive** –s
	Standard English forms for **verb inflections** instead of local spoken forms [for example, *we were* instead of *we was*, or *I did* instead of *I done*]
Sentence	Noun phrases expanded by the addition of modifying adjectives, nouns and preposition phrases (e.g. *the teacher* expanded to: *the strict maths teacher with curly hair*)
	Fronted adverbials [for example, *Later that day*, I heard the bad news.]
Text	Use of paragraphs to organise ideas around a theme
	Appropriate choice of **pronoun** or **noun** within and across **sentences** to aid **cohesion** and avoid repetition
Punctuation	Use of inverted commas and other **punctuation** to indicate direct speech [for example, a comma after the reporting clause; end punctuation within inverted commas: *The conductor shouted, "Sit down!"*]
	Apostrophes to mark **plural** possession [for example, *the girl's name, the girls' names*]
	Use of commas after **fronted adverbials**
Terminology for pupils	determiner
	pronoun, possessive pronoun
	adverbial

Year 5: Detail of content to be introduced (statutory requirement)	
Word	Converting **nouns** or **adjectives** into **verbs** using **suffixes** [for example, *–ate; –ise; –ify*]
	Verb prefixes [for example, *dis–, de–, mis–, over–* and *re–*]
Sentence	**Relative clauses** beginning with *who, which, where, when, whose, that*, or an omitted relative pronoun
	Indicating degrees of possibility using **adverbs** [for example, *perhaps, surely*] or **modal verbs** [for example, *might, should, will, must*]
Text	Devices to build **cohesion** within a paragraph [for example, *then, after that, this, firstly*]
	Linking ideas across paragraphs using **adverbials** of time [for example, *later*], place [for example, *nearby*] and number [for example, *secondly*] or tense choices [for example, he *had* seen her before]
Punctuation	Brackets, dashes or commas to indicate parenthesis
	Use of commas to clarify meaning or avoid ambiguity
Terminology for pupils	modal verb, relative pronoun
	relative clause
	parenthesis, bracket, dash
	cohesion, ambiguity

Year 6: Detail of content to be introduced (statutory requirement)	
Word	The difference between vocabulary typical of informal speech and vocabulary appropriate for formal speech and writing [for example, *find out – discover; ask for – request; go in – enter*]
	How words are related by meaning as synonyms and antonyms [for example, *big, large, little*].
Sentence	Use of the **passive** to affect the presentation of information in a **sentence** [for example, *I broke the window in the greenhouse* versus *The window in the greenhouse was broken (by me)*].
	The difference between structures typical of informal speech and structures appropriate for formal speech and writing [for example, the use of question tags: *He's your friend, isn't he?*, or the use of **subjunctive** forms such as *If I were* or *Were they to come* in some very formal writing and speech]
Text	Linking ideas across paragraphs using a wider range of **cohesive devices**: repetition of a **word** or phrase, grammatical connections [for example, the use of **adverbials** such as *on the other hand, in contrast*, or *as a consequence*], and **ellipsis**
	Layout devices [for example, headings, sub-headings, columns, bullets, or tables, to structure text]
Punctuation	Use of the semi-colon, colon and dash to mark the boundary between independent **clauses** [for example, *It's raining; I'm fed up*]
	Use of the colon to introduce a list and use of semi-colons within lists
	Punctuation of bullet points to list information
	How hyphens can be used to avoid ambiguity [for example, *man eating shark* versus *man-eating shark*, or *recover* versus *re-cover*]
Terminology for pupils	subject, object
	active, passive
	synonym, antonym
	ellipsis, hyphen, colon, semi-colon, bullet points

Key stages 3 and 4

Spoken language

The national curriculum for English reflects the importance of spoken language in pupils' development across the whole curriculum – cognitively, socially and linguistically. Spoken language continues to underpin the development of pupils' reading and writing during key stages 3 and 4 and teachers should therefore ensure pupils' confidence and competence in this area continue to develop. Pupils should be taught to understand and use the conventions for discussion and debate, as well as continuing to develop their skills in working collaboratively with their peers to discuss reading, writing and speech across the curriculum.

Reading and writing

Reading at key stages 3 and 4 should be wide, varied and challenging. Pupils should be expected to read whole books, to read in depth and to read for pleasure and information.

Pupils should continue to develop their knowledge of and skills in writing, refining their drafting skills and developing resilience to write at length. They should be taught to write formal and academic essays as well as writing imaginatively. They should be taught to write for a variety of purposes and audiences across a range of contexts. This requires an increasingly wide knowledge of vocabulary and grammar.

Opportunities for teachers to enhance pupils' vocabulary will arise naturally from their reading and writing. Teachers should show pupils how to understand the relationships between words, how to understand nuances in meaning, and how to develop their understanding of, and ability to use, figurative language.

Pupils should be taught to control their speaking and writing consciously, understand why sentences are constructed as they are and to use Standard English. They should understand and use age-appropriate vocabulary, including linguistic and literary terminology, for discussing their reading, writing and spoken language. This involves consolidation, practice and discussion of language. It is important that pupils learn the correct grammatical terms in English and that these terms are integrated within teaching.

Teachers should build on the knowledge and skills that pupils have been taught at earlier key stages. Decisions about progression should be based on the security of pupils' linguistic knowledge, skills and understanding and their readiness to progress to the next stage. Pupils whose linguistic development is more advanced should be challenged through being offered opportunities for increased breadth and depth in reading and writing. Those who are less fluent should consolidate their knowledge, understanding and skills, including through additional practice.

Glossary

A non-statutory Glossary is provided for teachers.

Key stage 3 subject content

Reading

Pupils should be taught to:

- develop an appreciation and love of reading, and read increasingly challenging material independently through:

- reading a wide range of fiction and non-fiction, including in particular whole books, short stories, poems and plays with a wide coverage of genres, historical periods, forms and authors. The range will include high-quality works from:

  - English literature, both pre-1914 and contemporary, including prose, poetry and drama
  - Shakespeare (two plays)
  - seminal world literature

- choosing and reading books independently for challenge, interest and enjoyment.
- re-reading books encountered earlier to increase familiarity with them and provide a basis for making comparisons.

- understand increasingly challenging texts through:

  - learning new vocabulary, relating it explicitly to known vocabulary and understanding it with the help of context and dictionaries
  - making inferences and referring to evidence in the text
  - knowing the purpose, audience for and context of the writing and drawing on this knowledge to support comprehension
  - checking their understanding to make sure that what they have read makes sense.

- read critically through:

  - knowing how language, including figurative language, vocabulary choice, grammar, text structure and organisational features, presents meaning
  - recognising a range of poetic conventions and understanding how these have been used
  - studying setting, plot, and characterisation, and the effects of these
  - understanding how the work of dramatists is communicated effectively through performance and how alternative staging allows for different interpretations of a play
  - making critical comparisons across texts
  - studying a range of authors, including at least two authors in depth each year.

Writing

Pupils should be taught to:

- write accurately, fluently, effectively and at length for pleasure and information through:

  - writing for a wide range of purposes and audiences, including:

    - well-structured formal expository and narrative essays
    - stories, scripts, poetry and other imaginative writing
    - notes and polished scripts for talks and presentations
    - a range of other narrative and non-narrative texts, including arguments, and personal and formal letters

  - summarising and organising material, and supporting ideas and arguments with any necessary factual detail
  - applying their growing knowledge of vocabulary, grammar and text structure to their writing and selecting the appropriate form
  - drawing on knowledge of literary and rhetorical devices from their reading and listening to enhance the impact of their writing

- plan, draft, edit and proof-read through:

  - considering how their writing reflects the audiences and purposes for which it was intended

- o amending the vocabulary, grammar and structure of their writing to improve its coherence and overall effectiveness
- o paying attention to accurate grammar, punctuation and spelling; applying the spelling patterns and rules set out in English Appendix 1 to the key stage 1 and 2 programmes of study for English.

Grammar and vocabulary

Pupils should be taught to:

- consolidate and build on their knowledge of grammar and vocabulary through:
  - o extending and applying the grammatical knowledge set out in English Appendix 2 to the key stage 1 and 2 programmes of study to analyse more challenging texts
  - o studying the effectiveness and impact of the grammatical features of the texts they read
  - o drawing on new vocabulary and grammatical constructions from their reading and listening, and using these consciously in their writing and speech to achieve particular effects
  - o knowing and understanding the differences between spoken and written language, including differences associated with formal and informal registers, and between Standard English and other varieties of English
  - o using Standard English confidently in their own writing and speech
  - o discussing reading, writing and spoken language with precise and confident use of linguistic and literary terminology.

Spoken English

Pupils should be taught to:

- speak confidently and effectively, including through:
  - o using Standard English confidently in a range of formal and informal contexts, including classroom discussion
  - o giving short speeches and presentations, expressing their own ideas and keeping to the point
  - o participating in formal debates and structured discussions, summarising and/or building on what has been said
  - o improvising, rehearsing and performing play scripts and poetry in order to generate language and discuss language use and meaning, using role, intonation, tone, volume, mood, silence, stillness and action to add impact.

Key stage 4 subject content

Reading

Pupils should be taught to:

- read and appreciate the depth and power of the English literary heritage through:
  - o reading a wide range of high-quality, challenging, classic literature and extended literary non-fiction, such as essays, reviews and journalism. This writing should include whole texts. The range will include:

- o   at least one play by Shakespeare
- o   works from the 19th, 20th and 21st centuries
- o   poetry since 1789, including representative Romantic poetry
- o   re-reading literature and other writing as a basis for making comparisons
- o   choosing and reading books independently for challenge, interest and enjoyment.

- understand and critically evaluate texts through:

  - o   reading in different ways for different purposes, summarising and synthesising ideas and information, and evaluating their usefulness for particular purposes
  - o   drawing on knowledge of the purpose, audience for and context of the writing, including its social, historical and cultural context and the literary tradition to which it belongs, to inform evaluation
  - o   identifying and interpreting themes, ideas and information
  - o   exploring aspects of plot, characterisation, events and settings, the relationships between them and their effects
  - o   seeking evidence in the text to support a point of view, including justifying inferences with evidence
  - o   distinguishing between statements that are supported by evidence and those that are not, and identifying bias and misuse of evidence
  - o   analysing a writer's choice of vocabulary, form, grammatical and structural features, and evaluating their effectiveness and impact
  - o   making critical comparisons, referring to the contexts, themes, characterisation, style and literary quality of texts, and drawing on knowledge and skills from wider reading

- make an informed personal response, recognising that other responses to a text are possible and evaluating these.

Writing

Pupils should be taught to:

- write accurately, fluently, effectively and at length for pleasure and information through:

  - o   adapting their writing for a wide range of purposes and audiences: to describe, narrate, explain, instruct, give and respond to information, and argue
  - o   selecting and organising ideas, facts and key points, and citing evidence, details and quotation effectively and pertinently for support and emphasis
  - o   selecting, and using judiciously, vocabulary, grammar, form, and structural and organisational features, including rhetorical devices, to reflect audience, purpose and context, and using Standard English where appropriate

- make notes, draft and write, including using information provided by others [e.g. writing a letter from key points provided; drawing on and using information from a presentation]
- revise, edit and proof-read through:

  - o   reflecting on whether their draft achieves the intended impact
  - o   restructuring their writing, and amending its grammar and vocabulary to improve coherence, consistency, clarity and overall effectiveness
  - o   paying attention to the accuracy and effectiveness of grammar, punctuation and spelling.

Grammar and vocabulary

Pupils should be taught to:

- consolidate and build on their knowledge of grammar and vocabulary through:
    - studying their effectiveness and impact in the texts they read
    - drawing on new vocabulary and grammatical constructions from their reading and listening, and using these consciously in their writing and speech to achieve particular effects
    - analysing some of the differences between spoken and written language, including differences associated with formal and informal registers, and between Standard English and other varieties of English
    - using linguistic and literary terminology accurately and confidently in discussing reading, writing and spoken language.

Spoken English

Pupils should be taught to:

- speak confidently, audibly and effectively, including through:
    - using Standard English when the context and audience require it
    - working effectively in groups of different sizes and taking on required roles, including leading and managing discussions, involving others productively, reviewing and summarising, and contributing to meeting goals/deadlines
    - listening to and building on the contributions of others, asking questions to clarify and inform, and challenging courteously when necessary
    - planning for different purposes and audiences, including selecting and organising information and ideas effectively and persuasively for formal spoken presentations and debates
    - listening and responding in a variety of different contexts, both formal and informal, and evaluating content, viewpoints, evidence and aspects of presentation
    - improvising, rehearsing and performing play scripts and poetry in order to generate language and discuss language use and meaning, using role, intonation, tone, volume, mood, silence, stillness and action to add impact.

Glossary for the programmes of study for English (non-statutory)

The following glossary includes all the technical grammatical terms used in the programmes of study for English, as well as others that might be useful. It is intended as an aid for teachers, not as the body of knowledge that should be learnt by pupils. Apart from a few which are used only in schools (for example, *root word*), the terms below are used with the meanings defined here in most modern books on English grammar. It is recognised that there are different schools of thought on grammar, but the terms defined here clarify those being used in the programmes of study. For further details, teachers should consult the many books that are available.

Terms in definitions

As in any tightly structured area of knowledge, grammar, vocabulary and spelling involve a network of technical concepts that help to define each other. Consequently, the definition of one concept builds on other concepts that are equally technical. Concepts that are defined elsewhere in the glossary are hyperlinked. For some concepts, the technical definition may be slightly different from the meaning that some teachers may have learnt at school or may have been using with their own pupils; in these cases, the more familiar meaning is also discussed.

Term	Guidance	Example
active voice	An active **verb** has its usual pattern of **subject** and **object** (in contrast with the **passive**).	Active: *The school arranged a visit.* Passive: *A visit was arranged by the school.*
adjective	The surest way to identify adjectives is by the ways they can be used: • before a noun, to make the noun's meaning more specific (i.e. to **modify** the noun), or • after the verb *be,* as its **complement**. Adjectives cannot be modified by other adjectives. This distinguishes them from **nouns**, which can be. Adjectives are sometimes called 'describing words' because they pick out single characteristics such as size or colour. This is often true, but it doesn't help to distinguish adjectives from other word classes, because **verbs**, **nouns** and **adverbs** can do the same thing.	*The pupils did some really <u>good</u> work.* [adjective used before a noun, to modify it] *Their work was <u>good</u>.* [adjective used after the verb *be*, as its complement] Not adjectives: *The lamp <u>glowed.</u>* [verb] *It was such a bright <u>red</u>!* [noun] *He spoke <u>loudly</u>.* [adverb] *It was a French <u>grammar</u> book.* [noun]
adverb	The surest way to identify adverbs is by the ways they can be used: they can **modify** a **verb**, an **adjective**, another adverb or even a whole clause.	*Usha <u>soon</u> started snoring <u>loudly</u>.* [adverbs modifying the verbs *started* and *snoring]*

	Adverbs are sometimes said to describe manner or time. This is often true, but it doesn't help to distinguish adverbs from other word classes that can be used as **adverbials**, such as **preposition phrases, noun phrases** and **subordinate clauses.**	*That match was <u>really</u> exciting!* [adverb modifying the adjective *exciting*] *We don't get to play games <u>very</u> often.* [adverb modifying the other adverb, *often*] <u>*Fortunately,*</u> *it didn't rain.* [adverb modifying the whole clause 'it didn't rain' by commenting on it] Not adverbs: • *Usha went <u>up the stairs</u>.* [preposition phrase used as adverbial] • *She finished her work <u>this evening</u>.* [noun phrase used as adverbial] • *She finished <u>when the teacher got cross</u>.* [subordinate clause used as adverbial]
adverbial	An adverbial is a word or phrase that is used, like an adverb, to modify a verb or clause. Of course, **adverbs** can be used as adverbials, but many other types of words and phrases can be used this way, including **preposition phrases** and **subordinate clauses.**	*The bus leaves in <u>five minutes</u>.* [preposition phrase as adverbial: modifies *leaves*] *She promised to see him <u>last night</u>.* [noun phrase modifying either *promised* or *see*, according to the intended meaning] *She worked until she had finished.* [subordinate clause as adverbial]
antonym	Two words are antonyms if their meanings are opposites.	*hot – cold* *light – dark* *light – heavy*
apostrophe	Apostrophes have two completely different uses: • showing the place of missing letters (e.g. *I'm* for *I am*) • marking **possessives** (e.g. *Hannah's mother).*	<u>*I'm*</u> *going out and I <u>won't</u> be long.* [showing missing letters] <u>*Hannah's*</u> *mother went to town in <u>Justin's</u> car.* [marking possessives]
article	The articles *the* (definite) and *a* or *an* (indefinite) are the most common type of **determiner.**	<u>*The*</u> *dog found <u>a</u> bone in <u>an</u> old box.*
auxiliary verb	The auxiliary **verbs** are: *be, have, do* and the **modal verbs**. They can be used to make questions and negative statements. In addition:	*They <u>are</u> winning the match.* [*be* used in the progressive]

Term	Guidance	Example
	• *be* is used in the **progressive** and **passive** • *have* is used in the **perfect** • *do* is used to form questions and negative statements if no other auxiliary verb is present	*Have* you finished your picture? [have used to make a question, and the perfect] No, I *don't* know him. [do used to make a negative; no other auxiliary is present] *Will* you come with me or not? [modal verb *will* used to make a question about the other person's willingness]
clause	A clause is a special type of **phrase** whose **head** is a **verb**. Clauses can sometimes be complete sentences. Clauses may be **main** or **subordinate**. Traditionally, a clause had to have a **finite verb**, but most modern grammarians also recognise non-finite clauses.	*It was raining.* [single-clause sentence] *It was raining but we were indoors.* [two finite clauses] *If you are coming to the party, please let us know.* [finite subordinate clause inside a finite main clause] *Usha went upstairs to play on her computer.* [non-finite clause]
cohesion	A text has cohesion if it is clear how the meanings of its parts fit together. **Cohesive devices** can help to do this. In the example, there are repeated references to the same thing (shown by the different style pairings), and the logical relations, such as time and cause, between different parts are clear.	**A visit** has been arranged for *Year 6*, to the <u>Mountain Peaks Field Study Centre</u>, leaving school at 9.30am. **This** is **an overnight visit.** <u>The centre</u> has beautiful grounds and *a nature trail.* During the afternoon, *<u>the children</u>* will follow *the trail.*
cohesive device	Cohesive devices are words used to show how the different parts of a text fit together. In other words, they create **cohesion**. Some examples of cohesive devices are: • **determiners** and **pronouns**, which can refer back to earlier words • **conjunctions** and **adverbs**, which can make relations between words clear • **ellipsis** of expected words.	*Julia's dad bought her a football.* *<u>The</u> football was expensive!* [determiner; refers us back to a particular football] *Joe was given a bike for Christmas. <u>He</u> liked <u>it</u> very much.* [the pronouns refer back to Joe and the bike] *We'll be going shopping <u>before</u> we go to the park.* [**conjunction**; makes a relationship of time clear] *I'm afraid we're going to have to wait for the next train. <u>Meanwhile</u>, we could have*

		a cup of tea. [**adverb**; refers back to the time of waiting] *Where are you going? [_] To school!* [ellipsis of the expected words *I'm going*; links the answer back to the question]
complement	A verb's subject complement adds more information about its **subject**, and its object complement does the same for its **object**. Unlike the verb's object, its complement may be an adjective. The verb *be* normally has a complement.	*She is <u>our teacher</u>.* [adds more information about the subject, *she*] *They seem very competent.* [adds more information about the subject, *they*] *Learning makes me <u>happy</u>.* [adds more information about the object, *me*]
compound, compounding	A compound word contains at least two **root words** in its **morphology**; e.g. *whiteboard, superman*. Compounding is very important in English.	*blackbird, blow-dry, bookshop, icecream, English teacher, inkjet, one-eyed, bone-dry, baby-sit, daydream, outgrow*
conjunction	A conjunction links two words or phrases together. There are two main types of conjunctions: • **co-ordinating** conjunctions (e.g. *and)* link two words or phrases together as an equal pair • subordinating conjunctions (e.g. *when)* introduce a **subordinate clause**.	*James bought a bat <u>and</u> ball.* [links the words *bat* and *ball* as an equal pair] *Kylie is young <u>but</u> she can kick the ball hard.* [links two clauses as an equal pair] *Everyone watches <u>when</u> Kyle does back-flips.* [introduces a subordinate clause] *Joe can't practise kicking <u>because</u> he's injured.* [introduces a subordinate clause]
consonant	A sound which is produced when the speaker closes off or obstructs the flow of air through the vocal tract, usually using lips, tongue or teeth. Most of the letters of the alphabet represent consonants. Only the letters a, e, *i, o, u* and *y* can represent **vowel** sounds.	/p/ [flow of air stopped by the lips, then released] /t/ [flow of air stopped by the tongue touching the roof of the mouth, then released] /f/ [flow of air obstructed by the bottom lip touching the top teeth] /s/ [flow of air obstructed by the tip of the tongue touching the gum line]
continuous	See **progressive**	

Term	Guidance	Example
co-ordinate, co-ordination	Words or phrases are co-ordinated if they are linked as an equal pair by a co-ordinating **conjunction** (i.e. *and, but, or*). In the examples on the right, the co-ordinated elements are shown in bold, and the conjunction is underlined. The difference between co-ordination and **subordination** is that, in subordination, the two linked elements are not equal.	***Susan*** <u>*and*</u> ***Amra*** *met in a café.* [links the words *Susan* and *Amra* as an equal pair] ***They talked*** <u>*and*</u> ***drank tea*** *for an hour.* [links two clauses as an equal pair] ***Susan got a bus*** <u>*but*</u> ***Amra walked.*** [links two clauses as an equal pair] Not co-ordination: *They ate* <u>*before*</u> *they met.* [*before* introduces a subordinate clause]
determiner	A determiner specifies a noun as known or unknown, and it goes before any modifiers (e.g. adjectives or other nouns). Some examples of determiners are: • **articles** (the, *a* or an) • demonstratives (e.g. *this, those*) • **possessives** (e.g. my, *your*) • quantifiers (e.g. *some, every*).	<u>*the*</u> *home team* [article, specifies the team as known] <u>*a*</u> *good team* [article, specifies the team as unknown] <u>*that*</u> *pupil* [demonstrative, known] <u>*Julia's*</u> *parents* [possessive, known] <u>*some*</u> *big boys* [quantifier, unknown] Contrast: *home* <u>*the*</u> *team, big* <u>*some*</u> *boys* [both incorrect, because the determiner should come before other modifiers]
digraph	A type of **grapheme** where two letters represent one **phoneme**. Sometimes, these two letters are not next to one another; this is called a split digraph.	The digraph <u>*ea*</u> in <u>*each*</u> is pronounced /iː/. The digraph <u>*sh*</u> in <u>*shed*</u> is pronounced /ʃ/. The split digraph <u>*i–e*</u> in <u>*line*</u> is pronounced /aɪ/.
ellipsis	Ellipsis is the omission of a word or phrase which is expected and predictable.	*Frankie waved to Ivana and* <u>*she*</u> *watched her drive away.* *She did it because she wanted to* ~~*do it*~~.
etymology	A word's etymology is its history: its origins in earlier forms of English or other languages, and how its form and meaning have changed. Many words in English have come from Greek, Latin or French.	The word *school* was borrowed from a Greek word ό÷ïëþ *(skholé)* meaning 'leisure'.

		The word *verb* comes from Latin *verbum*, meaning 'word'. The word *mutton* comes from French *mouton*, meaning 'sheep'.
finite verb	Every sentence typically has at least one verb which is either past or present tense. Such verbs are called 'finite'. The imperative verb in a command is also finite. Verbs that are not finite, such as participles or infinitives, cannot stand on their own: they are linked to another verb in the sentence.	*Lizzie does the dishes every day.* [**present tense**] *Even Hana did the dishes yesterday.* [**past tense**] *Do the dishes, Naser!* [imperative] Not finite verbs: • *I have done them.* [combined with the finite verb *have*] • *I will do them.* [combined with the finite verb *will*] • *I want to do them!* [combined with the finite verb *want*]
fronting, fronted	A word or phrase that normally comes after the **verb** may be moved before the verb: when this happens, we say it has been 'fronted'. For example, a fronted adverbial is an **adverbial** which has been moved before the verb. When writing fronted phrases, we often follow them with a comma.	*Before we begin, make sure you've got a pencil.* [Without fronting: *Make sure you've got a pencil before we begin.*] *The day after tomorrow, I'm visiting my granddad.* [Without fronting: *I'm visiting my granddad the day after tomorrow.*]
future	Reference to future time can be marked in a number of different ways in English. All these ways involve the use of a **present-tense verb**. See also **tense**. Unlike many other languages (such as French, Spanish or Italian), English has no distinct 'future tense' form of the verb comparable with its **present** and **past** tenses.	*He will leave tomorrow.* [present-tense *will* followed by infinitive *leave*] *He may leave tomorrow.* [present-tense *may* followed by infinitive *leave*] *He leaves tomorrow.* [present-tense *leaves*] *He is going to leave tomorrow.* [present tense *is* followed by *going to* plus the infinitive *leave*]
GPC	See **grapheme-phoneme correspondences**.	

Term	Guidance	Example
grapheme	A letter, or combination of letters, that corresponds to a single **phoneme** within a word.	The grapheme _t_ in the words _ten_, _bet_ and _ate_ corresponds to the phoneme /t/. The grapheme _ph_ in the word _dolphin_ corresponds to the phoneme /f/.
grapheme-phoneme correspondences	The links between letters, or combinations of letters (**graphemes**) and the speech sounds (**phonemes**) that they represent. In the English writing system, graphemes may correspond to different phonemes in different words.	The grapheme _s_ corresponds to the phoneme /s/ in the word _see_, but... ...it corresponds to the phoneme /z/ in the word _easy_.
head	See **phrase**.	
homonym	Two different words are homonyms if they both look exactly the same when written, and sound exactly the same when pronounced.	_Has he left yet? Yes – he went through the door on the left._ _The noise a dog makes is called a bark. Trees have bark._
homophone	Two different words are homophones if they sound exactly the same when pronounced.	_hear, here_ _some, sum_
infinitive	A verb's infinitive is the basic form used as the head-word in a dictionary (e.g. _walk, be_). Infinitives are often used: • after _to_ • after **modal verbs**.	_I want to walk._ _I will be quiet._
inflection	When we add _-ed_ to _walk_, or change _mouse_ to _mice_, this change of **morphology** produces an inflection ('bending') of the basic word which has special grammar (e.g. **past tense** or **plural**). In contrast, adding _-er_ to _walk_ produces a completely different word, _walker_, which is part of the same **word family**. Inflection is sometimes thought of as merely a change of ending, but, in fact, some words change completely when inflected.	_dogs_ is an inflection of _dog_. _went_ is an inflection of _go_. _better_ is an inflection of _good_.

intransitive verb	A verb which does not need an object in a sentence to complete its meaning is described as intransitive. See 'transitive verb'.	*We all <u>laughed</u>.* *We would like to stay longer, but we must <u>leave</u>.*
main clause	A **sentence** contains at least one **clause** which is not a **subordinate clause**; such a clause is a main clause. A main clause may contain any number of subordinate clauses.	*<u>It was raining</u> but <u>the sun was shining</u>.* [two main clauses] *<u>The man **who wrote it** told me **that it was true**</u>.* [one main clause containing two subordinate clauses.] *She said, "It rained all day."* [one main clause containing another.]
modal verb	Modal verbs are used to change the meaning of other **verbs**. They can express meanings such as certainty, ability, or obligation. The main modal verbs are *will, would, can, could, may, might, shall, should, must* and *ought*. A modal verb only has **finite** forms and has no **suffixes** (e.g. *I sing – he sings*, but not *I must – he musts*).	*I <u>can</u> do this maths work by myself.* *This ride <u>may</u> be too scary for you!* *You <u>should</u> help your little brother.* *Is it going to rain? Yes, it <u>might</u>.* *Canning swim is important.* [not possible because *can* must be finite; contrast: *Being able to swim is important*, where *being* is not a modal verb]
modify, modifier	One word or phrase modifies another by making its meaning more specific. Because the two words make a **phrase**, the 'modifier' is normally close to the modified word.	In the phrase *primary-school teacher*: • *teacher* is modified by *primary-school* (to mean a specific kind of teacher) • *school* is modified by *primary* (to mean a specific kind of school).
morphology	A word's morphology is its internal make-up in terms of **root words** and **suffixes** or **prefixes**, as well as other kinds of change such as the change of *mouse* to *mice*. Morphology may be used to produce different **inflections** of the same word (e.g. *boy – boys*), or entirely new words (e.g. *boy – boyish*) belonging to the same **word family**. A word that contains two or more root words is a **compound** (e.g. *news+paper, ice+cream*).	*dogs* has the morphological make-up: *dog* + s. *unhelpfulness* has the morphological make-up: *unhelpful* + *ness* • where *unhelpful* = *un* + *helpful* • and *helpful* = *help* + *ful*

Term	Guidance	Example
noun	The surest way to identify nouns is by the ways they can be used after **determiners** such as *the*: for example, most nouns will fit into the frame "The ____matters/ matter." Nouns are sometimes called 'naming words' because they name people, places and 'things'; this is often true, but it doesn't help to distinguish nouns from other **word classes**. For example, **prepositions** can name places and **verbs** can name 'things' such as actions. Nouns may be classified as **common** (e.g. *boy, day*) or **proper** (e.g. *Ivan, Wednesday*), and also as **countable** (e.g. *thing, boy*) or **non-countable** (e.g. *stuff, money*). These classes can be recognised by the determiners they combine with.	*Our <u>dog</u> bit the <u>burglar</u> on his <u>behind</u>!* *My big <u>brother</u> did an amazing <u>jump</u> on his <u>skateboard</u>.* *<u>Actions</u> speak louder than <u>words</u>.* Not nouns: • *He's <u>behind</u> you!* [this names a place, but is a preposition, not a noun] • *She can <u>jump</u> so high!* [this names an action, but is a verb, not a noun] common, countable: *a <u>book</u>, <u>books</u>, two <u>chocolates</u>, one <u>day</u>, fewer <u>ideas</u>* common, non-countable: *<u>money</u>, some <u>chocolate</u>, less <u>imagination</u>* proper, countable: *<u>Marilyn</u>, <u>London</u>, <u>Wednesday</u>*
noun phrase	A noun phrase is a **phrase** with a noun as its **head**, e.g. *some foxes, foxes with bushy tails*. Some grammarians recognise one-word phrases, so that *foxes are multiplying* would contain the noun *foxes* acting as the head of the noun phrase *foxes*.	*<u>Adult foxes</u> can jump.* [*adult* modifies *foxes*, so *adult* belongs to the noun phrase] *<u>Almost all healthy adult foxes in this area</u> can jump.* [all the other words help to modify *foxes*, so they all belong to the noun phrase]
object	An object is normally a **noun**, **pronoun** or **noun phrase** that comes straight after the **verb**, and shows what the verb is acting upon. Objects can be turned into the **subject** of a **passive** verb, and cannot be **adjectives** (contrast with **complements**).	*Year 2 designed <u>puppets</u>.* [noun acting as object] *I like <u>that</u>.* [pronoun acting as object] *Some people suggested a <u>pretty display</u>.* [noun phrase acting as object] Contrast: • *A display was suggested.* [object of active verb becomes the subject of the passive verb] • *Year 2 designed pretty.* [incorrect, because adjectives cannot be objects]

participle	Verbs in English have two participles, called 'present participle' (e.g. *walking, taking*) and 'past participle' (e.g. *walked, taken*). Unfortunately, these terms can be confusing to learners, because: • they don't necessarily have anything to do with present or past time • although past participles are used as **perfects** (e.g. *has eaten*) they are also used as **passives** (e.g. *was eaten*).	*He is <u>walking</u> to school.* [present participle in a **progressive**] *He has <u>taken</u> the bus to school.* [past participle in a **perfect**] *The photo was <u>taken</u> in the rain.* [past participle in a **passive**]
passive	The sentence *It was eaten by our dog* is the passive of *Our dog ate it.* A passive is recognisable from: • the past **participle** form *eaten* • the normal **object** (*it*) turned into the **subject** • the normal subject (*our dog*) turned into an optional **preposition phrase** with *by* as its **head** • the verb *be* (*was*), or some other verb such as *get*. Contrast **active**. A verb is not 'passive' just because it has a passive meaning: it must be the passive version of an active verb.	*A visit was <u>arranged</u> by the school. Our cat got <u>run</u> over by a bus.* Active versions: • *The school arranged a visit.* • *A bus ran over our cat.* Not passive: • *He received a warning.* [past tense, active *received*] • *We had an accident.* [past tense, active *had*]
past tense	**Verbs** in the past tense are commonly used to: • talk about the past • talk about imagined situations • make a request sound more polite. Most verbs take a **suffix** *–ed*, to form their past tense, but many commonly-used verbs are irregular. See also **tense**.	*Tom and Chris <u>showed</u> me their new TV.* [names an event in the past] *Antonio <u>went</u> on holiday to Brazil.* [names an event in the past; irregular past of *go*] *I wish I <u>had</u> a puppy.* [names an imagined situation, not a situation in the past] *I <u>was</u> hoping you'd help tomorrow.* [makes an implied request sound more polite]
perfect	The perfect form of a **verb** generally calls attention to the consequences of a prior event; for example, *he has gone to lunch* implies that he is still away, in contrast with *he went to lunch.* 'Had gone to lunch' takes a past time point (i.e. when we	*She <u>has downloaded</u> some songs.* [present perfect; now she has some songs]

Term	Guidance	Example
	arrived) as its reference point and is another way of establishing time relations in a text. The perfect tense is formed by: • turning the verb into its past **participle inflection** • adding a form of the verb *have* before it. It can also be combined with the **progressive** (e.g. *he has been going*).	*I had eaten lunch when you came.* [past perfect; I wasn't hungry when you came]
phoneme	A phoneme is the smallest unit of sound that signals a distinct, contrasting meaning. For example: • /t/ contrasts with /k/ to signal the difference between *tap* and *cap* • /t/ contrasts with /l/ to signal the difference between *bought* and *ball*. It is this contrast in meaning that tells us there are two distinct phonemes at work. There are around 44 phonemes in English; the exact number depends on regional accents. A single phoneme may be represented in writing by one, two, three or four letters constituting a single **grapheme**.	The word *cat* has three letters and three phonemes: /kæt/ The word *catch* has five letters and three phonemes: /katʃ/ The word *caught* has six letters and three phonemes: /kɔːt/
phrase	A phrase is a group of words that are grammatically connected so that they stay together, and that expand a single word, called the 'head'. The phrase is a **noun phrase** if its head is a noun, a **preposition phrase** if its head is a preposition, and so on; but if the head is a **verb**, the phrase is called a **clause**. Phrases can be made up of other phrases.	*She waved to her mother.* [a noun phrase, with the noun *mother* as its head] *She waved to her mother.* [a preposition phrase, with the preposition *to* as its head] *She waved to her mother.* [a clause, with the verb *waved* as its head]
plural	A plural **noun** normally has a **suffix** –s or –es and means 'more than one'. There are a few nouns with different **morphology** in the plural (e.g. *mice, formulae*).	*dogs* [more than one dog]; *boxes* [more than one box] *mice* [more than one mouse]
possessive	A possessive can be: • a **noun** followed by an **apostrophe**, with or without s • a possessive **pronoun**.	*Tariq's* book [Tariq has the book]

	The relation expressed by a possessive goes well beyond ordinary ideas of 'possession'. A possessive may act as a **determiner**.	*The <u>boys'</u> arrival* [the boys arrive] *<u>His</u> obituary* [the obituary is about him] *That essay is <u>mine</u>.* [I wrote the essay]
prefix	A prefix is added at the beginning of a **word** in order to turn it into another word. Contrast **suffix**.	*<u>over</u>take, <u>dis</u>appear*
preposition	A preposition links a following **noun, pronoun** or **noun phrase** to some other word in the sentence. Prepositions often describe locations or directions, but can describe other things, such as relations of time. Words like *before* or *since* can act either as prepositions or as **conjunctions**.	*Tom waved goodbye <u>to</u> Christy.* *She'll be back <u>from</u> Australia <u>in</u> two weeks.* *I haven't seen my dog <u>since</u> this morning.* Contrast: *I'm going, <u>since</u> no-one wants me here!* [conjunction: links two clauses]
preposition phrase	A preposition phrase has a preposition as its head followed by a noun, pronoun or noun phrase.	*He was <u>in bed</u>.* *I met them <u>after the party</u>.*
present tense	**Verbs** in the present tense are commonly used to: • talk about the present • talk about the **future**. They may take a suffix *–s* (depending on the **subject**). See also **tense**.	*Jamal <u>goes</u> to the pool every day.* [describes a habit that exists now] *He <u>can</u> swim.* [describes a state that is true now] *The bus <u>arrives</u> at three.* [scheduled now] *My friends <u>are</u> coming to play.* [describes a plan in progress now]
progressive	The progressive (also known as the 'continuous') form of a **verb** generally describes events in progress. It is formed by combining the verb's present **participle** (e.g. *singing*) with a form of the verb *be* (e.g. *he was singing*). The progressive can also be combined with the **perfect** (e.g. *he has been singing*).	*Michael <u>is singing</u> in the store room.* [present progressive] *Amanda <u>was making</u> a patchwork quilt.* [past progressive] *Usha <u>had been practising</u> for an hour when I called.* [past perfect progressive]
pronoun	Pronouns are normally used like **nouns**, except that: • they are grammatically more specialised • it is harder to **modify** them	***Amanda** waved to **Michael**. **She** waved to **<u>him</u>**.* ***John's** mother is over there. **His** mother is over there.*

Term	Guidance	Example
	In the examples, each sentence is written twice: once with nouns, and once with pronouns (underlined). Where the same thing is being talked about, the words are shown in bold.	*The **visit** will be an overnight **visit**. **This** will be an overnight **visit**.* ***Simon** is the person: **Simon** broke it. **He** is the one **who** broke it.*
punctuation	Punctuation includes any conventional features of writing other than spelling and general layout: the standard punctuation marks . , ; : ? ! - – ( ) " " ' ' , and also word-spaces, capital letters, apostrophes, paragraph breaks and bullet points. One important role of punctuation is to indicate **sentence** boundaries.	*"I'm_going_out,_Usha,_and I won't be long," Mum said.*
Received Pronunciation	Received Pronunciation (often abbreviated to RP) is an accent which is used only by a small minority of English speakers in England. It is not associated with any one region. Because of its regional neutrality, it is the accent which is generally shown in dictionaries in the UK (but not, of course, in the USA). RP has no special status in the national curriculum.	
register	Classroom lessons, football commentaries and novels use different registers of the same language, recognised by differences of vocabulary and grammar. Registers are 'varieties' of a language which are each tied to a range of uses, in contrast with dialects, which are tied to groups of users.	*I regret to inform you that Mr Joseph Smith has passed away.* [formal letter] *Have you heard that Joe has died?* [casual speech] *Joe falls down and dies, centre stage.* [stage direction]
relative clause	A relative clause is a special type of **subordinate clause** that modifies a **noun**. It often does this by using a relative **pronoun** such as *who* or *that* to refer back to that noun, though the relative pronoun *that* is often omitted. A relative **clause** may also be attached to a clause. In that case, the pronoun refers back to the whole clause, rather than referring back to a noun. In the examples, the relative clauses are underlined, and both the pronouns and the words they refer back to are in bold.	*That's the **boy who** lives near school.* [*who* refers back to boy] *The **prize that** I won was a book.* [*that* refers back to prize] *The **prize** I won was a book.* [the pronoun *that* is omitted] *Tom broke the game, **which** annoyed Ali.* [*which* refers back to the whole clause]

root word	**Morphology** breaks words down into root words, which can stand alone, and **suffixes** or **prefixes** which can't. For example, *help* is the root word for other words in its **word family** such as *helpful* and *helpless,* and also for its **inflections** such as *helping.* **Compound** words (e.g. *help-desk)* contain two or more root words. When looking in a dictionary, we sometimes have to look for the root word (or words) of the word we are interested in.	*pl<u>ay</u>ed* [the root word is *play*] *un<u>fair</u>* [the root word is *fair*] *football* [the root words are *foot* and *ball*]
schwa	The name of a vowel sound that is found only in unstressed positions in English. It is the most common vowel sound in English. It is written as /ə/ in the International Phonetic Alphabet. In the English writing system, it can be written in many different ways.	/əlɒŋ/ *[<u>a</u>long]* /bʌtə/ *[butt<u>er</u>]* /dɒktə/ *[doct<u>or</u>]*
sentence	A sentence is a group of **words** which are grammatically connected to each other but not to any words outside the sentence. The form of a sentence's main clause shows whether it is being used as a statement, a question, a command or an exclamation. A sentence may consist of a single clause or it may contain several clauses held together by subordination or co-ordination. Classifying sentences as 'simple', 'complex' or 'compound' can be confusing, because a 'simple' sentence may be complicated, and a 'complex' one may be straightforward. The terms '**single-clause sentence**' and '**multi-clause sentence**' may be more helpful.	*<u>John went to his friend's house. He stayed there till tea-time</u>.* *John went to his friend's house, he stayed there till tea-time.* [This is a 'comma splice', a common error in which a comma is used where either a full stop or a semi-colon is needed to indicate the lack of any grammatical connection between the two clauses.] *You are my friend.* [statement] *Are you my friend?* [question] *Be my friend!* [command] *What a good friend you are!* [exclamation] *Ali went home on his bike to his goldfish and his current library book about pets.* [single-clause sentence] *She went shopping but took back everything she had bought because she didn't like any of it.* [multi-clause sentence]
split digraph	See **digraph**.	

Term	Guidance	Example
Standard English	Standard English can be recognised by the use of a very small range of forms such as *those books, I did it* and *I wasn't doing anything* (rather than their non-Standard equivalents); it is not limited to any particular accent. It is the variety of English which is used, with only minor variation, as a major world language. Some people use Standard English all the time, in all situations from the most casual to the most formal, so it covers most **registers**. The aim of the national curriculum is that everyone should be able to use Standard English as needed in writing and in relatively formal speaking.	*I did it because they were not willing to undertake any more work on those houses.* [formal Standard English] *I did it cos they wouldn't do any more work on those houses.* [casual Standard English] *I done it cos they wouldn't do no more work on them houses.* [casual non-Standard English]
stress	A **syllable** is stressed if it is pronounced more forcefully than the syllables next to it. The other syllables are unstressed.	a<u>bout</u> <u>vis</u>it
subject	The subject of a verb is normally the **noun**, **noun phrase** or **pronoun** that names the 'do-er' or 'be-er'. The subject's normal position is: • just before the **verb** in a statement • just after the **auxiliary verb**, in a question. Unlike the verb's **object** and **complement**, the subject can determine the form of the verb (e.g. *I am*, *you are*).	<u>Rula's mother</u> *went out.* <u>That</u> *is uncertain.* <u>The children</u> *will study the animals.* *Will* <u>the children</u> *study the animals?*
subjunctive	In some languages, the **inflections** of a **verb** include a large range of special forms which are used typically in **subordinate clauses**, and are called 'subjunctives'. English has very few such forms and those it has tend to be used in rather formal styles.	*The school requires that all pupils* <u>be</u> *honest.* *The school rules demand that pupils not* <u>enter</u> *the gym at lunchtime.* *If Zoë* <u>were</u> *the class president, things would be much better.*
subordinate, subordination	A subordinate word or phrase tells us more about the meaning of the word it is subordinate to. Subordination can be thought of as an unequal relationship between a subordinate word and a main word. For example:	<u>big</u> *dogs* [*big* is subordinate to *dogs*] <u>Big dogs</u> *need* <u>long walks</u>. [*big dogs* and *long walks* are subordinate to *need*]

	• an adjective is subordinate to the noun it **modifies** • **subjects** and **objects** are subordinate to their **verbs**. Subordination is much more common than the equal relationship of **co-ordination**. See also **subordinate clause**.	*We can watch TV <u>when we've finished</u>.* [*when we've finished* is subordinate to *watch*]
subordinate clause	A clause which is **subordinate** to some other part of the same **sentence** is a subordinate clause; for example, in *The apple that I ate was sour*, the clause *that I ate* is subordinate to *apple* (which it **modifies**). Subordinate clauses contrast with **co-ordinate** clauses as in *It was sour but looked very tasty*. (Contrast: **main clause**) However, clauses that are directly quoted as direct speech are not subordinate clauses.	*That's the street where Ben lives.* [**relative clause**; modifies *street*] *He watched her <u>as she disappeared</u>.* [**adverbial**; modifies *watched*] *<u>What you said</u> was very nice.* [acts as **subject** of *was*] *She noticed <u>an hour had passed</u>.* [acts as **object** of *noticed*] Not subordinate: *He shouted, <u>"Look out!"</u>*
suffix	A suffix is an 'ending', used at the end of one word to turn it into another word. Unlike **root words**, suffixes cannot stand on their own as a complete word. Contrast **prefix**.	*call – call<u>ed</u>* *teach – teach<u>er</u>* [turns a **verb** into a **noun**] *terror – terror<u>ise</u>* [turns a noun into a verb] *green – green<u>ish</u>* [leaves **word class** unchanged]
syllable	A syllable sounds like a beat in a **word**. Syllables consist of at least one **vowel**, and possibly one or more **consonants**.	*Cat* has one syllable. *Fairy* has two syllables. *Hippopotamus* has five syllables.
synonym	Two words are synonyms if they have the same meaning, or similar meanings. Contrast **antonym**.	*talk – speak* *old – elderly*
tense	In English, tense is the choice between **present** and **past verbs**, which is special because it is signalled by **inflections** and normally indicates differences of time. In contrast, languages like French, Spanish and Italian, have three or more distinct tense forms, including a future tense. (See also: **future**.)	*He <u>studies</u>.* [present tense – present time] *He <u>studied</u> yesterday.* [past tense – past time] *He <u>studies</u> tomorrow, or else!* [present tense – future time] *He <u>may study</u> tomorrow.* [present tense + infinitive – future time]

Term	Guidance	Example
	The simple tenses (present and past) may be combined in English with the **perfect** and **progressive**.	*He plans to study tomorrow.* [present tense + infinitive – future time] *If he studied tomorrow, he'd see the difference!* [past tense – imagined future] Contrast three distinct tense forms in Spanish: • *Estudia.* [present tense] • *Estudió.* [past tense] • *Estudiará.* [future tense]
transitive verb	A transitive verb takes at least one object in a sentence to complete its meaning, in contrast to an **intransitive verb**, which does not.	*He loves Juliet.* *She understands English grammar.*
trigraph	A type of **grapheme** where three letters represent one **phoneme**.	*High, pure, patch, hedge*
unstressed	See **stressed**.	
verb	The surest way to identify verbs is by the ways they can be used: they can usually have a **tense**, either **present** or **past** (see also **future**). Verbs are sometimes called 'doing words' because many verbs name an action that someone does; while this can be a way of recognising verbs, it doesn't distinguish verbs from **nouns** (which can also name actions). Moreover many verbs name states or feelings rather than actions. Verbs can be classified in various ways: for example, as **auxiliary**, or **modal**; as **transitive** or **intransitive**; and as states or events.	*He lives in Birmingham.* [present tense] *The teacher wrote a song for the class.* [past tense] *He likes chocolate.* [present tense; not an action] *He knew my father.* [past tense; not an action] Not verbs: • *The walk to Halina's house will take an hour.* [noun] • *All that surfing makes Morwenna so sleepy!* [noun]
vowel	A vowel is a speech sound which is produced without any closure or obstruction of the vocal tract. Vowels can form **syllables** by themselves, or they may combine with **consonants**. In the English writing system, the letters *a, e, i, o, u* and *y* can represent vowels.	

word	A word is a unit of grammar: it can be selected and moved around relatively independently, but cannot easily be split. In punctuation, words are normally separated by word spaces. Sometimes, a sequence that appears grammatically to be two words is collapsed into a single written word, indicated with a hyphen or apostrophe (e.g. *well-built, he's*).	*headteacher* or *head teacher* [can be written with or without a space] *I'm* going out. *9.30 am*
word class	Every **word** belongs to a word class which summarises the ways in which it can be used in grammar. The major word classes for English are: **noun, verb, adjective, adverb, preposition, determiner, pronoun, conjunction**. Word classes are sometimes called 'parts of speech'.	
word family	The **words** in a word family are normally related to each other by a combination of **morphology**, grammar and meaning.	*teach – teacher* *extend – extent – extensive* *grammar – grammatical – grammarian*

MATHEMATICS

Purpose of study

Mathematics is a creative and highly inter-connected discipline that has been developed over centuries, providing the solution to some of history's most intriguing problems. It is essential to everyday life, critical to science, technology and engineering, and necessary for financial literacy and most forms of employment. A high-quality mathematics education therefore provides a foundation for understanding the world, the ability to reason mathematically, an appreciation of the beauty and power of mathematics, and a sense of enjoyment and curiosity about the subject.

Aims

The national curriculum for mathematics aims to ensure that all pupils:

- become **fluent** in the fundamentals of mathematics, including through varied and frequent practice with increasingly complex problems over time, so that pupils develop conceptual understanding and the ability to recall and apply knowledge rapidly and accurately.
- **reason mathematically** by following a line of enquiry, conjecturing relationships and generalisations, and developing an argument, justification or proof using mathematical language
- can **solve problems** by applying their mathematics to a variety of routine and non-routine problems with increasing sophistication, including breaking down problems into a series of simpler steps and persevering in seeking solutions.

Mathematics is an interconnected subject in which pupils need to be able to move fluently between representations of mathematical ideas. The programmes of study are, by necessity, organised into apparently distinct domains, but pupils should make rich connections across mathematical ideas to develop fluency, mathematical reasoning and competence in solving increasingly sophisticated problems. They should also apply their mathematical knowledge to science and other subjects.

The expectation is that the majority of pupils will move through the programmes of study at broadly the same pace. However, decisions about when to progress should always be based on the security of pupils' understanding and their readiness to progress to the next stage. Pupils who grasp concepts rapidly should be challenged through being offered rich and sophisticated problems before any acceleration through new content. Those who are not sufficiently fluent with earlier material should consolidate their understanding, including through additional practice, before moving on.

Information and communication technology (ICT)

Calculators should not be used as a substitute for good written and mental arithmetic. They should therefore only be introduced near the end of key stage 2 to support pupils' conceptual understanding and exploration of more complex number problems, if written and mental arithmetic are secure. In both primary and secondary schools, teachers should use their judgement about when ICT tools should be used.

Spoken language

The national curriculum for mathematics reflects the importance of spoken language in pupils' development across the whole curriculum – cognitively, socially and linguistically. The quality and variety of language that pupils hear and speak are key factors in developing their mathematical vocabulary and presenting a mathematical justification, argument or proof. They must be assisted in making their thinking clear to themselves as well as others and teachers should ensure that pupils build secure foundations by using discussion to probe and remedy their misconceptions.

School curriculum

The programmes of study for mathematics are set out year by year for key stages 1 and 2. Schools are, however, only required to teach the relevant programme of study by the end of the key stage. Within each key stage, schools therefore have the flexibility to introduce content earlier or later than set out in the programme of study. In addition, schools can introduce key stage content during an earlier key stage, if appropriate. All schools are also required to set out their school curriculum for mathematics on a year-by-year basis and make this information available online.

Attainment targets

By the end of each key stage, pupils are expected to know, apply and understand the matters, skills and processes specified in the relevant programme of study.

Schools are not required by law to teach the example content in [square brackets] or the content indicated as being 'non-statutory'.

Key stage 1 – years 1 and 2

The principal focus of mathematics teaching in key stage 1 is to ensure that pupils develop confidence and mental fluency with whole numbers, counting and place value. This should involve working with numerals, words and the four operations, including with practical resources [for example, concrete objects and measuring tools].

At this stage, pupils should develop their ability to recognise, describe, draw, compare and sort different shapes and use the related vocabulary. Teaching should also involve using a range of measures to describe and compare different quantities such as length, mass, capacity/volume, time and money.

By the end of year 2, pupils should know the number bonds to 20 and be precise in using and understanding place value. An emphasis on practice at this early stage will aid fluency.

Pupils should read and spell mathematical vocabulary, at a level consistent with their increasing word reading and spelling knowledge at key stage 1.

Year 1 programme of study

Number – number and place value

Statutory requirements

Pupils should be taught to:

- count to and across 100, forwards and backwards, beginning with 0 or 1, or from any given number
- count, read and write numbers to 100 in numerals; count in multiples of twos, fives and tens
- given a number, identify one more and one less
- identify and represent numbers using objects and pictorial representations including the number line, and use the language of: equal to, more than, less than (fewer), most, least
- read and write numbers from 1 to 20 in numerals and words.

Notes and guidance (non-statutory)

Pupils practise counting (1, 2, 3...), ordering (for example, first, second, third...), and to indicate a quantity (for example, 3 apples, 2 centimetres), including solving simple concrete problems, until they are fluent.

Pupils begin to recognise place value in numbers beyond 20 by reading, writing, counting and comparing numbers up to 100, supported by objects and pictorial representations.

They practise counting as reciting numbers and counting as enumerating objects, and counting in twos, fives and tens from different multiples to develop their recognition of patterns in the number system (for example, odd and even numbers), including varied and frequent practice through increasingly complex questions.

They recognise and create repeating patterns with objects and with shapes.

Number – addition and subtraction

Statutory requirements

Pupils should be taught to:

- read, write and interpret mathematical statements involving addition (+), subtraction (–) and equals (=) signs
- represent and use number bonds and related subtraction facts within 20
- add and subtract one-digit and two-digit numbers to 20, including zero
- solve one-step problems that involve addition and subtraction, using concrete objects and pictorial representations, and missing number problems such as $7 = \square - 9$.

Number – multiplication and division

Statutory requirements

Pupils should be taught to:

- solve one-step problems involving multiplication and division, by calculating the answer using concrete objects, pictorial representations and arrays with the support of the teacher.

Notes and guidance (non-statutory)

Through grouping and sharing small quantities, pupils begin to understand: multiplication and division; doubling numbers and quantities; and finding simple fractions of objects, numbers and quantities.

They make connections between arrays, number patterns, and counting in twos, fives and tens.

Number – fractions

Statutory requirements

Pupils should be taught to:

- recognise, find and name a half as one of two equal parts of an object, shape or quantity
- recognise, find and name a quarter as one of four equal parts of an object, shape or quantity.

> **Notes and guidance (non-statutory)**
>
> Pupils are taught half and quarter as 'fractions of' discrete and continuous quantities by solving problems using shapes, objects and quantities. For example, they could recognise and find half a length, quantity, set of objects or shape. Pupils connect halves and quarters to the equal sharing and grouping of sets of objects and to measures, as well as recognising and combining halves and quarters as parts of a whole.

Measurement

Statutory requirements

Pupils should be taught to:

- compare, describe and solve practical problems for:

  - lengths and heights [for example, long/short, longer/shorter, tall/short, double/half]
  - mass/weight [for example, heavy/light, heavier than, lighter than]
  - capacity and volume [for example, full/empty, more than, less than, half, half full, quarter]
  - time [for example, quicker, slower, earlier, later]

- measure and begin to record the following:

  - lengths and heights
  - mass/weight
  - capacity and volume
  - time (hours, minutes, seconds)

- recognise and know the value of different denominations of coins and notes
- sequence events in chronological order using language [for example, before and after, next, first, today, yesterday, tomorrow, morning, afternoon and evening]
- recognise and use language relating to dates, including days of the week, weeks, months and years
- tell the time to the hour and half past the hour and draw the hands on a clock face to show these times.

> **Notes and guidance (non-statutory)**
>
> The pairs of terms: mass and weight, volume and capacity, are used interchangeably at this stage.
>
> Pupils move from using and comparing different types of quantities and measures using non-standard units, including discrete (for example, counting) and continuous (for example, liquid) measurement, to using manageable common standard units.
>
> In order to become familiar with standard measures, pupils begin to use measuring tools such as a ruler, weighing scales and containers.
>
> Pupils use the language of time, including telling the time throughout the day, first using o'clock and then half past.

Geometry – properties of shapes

Statutory requirements

Pupils should be taught to:

- recognise and name common 2-D and 3-D shapes, including:

  o   2-D shapes [for example, rectangles (including squares), circles and triangles]
  o   3-D shapes [for example, cuboids (including cubes), pyramids and spheres].

Notes and guidance (non-statutory)

Pupils handle common 2-D and 3-D shapes, naming these and related everyday objects fluently. They recognise these shapes in different orientations and sizes, and know that rectangles, triangles, cuboids and pyramids are not always similar to each other.

Geometry – position and direction

Statutory requirements

Pupils should be taught to:

- describe position, direction and movement, including whole, half, quarter and three-quarter turns.

Notes and guidance (non-statutory)

Pupils use the language of position, direction and motion, including: left and right, top, middle and bottom, on top of, in front of, above, between, around, near, close and far, up and down, forwards and backwards, inside and outside.

   Pupils make whole, half, quarter and three-quarter turns in both directions and connect turning clockwise with movement on a clock face.

Year 2 programme of study

Number – number and place value

Statutory requirements

Pupils should be taught to:

- count in steps of 2, 3, and 5 from 0, and in tens from any number, forward and backward
- recognise the place value of each digit in a two-digit number (tens, ones)

(Continued)

(Continued)

- identify, represent and estimate numbers using different representations, including the number line
- compare and order numbers from 0 up to 100; use <, > and = signs
- read and write numbers to at least 100 in numerals and in words
- use place value and number facts to solve problems.

Notes and guidance (non-statutory)

Using materials and a range of representations, pupils practise counting, reading, writing and comparing numbers to at least 100 and solving a variety of related problems to develop fluency. They count in multiples of three to support their later understanding of a third.

As they become more confident with numbers up to 100, pupils are introduced to larger numbers to develop further their recognition of patterns within the number system and represent them in different ways, including spatial representations.

Pupils should partition numbers in different ways (for example, $23 = 20 + 3$ and $23 = 10 + 13$) to support subtraction. They become fluent and apply their knowledge of numbers to reason with, discuss and solve problems that emphasise the value of each digit in two-digit numbers. They begin to understand zero as a place holder.

Number – addition and subtraction

Statutory requirements

Pupils should be taught to:

- solve problems with addition and subtraction:

  o using concrete objects and pictorial representations, including those involving numbers, quantities and measures
  o applying their increasing knowledge of mental and written methods

- recall and use addition and subtraction facts to 20 fluently, and derive and use related facts up to 100
- add and subtract numbers using concrete objects, pictorial representations, and mentally, including:

  o a two-digit number and ones
  o a two-digit number and tens
  o two two-digit numbers
  o adding three one-digit numbers

- show that addition of two numbers can be done in any order (commutative) and subtraction of one number from another cannot
- recognise and use the inverse relationship between addition and subtraction and use this to check calculations and solve missing number problems.

Number – multiplication and division

Statutory requirements

Pupils should be taught to:

- recall and use multiplication and division facts for the 2, 5 and 10 multiplication tables, including recognising odd and even numbers
- calculate mathematical statements for multiplication and division within the multiplication tables and write them using the multiplication (×), division (÷) and equals (=) signs
- show that multiplication of two numbers can be done in any order (commutative) and division of one number by another cannot
- solve problems involving multiplication and division, using materials, arrays, repeated addition, mental methods, and multiplication and division facts, including problems in contexts.

Notes and guidance (non-statutory)

Pupils use a variety of language to describe multiplication and division.

Pupils are introduced to the multiplication tables. They practise to become fluent in the 2, 5 and 10 multiplication tables and connect them to each other. They connect the 10 multiplication table to place value, and the 5 multiplication table to the divisions on the clock face. They begin to use other multiplication tables and recall multiplication facts, including using related division facts to perform written and mental calculations.

Pupils work with a range of materials and contexts in which multiplication and division relate to grouping and sharing discrete and continuous quantities, to arrays and to repeated addition. They begin to relate these to fractions and measures (for example, $40 \div 2 = 20$, 20 is a half of 40). They use commutativity and inverse relations to develop multiplicative reasoning (for example, $4 \times 5 = 20$ and $20 \div 5 = 4$).

Number – fractions

Statutory requirements

Pupils should be taught to:

- recognise, find, name and write fractions $\frac{1}{3}, \frac{1}{4}, \frac{2}{4}$ and $\frac{3}{4}$, of a length, shape, set of objects or quantity
- write simple fractions for example, $\frac{1}{2}$ of 6 = 3 and recognise the equivalence of $\frac{2}{4}$ and $\frac{1}{2}$.

Notes and guidance (non-statutory)

Pupils use fractions as 'fractions of' discrete and continuous quantities by solving problems using shapes, objects and quantities. They connect unit fractions to equal sharing and grouping, to numbers when they can be calculated, and to measures, finding fractions of lengths, quantities, sets of objects or shapes. They meet $\frac{3}{4}$ as the first example of a non-unit fraction.

Pupils should count in fractions up to 10, starting from any number and using the $\frac{1}{2}$ and $\frac{2}{4}$ equivalence on the number line (for example, $1\frac{1}{4}, 1\frac{2}{4}$ (or $1\frac{1}{2}$), $1\frac{3}{4}$, 2). This reinforces the concept of fractions as numbers and that they can add up to more than one.

Measurement

Statutory requirements

Pupils should be taught to:

- choose and use appropriate standard units to estimate and measure length/height in any direction (m/cm); mass (kg/g); temperature (°C); capacity (litres/ml) to the nearest appropriate unit, using rulers, scales, thermometers and measuring vessels
- compare and order lengths, mass, volume/capacity and record the results using >, < and =
- recognise and use symbols for pounds (£) and pence (p); combine amounts to make a particular value
- find different combinations of coins that equal the same amounts of money
- solve simple problems in a practical context involving addition and subtraction of money of the same unit, including giving change
- compare and sequence intervals of time
- tell and write the time to five minutes, including quarter past/to the hour and draw the hands on a clock face to show these times
- know the number of minutes in an hour and the number of hours in a day.

Notes and guidance (non-statutory)

Pupils use standard units of measurement with increasing accuracy, using their knowledge of the number system. They use the appropriate language and record using standard abbreviations.

Comparing measures includes simple multiples such as 'half as high'; 'twice as wide'.

They become fluent in telling the time on analogue clocks and recording it.

Pupils become fluent in counting and recognising coins. They read and say amounts of money confidently and use the symbols £ and p accurately, recording pounds and pence separately.

Geometry – properties of shapes

Statutory requirements

Pupils should be taught to:

- identify and describe the properties of 2-D shapes, including the number of sides and line symmetry in a vertical line
- identify and describe the properties of 3-D shapes, including the number of edges, vertices and faces
- identify 2-D shapes on the surface of 3-D shapes [for example, a circle on a cylinder and a triangle on a pyramid]
- compare and sort common 2-D and 3-D shapes and everyday objects.

Notes and guidance (non-statutory)

Pupils handle and name a wide variety of common 2-D and 3-D shapes including: quadrilaterals and polygons, and cuboids, prisms and cones, and identify the properties of each shape (for example, number of sides, number of faces). Pupils identify, compare and sort shapes on the basis of their properties and use vocabulary precisely, such as sides, edges, vertices and faces.

Pupils read and write names for shapes that are appropriate for their word reading and spelling.

Pupils draw lines and shapes using a straight edge.

Geometry – position and direction

Statutory requirements

Pupils should be taught to:

- order and arrange combinations of mathematical objects in patterns and sequences
- use mathematical vocabulary to describe position, direction and movement, including movement in a straight line and distinguishing between rotation as a turn and in terms of right angles for quarter, half and three-quarter turns (clockwise and anti-clockwise).

Notes and guidance (non-statutory)

Pupils should work with patterns of shapes, including those in different orientations.
Pupils use the concept and language of angles to describe 'turn' by applying rotations, including in practical contexts (for example, pupils themselves moving in turns, giving instructions to other pupils to do so, and programming robots using instructions given in right angles).

Statistics

Statutory requirements

Pupils should be taught to:

- interpret and construct simple pictograms, tally charts, block diagrams and simple tables
- ask and answer simple questions by counting the number of objects in each category and sorting the categories by quantity
- ask and answer questions about totalling and comparing categorical data.

Notes and guidance (non-statutory)

Pupils record, interpret, collate, organise and compare information (for example, using many-to-one correspondence in pictograms with simple ratios 2, 5, 10).

Lower key stage 2 – years 3 and 4

The principal focus of mathematics teaching in lower key stage 2 is to ensure that pupils become increasingly fluent with whole numbers and the four operations, including number facts and the concept of place value. This should ensure that pupils develop efficient written and mental methods and perform calculations accurately with increasingly large whole numbers.

At this stage, pupils should develop their ability to solve a range of problems, including with simple fractions and decimal place value. Teaching should also ensure that pupils draw with increasing accuracy and develop mathematical reasoning so they can analyse shapes and their properties, and confidently describe the relationships between them. It should ensure that they can use measuring instruments with accuracy and make connections between measure and number.

By the end of year 4, pupils should have memorised their multiplication tables up to and including the 12 multiplication table and show precision and fluency in their work.

Pupils should read and spell mathematical vocabulary correctly and confidently, using their growing word reading knowledge and their knowledge of spelling.

Year 3 programme of study

Number – number and place value

Statutory requirements

Pupils should be taught to:

- count from 0 in multiples of 4, 8, 50 and 100; find 10 or 100 more or less than a given number
- recognise the place value of each digit in a three-digit number (hundreds, tens, ones)
- compare and order numbers up to 1000
- identify, represent and estimate numbers using different representations
- read and write numbers up to 1000 in numerals and in words
- solve number problems and practical problems involving these ideas.

Notes and guidance (non-statutory)

Pupils now use multiples of 2, 3, 4, 5, 8, 10, 50 and 100.

They use larger numbers to at least 1000, applying partitioning related to place value using varied and increasingly complex problems, building on work in year 2 (for example, 146 = 100 + 40 and 6, 146 = 130 + 16).

Using a variety of representations, including those related to measure, pupils continue to count in ones, tens and hundreds, so that they become fluent in the order and place value of numbers to 1000.

Number – addition and subtraction

Statutory requirements

Pupils should be taught to:

- add and subtract numbers mentally, including:

  o   a three-digit number and ones
  o   a three-digit number and tens
  o   a three-digit number and hundreds

- add and subtract numbers with up to three digits, using formal written methods of columnar addition and subtraction
- estimate the answer to a calculation and use inverse operations to check answers
- solve problems, including missing number problems, using number facts, place value, and more complex addition and subtraction.

Notes and guidance (non-statutory)

Pupils practise solving varied addition and subtraction questions. For mental calculations with two-digit numbers, the answers could exceed 100.

Pupils use their understanding of place value and partitioning, and practise using columnar addition and subtraction with increasingly large numbers up to three digits to become fluent (see Mathematics Appendix 1).

Number – multiplication and division

Statutory requirements

Pupils should be taught to:

- recall and use multiplication and division facts for the 3, 4 and 8 multiplication tables
- write and calculate mathematical statements for multiplication and division using the multiplication tables that they know, including for two-digit numbers times one-digit numbers, using mental and progressing to formal written methods
- solve problems, including missing number problems, involving multiplication and division, including positive integer scaling problems and correspondence problems in which n objects are connected to m objects.

Notes and guidance (non-statutory)

Pupils continue to practise their mental recall of multiplication tables when they are calculating mathematical statements in order to improve fluency. Through doubling, they connect the 2, 4 and 8 multiplication tables.

Pupils develop efficient mental methods, for example, using commutativity and associativity (for example, $4 \times 12 \times 5 = 4 \times 5 \times 12 = 20 \times 12 = 240$) and multiplication and division facts (for example, using $3 \times 2 = 6$, $6 \div 3 = 2$ and $2 = 6 \div 3$) to derive related facts (for example, $30 \times 2 = 60$, $60 \div 3 = 20$ and $20 = 60 \div 3$).

Pupils develop reliable written methods for multiplication and division, starting with calculations of two-digit numbers by one-digit numbers and progressing to the formal written methods of short multiplication and division.

Pupils solve simple problems in contexts, deciding which of the four operations to use and why. These include measuring and scaling contexts, (for example, four times as high, eight times as long etc.) and correspondence problems in which m objects are connected to n objects (for example, 3 hats and 4 coats, how many different outfits?; 12 sweets shared equally between 4 children; 4 cakes shared equally between 8 children).

Number – fractions

Statutory requirements

Pupils should be taught to:

- count up and down in tenths; recognise that tenths arise from dividing an object into 10 equal parts and in dividing one-digit numbers or quantities by 10
- recognise, find and write fractions of a discrete set of objects: unit fractions and non-unit fractions with small denominators

- recognise and use fractions as numbers: unit fractions and non-unit fractions with small denominators
- recognise and show, using diagrams, equivalent fractions with small denominators
- add and subtract fractions with the same denominator within one whole [for example, $\frac{5}{7} + \frac{1}{7} = \frac{6}{7}$]
- compare and order unit fractions, and fractions with the same denominators
- solve problems that involve all of the above.

Notes and guidance (non-statutory)

Pupils connect tenths to place value, decimal measures and to division by 10.

They begin to understand unit and non-unit fractions as numbers on the number line, and deduce relations between them, such as size and equivalence. They should go beyond the [0, 1] interval, including relating this to measure.

Pupils understand the relation between unit fractions as operators (fractions of), and division by integers.

They continue to recognise fractions in the context of parts of a whole, numbers, measurements, a shape, and unit fractions as a division of a quantity.

Pupils practise adding and subtracting fractions with the same denominator through a variety of increasingly complex problems to improve fluency.

Measurement

Statutory requirements

Pupils should be taught to:

- measure, compare, add and subtract: lengths (m/cm/mm); mass (kg/g); volume/capacity (l/ml)
- measure the perimeter of simple 2-D shapes
- add and subtract amounts of money to give change, using both £ and p in practical contexts
- tell and write the time from an analogue clock, including using Roman numerals from I to XII, and 12-hour and 24-hour clocks
- estimate and read time with increasing accuracy to the nearest minute; record and compare time in terms of seconds, minutes and hours; use vocabulary such as o'clock, a.m./p.m., morning, afternoon, noon and midnight
- know the number of seconds in a minute and the number of days in each month, year and leap year
- compare durations of events [for example to calculate the time taken by particular events or tasks].

Notes and guidance (non-statutory)

Pupils continue to measure using the appropriate tools and units, progressing to using a wider range of measures, including comparing and using mixed units (for example, 1 kg and 200g) and simple equivalents of mixed units (for example, 5m = 500cm).

(Continued)

(Continued)

The comparison of measures includes simple scaling by integers (for example, a given quantity or measure is twice as long or five times as high) and this connects to multiplication.

Pupils continue to become fluent in recognising the value of coins, by adding and subtracting amounts, including mixed units, and giving change using manageable amounts. They record £ and p separately. The decimal recording of money is introduced formally in year 4.

Pupils use both analogue and digital 12-hour clocks and record their times. In this way they become fluent in and prepared for using digital 24-hour clocks in year 4.

Geometry – properties of shapes

Statutory requirements

Pupils should be taught to:

- draw 2-D shapes and make 3-D shapes using modelling materials; recognise 3-D shapes in different orientations and describe them
- recognise angles as a property of shape or a description of a turn
- identify right angles, recognise that two right angles make a half-turn, three make three-quarters of a turn and four a complete turn; identify whether angles are greater than or less than a right angle
- identify horizontal and vertical lines and pairs of perpendicular and parallel lines.

Notes and guidance (non-statutory)

Pupils' knowledge of the properties of shapes is extended at this stage to symmetrical and non-symmetrical polygons and polyhedra. Pupils extend their use of the properties of shapes. They should be able to describe the properties of 2-D and 3-D shapes using accurate language, including lengths of lines and acute and obtuse for angles greater or lesser than a right angle.

Pupils connect decimals and rounding to drawing and measuring straight lines in centimetres, in a variety of contexts.

Statutory requirements

Pupils should be taught to:

- interpret and present data using bar charts, pictograms and tables
- solve one-step and two-step questions [for example, 'How many more?' and 'How many fewer?'] using information presented in scaled bar charts and pictograms and tables.

Notes and guidance (non-statutory)

Pupils understand and use simple scales (for example, 2, 5, 10 units per cm) in pictograms and bar charts with increasing accuracy.

They continue to interpret data presented in many contexts.

Year 4 programme of study

Number – number and place value

Statutory requirements

Pupils should be taught to

- count in multiples of 6, 7, 9, 25 and 1000
- find 1000 more or less than a given number
- count backwards through zero to include negative numbers
- recognise the place value of each digit in a four-digit number (thousands, hundreds, tens, and ones)
- order and compare numbers beyond 1000
- identify, represent and estimate numbers using different representations
- round any number to the nearest 10, 100 or 1000
- solve number and practical problems that involve all of the above and with increasingly large positive numbers
- read Roman numerals to 100 (I to C) and know that over time, the numeral system changed to include the concept of zero and place value.

Notes and guidance (non-statutory)

Using a variety of representations, including measures, pupils become fluent in the order and place value of numbers beyond 1000, including counting in tens and hundreds, and maintaining fluency in other multiples through varied and frequent practice.

They begin to extend their knowledge of the number system to include the decimal numbers and fractions that they have met so far.

They connect estimation and rounding numbers to the use of measuring instruments.

Roman numerals should be put in their historical context so pupils understand that there have been different ways to write whole numbers and that the important concepts of zero and place value were introduced over a period of time.

Number – addition and subtraction

Statutory requirements

Pupils should be taught to:

- add and subtract numbers with up to 4 digits using the formal written methods of columnar addition and subtraction where appropriate
- estimate and use inverse operations to check answers to a calculation
- solve addition and subtraction two-step problems in contexts, deciding which operations and methods to use and why.

Notes and guidance (non-statutory)

Pupils continue to practise both mental methods and columnar addition and subtraction with increasingly large numbers to aid fluency (see Mathematics Appendix 1).

Number – multiplication and division

Statutory requirements

Pupils should be taught to:

- recall multiplication and division facts for multiplication tables up to 12 × 12
- use place value, known and derived facts to multiply and divide mentally, including: multiplying by 0 and 1; dividing by 1; multiplying together three numbers
- recognise and use factor pairs and commutativity in mental calculations
- multiply two-digit and three-digit numbers by a one-digit number using formal written layout
- solve problems involving multiplying and adding, including using the distributive law to multiply two digit numbers by one digit, integer scaling problems and harder correspondence problems such as n objects are connected to m objects.

Notes and guidance (non-statutory)

Pupils continue to practise recalling and using multiplication tables and related division facts to aid fluency.

Pupils practise mental methods and extend this to three-digit numbers to derive facts, (for example 600 ÷ 3 = 200 can be derived from 2 × 3 = 6).

Pupils practise to become fluent in the formal written method of short multiplication and short division with exact answers (see Mathematics Appendix 1).

Pupils write statements about the equality of expressions (for example, use the distributive law $39 \times 7 = 30 \times 7 + 9 \times 7$ and associative law $(2 \times 3) \times 4 = 2 \times (3 \times 4)$). They combine their knowledge of number facts and rules of arithmetic to solve mental and written calculations for example, $2 \times 6 \times 5 = 10 \times 6 = 60$.

Pupils solve two-step problems in contexts, choosing the appropriate operation, working with increasingly harder numbers. This should include correspondence questions such as the numbers of choices of a meal on a menu, or three cakes shared equally between 10 children.

Number – fractions (including decimals)

Statutory requirements

Pupils should be taught to:

- recognise and show, using diagrams, families of common equivalent fractions
- count up and down in hundredths; recognise that hundredths arise when dividing an object by one hundred and dividing tenths by ten
- solve problems involving increasingly harder fractions to calculate quantities, and fractions to divide quantities, including non-unit fractions where the answer is a whole number
- add and subtract fractions with the same denominator
- recognise and write decimal equivalents of any number of tenths or hundredths
- recognise and write decimal equivalents to $\frac{1}{4}, \frac{1}{2}, \frac{3}{4}$

- find the effect of dividing a one- or two-digit number by 10 and 100, identifying the value of the digits in the answer as ones, tenths and hundredths
- round decimals with one decimal place to the nearest whole number
- compare numbers with the same number of decimal places up to two decimal places
- solve simple measure and money problems involving fractions and decimals to two decimal places.

Notes and guidance (non-statutory)

Pupils should connect hundredths to tenths and place value and decimal measure.

They extend the use of the number line to connect fractions, numbers and measures.

Pupils understand the relation between non-unit fractions and multiplication and division of quantities, with particular emphasis on tenths and hundredths.

Pupils make connections between fractions of a length, of a shape and as a representation of one whole or set of quantities. Pupils use factors and multiples to recognise equivalent fractions and simplify where appropriate (for example, $\frac{6}{9} = \frac{2}{3}$ or $\frac{1}{4} = \frac{2}{8}$)

Pupils continue to practise adding and subtracting fractions with the same denominator, to become fluent through a variety of increasingly complex problems beyond one whole.

Pupils are taught throughout that decimals and fractions are different ways of expressing numbers and proportions.

Pupils' understanding of the number system and decimal place value is extended at this stage to tenths and then hundredths. This includes relating the decimal notation to division of whole number by 10 and later 100.

They practise counting using simple fractions and decimals, both forwards and backwards.

Pupils learn decimal notation and the language associated with it, including in the context of measurements. They make comparisons and order decimal amounts and quantities that are expressed to the same number of decimal places. They should be able to represent numbers with one or two decimal places in several ways, such as on number lines.

Measurement

Statutory requirements

Pupils should be taught to:

- Convert between different units of measure [for example, kilometre to metre; hour to minute]
- measure and calculate the perimeter of a rectilinear figure (including squares) in centimetres and metres
- find the area of rectilinear shapes by counting squares
- estimate, compare and calculate different measures, including money in pounds and pence
- read, write and convert time between analogue and digital 12- and 24-hour clocks
- solve problems involving converting from hours to minutes; minutes to seconds; years to months; weeks to days.

Notes and guidance (non-statutory)

Pupils build on their understanding of place value and decimal notation to record metric measures, including money.

They use multiplication to convert from larger to smaller units.

Perimeter can be expressed algebraically as $2(a + b)$ where a and b are the dimensions in the same unit.

They relate area to arrays and multiplication.

Geometry – properties of shapes

Statutory requirements

Pupils should be taught to:

- compare and classify geometric shapes, including quadrilaterals and triangles, based on their properties and sizes
- identify acute and obtuse angles and compare and order angles up to two right angles by size
- identify lines of symmetry in 2-D shapes presented in different orientations
- complete a simple symmetric figure with respect to a specific line of symmetry.

Notes and guidance (non-statutory)

Pupils continue to classify shapes using geometrical properties, extending to classifying different triangles (for example, isosceles, equilateral, scalene) and quadrilaterals (for example, parallelogram, rhombus, trapezium).

Pupils compare and order angles in preparation for using a protractor and compare lengths and angles to decide if a polygon is regular or irregular.

Pupils draw symmetric patterns using a variety of media to become familiar with different orientations of lines of symmetry; and recognise line symmetry in a variety of diagrams, including where the line of symmetry does not dissect the original shape.

Geometry – position and direction

Statutory requirements

Pupils should be taught to:

- describe positions on a 2-D grid as coordinates in the first quadrant
- describe movements between positions as translations of a given unit to the left/ right and up/down
- plot specified points and draw sides to complete a given polygon.

Notes and guidance (non-statutory)

Pupils draw a pair of axes in one quadrant, with equal scales and integer labels. They read, write and use pairs of coordinates, for example (2, 5), including using coordinate-plotting ICT tools.

Statistics

Statutory requirements

Pupils should be taught to:

*   interpret and present discrete and continuous data using appropriate graphical methods, including bar charts and time graphs.
*   solve comparison, sum and difference problems using information presented in bar charts, pictograms, tables and other graphs.

Notes and guidance (non-statutory)

Pupils understand and use a greater range of scales in their representations.
    Pupils begin to relate the graphical representation of data to recording change over time.

Upper key stage 2 – years 5 and 6

The principal focus of mathematics teaching in upper key stage 2 is to ensure that pupils extend their understanding of the number system and place value to include larger integers. This should develop the connections that pupils make between multiplication and division with fractions, decimals, percentages and ratio.

At this stage, pupils should develop their ability to solve a wider range of problems, including increasingly complex properties of numbers and arithmetic, and problems demanding efficient written and mental methods of calculation. With this foundation in arithmetic, pupils are introduced to the language of algebra as a means for solving a variety of problems. Teaching in geometry and measures should consolidate and extend knowledge developed in number. Teaching should also ensure that pupils classify shapes with increasingly complex geometric properties and that they learn the vocabulary they need to describe them.

By the end of year 6, pupils should be fluent in written methods for all four operations, including long multiplication and division, and in working with fractions, decimals and percentages.

Pupils should read, spell and pronounce mathematical vocabulary correctly.

Year 5 programme of study

Number – number and place value

> **Statutory requirements**
>
> Pupils should be taught to:
>
> - read, write, order and compare numbers to at least 1 000 000 and determine the value of each digit
> - count forwards or backwards in steps of powers of 10 for any given number up to 1 000 000
> - interpret negative numbers in context, count forwards and backwards with positive and negative whole numbers, including through zero
> - round any number up to 1 000 000 to the nearest 10, 100, 1000, 10 000 and 100 000
> - solve number problems and practical problems that involve all of the above
> - read Roman numerals to 1000 (M) and recognise years written in Roman numerals.

> **Notes and guidance (non-statutory)**
>
> Pupils identify the place value in large whole numbers.
>
> They continue to use number in context, including measurement. Pupils extend and apply their understanding of the number system to the decimal numbers and fractions that they have met so far.
>
> They should recognise and describe linear number sequences, including those involving fractions and decimals, and find the term-to-term rule.
>
> They should recognise and describe linear number sequences (for example, 3, $3\frac{1}{2}$, 4, $4\frac{1}{2}$ ...), including those involving fractions and decimals, and find the term-to-term rule in words (for example, add $\frac{1}{2}$).

Number – addition and subtraction

> **Statutory requirements**
>
> Pupils should be taught to:
>
> - add and subtract whole numbers with more than 4 digits, including using formal written methods (columnar addition and subtraction)
> - add and subtract numbers mentally with increasingly large numbers
> - use rounding to check answers to calculations and determine, in the context of a problem, levels of accuracy
> - solve addition and subtraction multi-step problems in contexts, deciding which operations and methods to use and why.

Notes and guidance (non-statutory)

Pupils practise using the formal written methods of columnar addition and subtraction with increasingly large numbers to aid fluency (see Mathematics Appendix 1).

They practise mental calculations with increasingly large numbers to aid fluency (for example, 12 462 − 2300 = 10 162).

Number – multiplication and division

Statutory requirements

Pupils should be taught to:

- identify multiples and factors, including finding all factor pairs of a number, and common factors of two numbers
- know and use the vocabulary of prime numbers, prime factors and composite (non-prime) numbers
- establish whether a number up to 100 is prime and recall prime numbers up to 19
- multiply numbers up to 4 digits by a one- or two-digit number using a formal written method, including long multiplication for two-digit numbers
- multiply and divide numbers mentally drawing upon known facts
- divide numbers up to 4 digits by a one-digit number using the formal written method of short division and interpret remainders appropriately for the context
- multiply and divide whole numbers and those involving decimals by 10, 100 and 1000
- recognise and use square numbers and cube numbers, and the notation for squared (^{2}) and cubed (^{3})
- solve problems involving multiplication and division including using their knowledge of factors and multiples, squares and cubes
- solve problems involving addition, subtraction, multiplication and division and a combination of these, including understanding the meaning of the equals sign
- solve problems involving multiplication and division, including scaling by simple fractions and problems involving simple rates.

Notes and guidance (non-statutory)

Pupils practise and extend their use of the formal written methods of short multiplication and short division (see Mathematics Appendix 1). They apply all the multiplication tables and related division facts frequently, commit them to memory and use them confidently to make larger calculations.

They use and understand the terms factor, multiple and prime, square and cube numbers.

Pupils interpret non-integer answers to division by expressing results in different ways according to the context, including with remainders, as fractions, as decimals or by rounding (for example, $98 \div 4 = \frac{98}{4} = 24 \text{ r } 2 = 24\frac{1}{2} = 24.5 \approx 25$).

(Continued)

(Continued)

Pupils use multiplication and division as inverses to support the introduction of ratio in year 6, for example, by multiplying and dividing by powers of 10 in scale drawings or by multiplying and dividing by powers of a 1000 in converting between units such as kilometres and metres.

Distributivity can be expressed as $a(b + c) = ab + ac$.

They understand the terms factor, multiple and prime, square and cube numbers and use them to construct equivalence statements (for example, $4 \times 35 = 2 \times 2 \times 35$; $3 \times 270 = 3 \times 3 \times 9 \times 10 = 9^2 \times 10$).

Pupils use and explain the equals sign to indicate equivalence, including in missing number problems (for example, $13 + 24 = 12 + 25$; $33 = 5 \times \square$).

Number – fractions (including decimals and percentages)

Statutory requirements

Pupils should be taught to:

- compare and order fractions whose denominators are all multiples of the same number
- identify, name and write equivalent fractions of a given fraction, represented visually, including tenths and hundredths
- recognise mixed numbers and improper fractions and convert from one form to the other and write mathematical statements > 1 as a mixed number [for example, $\frac{2}{5} + \frac{4}{5} = \frac{6}{5} = 1\frac{1}{5}$]
- add and subtract fractions with the same denominator and denominators that are multiples of the same number
- multiply proper fractions and mixed numbers by whole numbers, supported by materials and diagrams
- read and write decimal numbers as fractions [for example, $0.71 = \frac{71}{100}$]
- recognise and use thousandths and relate them to tenths, hundredths and decimal equivalents
- round decimals with two decimal places to the nearest whole number and to one decimal place
- read, write, order and compare numbers with up to three decimal places
- solve problems involving number up to three decimal places
- recognise the per cent symbol (%) and understand that per cent relates to 'number of parts per hundred', and write percentages as a fraction with denominator 100, and as a decimal
- solve problems which require knowing percentage and decimal equivalents of $\frac{1}{2}, \frac{1}{4}, \frac{1}{5}, \frac{2}{5}, \frac{4}{5}$ and those fractions with a denominator of a multiple of 10 or 25.

Notes and guidance (non-statutory)

Pupils should be taught throughout that percentages, decimals and fractions are different ways of expressing proportions.

They extend their knowledge of fractions to thousandths and connect to decimals and measures.

Pupils connect equivalent fractions > 1 that simplify to integers with division and other fractions > 1 to division with remainders, using the number line and other models, and hence move from these to improper and mixed fractions.

Pupils connect multiplication by a fraction to using fractions as operators (fractions of), and to division, building on work from previous years. This relates to scaling by simple fractions, including fractions > 1.

Pupils practise adding and subtracting fractions to become fluent through a variety of increasingly complex problems. They extend their understanding of adding and subtracting fractions to calculations that exceed 1 as a mixed number.

Pupils continue to practise counting forwards and backwards in simple fractions.

Pupils continue to develop their understanding of fractions as numbers, measures and operators by finding fractions of numbers and quantities.

Pupils extend counting from year 4, using decimals and fractions including bridging zero, for example on a number line.

Pupils say, read and write decimal fractions and related tenths, hundredths and thousandths accurately and are confident in checking the reasonableness of their answers to problems.

They mentally add and subtract tenths, and one-digit whole numbers and tenths.

They practise adding and subtracting decimals, including a mix of whole numbers and decimals, decimals with different numbers of decimal places, and complements of 1 (for example, $0.83 + 0.17 = 1$).

Pupils should go beyond the measurement and money models of decimals, for example, by solving puzzles involving decimals.

Pupils should make connections between percentages, fractions and decimals (for example, 100% represents a whole quantity and 1% is $\frac{1}{100}$, 50% is $\frac{50}{100}$, 25% is $\frac{25}{100}$) and relate this to finding 'fractions of'.

Measurement

Statutory requirements

Pupils should be taught to:

- convert between different units of metric measure (for example, kilometre and metre; centimetre and metre; centimetre and millimetre; gram and kilogram; litre and millilitre)
- understand and use approximate equivalences between metric units and common imperial units such as inches, pounds and pints
- measure and calculate the perimeter of composite rectilinear shapes in centimetres and metres
- calculate and compare the area of rectangles (including squares), and including using standard units, square centimetres (cm²) and square metres (m²) and estimate the area of irregular shapes
- estimate volume [for example, using 1 cm³ blocks to build cuboids (including cubes)] and capacity [for example, using water]
- solve problems involving converting between units of time
- use all four operations to solve problems involving measure [for example, length, mass, volume, money] using decimal notation, including scaling.

Notes and guidance (non-statutory)

Pupils use their knowledge of place value and multiplication and division to convert between standard units.

Pupils calculate the perimeter of rectangles and related composite shapes, including using the relations of perimeter or area to find unknown lengths. Missing measures questions such as these can be expressed algebraically, for example $4 + 2b = 20$ for a rectangle of sides 2 cm and b cm and perimeter of 20cm.

Pupils calculate the area from scale drawings using given measurements.

Pupils use all four operations in problems involving time and money, including conversions (for example, days to weeks, expressing the answer as weeks and days).

Geometry – properties of shapes

Statutory requirements

Pupils should be taught to:

- identify 3-D shapes, including cubes and other cuboids, from 2-D representations
- know angles are measured in degrees: estimate and compare acute, obtuse and reflex angles
- draw given angles, and measure them in degrees (°)
- identify:

  - angles at a point and one whole turn (total 360°)
  - angles at a point on a straight line and $\frac{1}{2}$ a turn (total 180°)
  - other multiples of 90°

- use the properties of rectangles to deduce related facts and find missing lengths and angles
- distinguish between regular and irregular polygons based on reasoning about equal sides and angles.

Notes and guidance (non-statutory)

Pupils become accurate in drawing lines with a ruler to the nearest millimetre, and measuring with a protractor. They use conventional markings for parallel lines and right angles.

Pupils use the term diagonal and make conjectures about the angles formed between sides, and between diagonals and parallel sides, and other properties of quadrilaterals, for example using dynamic geometry ICT tools.

Pupils use angle sum facts and other properties to make deductions about missing angles and relate these to missing number problems.

Geometry – position and direction

Statutory requirements

Pupils should be taught to:

- identify, describe and represent the position of a shape following a reflection or translation, using the appropriate language, and know that the shape has not changed.

Notes and guidance(non-statutory)

Pupils recognise and use reflection and translation in a variety of diagrams, including continuing to use a 2-D grid and coordinates in the first quadrant. Reflection should be in lines that are parallel to the axes.

Statistics

Statutory requirements

Pupils should be taught to:

- solve comparison, sum and difference problems using information presented in a line graph
- complete, read and interpret information in tables, including timetables.

Notes and guidance (non-statutory)

Pupils connect their work on coordinates and scales to their interpretation of time graphs. They begin to decide which representations of data are most appropriate and why.

Year 6 programme of study

Number – number and place value

Statutory requirements

Pupils should be taught to:

- read, write, order and compare numbers up to 10 000 000 and determine the value of each digit
- round any whole number to a required degree of accuracy
- use negative numbers in context, and calculate intervals across zero
- solve number and practical problems that involve all of the above.

Number – addition, subtraction, multiplication and division

Statutory requirements

Pupils should be taught to:

- multiply multi-digit numbers up to 4 digits by a two-digit whole number using the formal written method of long multiplication
- divide numbers up to 4 digits by a two-digit whole number using the formal written method of long division, and interpret remainders as whole number remainders, fractions, or by rounding, as appropriate for the context
- divide numbers up to 4 digits by a two-digit number using the formal written method of short division where appropriate, interpreting remainders according to the context
- perform mental calculations, including with mixed operations and large numbers
- identify common factors, common multiples and prime numbers
- use their knowledge of the order of operations to carry out calculations involving the four operations
- solve addition and subtraction multi-step problems in contexts, deciding which operations and methods to use and why
- solve problems involving addition, subtraction, multiplication and division
- use estimation to check answers to calculations and determine, in the context of a problem, an appropriate degree of accuracy.

Notes and guidance (non-statutory)

Pupils practise addition, subtraction, multiplication and division for larger numbers, using the formal written methods of columnar addition and subtraction, short and long multiplication, and short and long division (see Mathematics Appendix 1).

They undertake mental calculations with increasingly large numbers and more complex calculations.

Pupils continue to use all the multiplication tables to calculate mathematical statements in order to maintain their fluency.

Pupils round answers to a specified degree of accuracy, for example, to the nearest 10, 20, 50 etc., but not to a specified number of significant figures.

Pupils explore the order of operations using brackets; for example, $2 + 1 \times 3 = 5$ and $(2 + 1) \times 3 = 9$.

Common factors can be related to finding equivalent fractions.

Number – fractions (including decimals and percentages)

Statutory requirements

Pupils should be taught to:

- use common factors to simplify fractions; use common multiples to express fractions in the same denomination
- compare and order fractions, including fractions > 1
- add and subtract fractions with different denominators and mixed numbers, using the concept of equivalent fractions
- multiply simple pairs of proper fractions, writing the answer in its simplest form [for example, $\frac{1}{4} \times \frac{1}{2} = \frac{1}{8}$]
- divide proper fractions by whole numbers [for example, $\frac{1}{3} \div 2 = \frac{1}{6}$]
- associate a fraction with division and calculate decimal fraction equivalents [for example, 0.375] for a simple fraction [for example, $\frac{3}{8}$]
- identify the value of each digit in numbers given to three decimal places and multiply and divide numbers by 10, 100 and 1000 giving answers up to three decimal places
- multiply one-digit numbers with up to two decimal places by whole numbers
- use written division methods in cases where the answer has up to two decimal places
- solve problems which require answers to be rounded to specified degrees of accuracy
- recall and use equivalences between simple fractions, decimals and percentages, including in different contexts.

Notes and guidance (non-statutory)

Pupils should practise, use and understand the addition and subtraction of fractions with different denominators by identifying equivalent fractions with the same denominator. They should start with fractions where the denominator of one fraction is a multiple of the other (for example, $\frac{1}{2} + \frac{1}{8} = \frac{5}{8}$) and progress to varied and increasingly complex problems.

Pupils should use a variety of images to support their understanding of multiplication with fractions. This follows earlier work about fractions as operators (fractions of), as numbers, and as equal parts of objects, for example as parts of a rectangle.

Pupils use their understanding of the relationship between unit fractions and division to work backwards by multiplying a quantity that represents a unit fraction to find the whole quantity (for example, if $\frac{1}{4}$ of a length is 36cm, then the whole length is 36 × 4 = 144cm).

They practise calculations with simple fractions and decimal fraction equivalents to aid fluency, including listing equivalent fractions to identify fractions with common denominators.

Pupils can explore and make conjectures about converting a simple fraction to a decimal fraction (for example, 3 ÷ 8 = 0.375). For simple fractions with recurring decimal

(Continued)

(Continued)

appropriate approximations depending on the context. Pupils multiply and divide numbers with up to two decimal places by one-digit and two-digit whole numbers. Pupils multiply decimals by whole numbers, starting with the simplest cases, such as $0.4 \times 2 = 0.8$, and in practical contexts, such as measures and money.

Pupils are introduced to the division of decimal numbers by one-digit whole number, initially, in practical contexts involving measures and money. They recognise division calculations as the inverse of multiplication.

Pupils also develop their skills of rounding and estimating as a means of predicting and checking the order of magnitude of their answers to decimal calculations. This includes rounding answers to a specified degree of accuracy and checking the reasonableness of their answers.

Ratio and proportion

Statutory requirements

Pupils should be taught to:

- solve problems involving the relative sizes of two quantities where missing values can be found by using integer multiplication and division facts
- solve problems involving the calculation of percentages [for example, of measures, and such as 15% of 360] and the use of percentages for comparison
- solve problems involving similar shapes where the scale factor is known or can be found
- solve problems involving unequal sharing and grouping using knowledge of fractions and multiples.

Notes and guidance (non-statutory)

Pupils recognise proportionality in contexts when the relations between quantities are in the same ratio (for example, similar shapes and recipes).

Pupils link percentages or 360° to calculating angles of pie charts.

Pupils should consolidate their understanding of ratio when comparing quantities, sizes and scale drawings by solving a variety of problems. They might use the notation *a:b* to record their work.

Pupils solve problems involving unequal quantities, for example, 'for every egg you need three spoonfuls of flour', '$\frac{3}{5}$ of the class are boys'. These problems are the foundation for later formal approaches to ratio and proportion.

Algebra

Statutory requirements

Pupils should be taught to:

- use simple formulae
- generate and describe linear number sequences

- express missing number problems algebraically
- find pairs of numbers that satisfy an equation with two unknowns
- enumerate possibilities of combinations of two variables.

Notes and guidance (non-statutory)

Pupils should be introduced to the use of symbols and letters to represent variables and unknowns in mathematical situations that they already understand, such as:

- missing numbers, lengths, coordinates and angles
- formulae in mathematics and science
- equivalent expressions (for example, $a + b = b + a$)
- generalisations of number patterns
- number puzzles (for example, what two numbers can add up to).

Measurement

Statutory requirements

Pupils should be taught to:

- solve problems involving the calculation and conversion of units of measure, using decimal notation up to three decimal places where appropriate
- use, read, write and convert between standard units, converting measurements of length, mass, volume and time from a smaller unit of measure to a larger unit, and vice versa, using decimal notation to up to three decimal places
- convert between miles and kilometres
- recognise that shapes with the same areas can have different perimeters and vice versa
- recognise when it is possible to use formulae for area and volume of shapes
- calculate the area of parallelograms and triangles
- calculate, estimate and compare volume of cubes and cuboids using standard units, including cubic centimetres (cm^3) and cubic metres (m^3), and extending to other units [for example, mm^3 and km^3].

Notes and guidance (non-statutory)

Pupils connect conversion (for example, from kilometres to miles) to a graphical representation as preparation for understanding linear/proportional graphs.

They know approximate conversions and are able to tell if an answer is sensible.

Using the number line, pupils use, add and subtract positive and negative integers for measures such as temperature.

They relate the area of rectangles to parallelograms and triangles, for example, by dissection, and calculate their areas, understanding and using the formulae (in words or symbols) to do this.

Pupils could be introduced to compound units for speed, such as miles per hour, and apply their knowledge in science or other subjects as appropriate.

Geometry – properties of shapes

Statutory requirements

Pupils should be taught to:

- draw 2-D shapes using given dimensions and angles
- recognise, describe and build simple 3-D shapes, including making nets
- compare and classify geometric shapes based on their properties and sizes and find unknown angles in any triangles, quadrilaterals, and regular polygons
- illustrate and name parts of circles, including radius, diameter and circumference and know that the diameter is twice the radius
- recognise angles where they meet at a point, are on a straight line, or are vertically opposite, and find missing angles.

Notes and guidance (non-statutory)

Pupils draw shapes and nets accurately, using measuring tools and conventional markings and labels for lines and angles.

Pupils describe the properties of shapes and explain how unknown angles and lengths can be derived from known measurements.

These relationships might be expressed algebraically for example, $d = 2 \times r$, $a = 180 - (b + c)$.

Geometry – position and direction

Statutory requirements

Pupils should be taught to:

- describe positions on the full coordinate grid (all four quadrants)
- draw and translate simple shapes on the coordinate plane, and reflect them in the axes.

Notes and guidance (non-statutory)

Pupils draw and label a pair of axes in all four quadrants with equal scaling. This extends their knowledge of one quadrant to all four quadrants, including the use of negative numbers.

Pupils draw and label rectangles (including squares), parallelograms and rhombuses, specified by coordinates in the four quadrants, predicting missing coordinates using the properties of shapes. These might be expressed algebraically for example, translating vertex (a, b) to $(a - 2, b + 3)$; (a, b) and $(a + d, b + d)$ being opposite vertices of a square of side d.

Statistics

Notes and guidance (non-statutory)

Pupils connect their work on angles, fractions and percentages to the interpretation of pie charts.

Pupils both encounter and draw graphs relating two variables, arising from their own enquiry and in other subjects.

They should connect conversion from kilometres to miles in measurement to its graphical representation.

Pupils know when it is appropriate to find the mean of a data set.

Mathematics Appendix 1: Examples of formal written methods for addition, subtraction, multiplication and division

This appendix sets out some examples of formal written methods for all four operations to illustrate the range of methods that could be taught. It is not intended to be an exhaustive list, nor is it intended to show progression in formal written methods. For example, the exact position of intermediate calculations (superscript and subscript digits) will vary depending on the method and format used.

For multiplication, some pupils may include an addition symbol when adding partial products. For division, some pupils may include a subtraction symbol when subtracting multiples of the divisor.

Addition and subtraction

789 + 642 becomes   874 − 523 becomes   932 − 457 becomes   932 − 457 becomes

$$789$$
$$+642$$
$$\overline{1431}$$
$$1\ 1$$

Answer: 1431

$$874$$
$$-523$$
$$\overline{351}$$

Answer: 351

$$^8\cancel{9}\,^{12}\cancel{3}\,^1 2$$
$$-4\ 5\ 7$$
$$\overline{4\ 7\ 5}$$

Answer: 475

$$9\,^1 3\,^1 2$$
$$-\cancel{4}_5\,\cancel{5}_6\,7$$
$$\overline{4\ 7\ 5}$$

Answer: 475

Short multiplication

24 × 6 becomes   342 × 7 becomes   2741 × 6 becomes

$$2\ 4$$
$$\times\ \ 6$$
$$\overline{1\ 4\ 4}$$
$$\ \ 2$$

Answer: 144

$$3\ 4\ 2$$
$$\times\ \ \ 7$$
$$\overline{2\ 3\ 9\ 4}$$
$$\ \ 2\ \ 1$$

Answer: 2394

$$2\ 7\ 4\ 1$$
$$\times\ \ \ \ 6$$
$$\overline{1\ 6\ 4\ 4\ 6}$$
$$\ \ 4\ \ 2$$

Answer: 16 446

Long multiplication

24 × 16 becomes

```
    2
    2 4
  × 1 6
  ─────
  2 4 0
  1 4 4
  ─────
  3 8 4
```

Answer: 384

124 × 26 becomes

```
      1 2
    1 2 4
  ×     2 6
  ───────
  2 4 8 0
      7 4 4
  ───────
  3 2 2 4
      1   1
```

Answer: 3224

124 × 26 becomes

```
      1 2
  1   2 4
  ×     2 6
  ───────
      7 4 4
  2 4 8 0
  ───────
  3 2 2 4
  1   1
```

Answer: 3224

Short division

98 ÷ 7 becomes

```
   1 4
 7│9 ²8
```

Answer: 14

432 ÷ 5 becomes

```
   8 6 r 2
 5│4 3 ³2
```

Answer: 86 remainder 2

496 ÷ 11 becomes

```
    4 5 r 1
 11│4 9 ⁵6
```

Answer: 45 $\frac{1}{11}$

Long division

432 ÷ 15 becomes

```
     2 8 r 12
 15│4 3 2
   3 0 0
   ─────
   1 3 2
   1 2 0
   ─────
     1 2
```

Answer: 28 remainder 12

432 ÷ 15 becomes

```
       2 8
 15│4 3 2
   3 0 0    15 × 20
   ─────
   1 3 2
            15 × 8
   1 2 0
   ─────
     1 2
```

$\frac{12}{15} = \frac{4}{5}$

Answer: 28 $\frac{4}{5}$

432 ÷ 15 becomes

```
       2 8 . 8
 15│4 3 2 . 0
   3 0 ↓
   ───
   1 3 2
   1 2 0 ↓
   ─────
     1 2 0
     1 2 0
     ─────
         0
```

Answer: 28 .8

Key stage 3

Introduction

Mathematics is an interconnected subject in which pupils need to be able to move fluently between representations of mathematical ideas. The programme of study for key stage 3 is organised into apparently distinct domains, but pupils should build on key stage 2 and connections across mathematical ideas to develop fluency, mathematical reasoning and competence in solving increasingly sophisticated problems. They should also apply their mathematical knowledge in science, geography, computing and other subjects.

The expectation is that the majority of pupils will move through the programme of study at broadly the same pace. However, decisions about progression should be based on the security of pupils' understanding and their readiness to progress to the next stage. Pupils who grasp concepts rapidly should be challenged through being offered rich and sophisticated problems before any acceleration through new content in preparation for key stage 4. Those who are not sufficiently fluent should consolidate their understanding, including through additional practice, before moving on.

Working mathematically

Through the mathematics content, pupils should be taught to:

Develop fluency

- consolidate their numerical and mathematical capability from key stage 2 and extend their understanding of the number system and place value to include decimals, fractions, powers and roots
- select and use appropriate calculation strategies to solve increasingly complex problems
- use algebra to generalise the structure of arithmetic, including to formulate mathematical relationships
- substitute values in expressions, rearrange and simplify expressions, and solve equations
- move freely between different numerical, algebraic, graphical and diagrammatic representations [for example, equivalent fractions, fractions and decimals, and equations and graphs]
- develop algebraic and graphical fluency, including understanding linear and simple quadratic functions
- use language and properties precisely to analyse numbers, algebraic expressions, 2-D and 3-D shapes, probability and statistics.

Reason mathematically

- extend their understanding of the number system; make connections between number relationships, and their algebraic and graphical representations
- extend and formalise their knowledge of ratio and proportion in working with measures and geometry, and in formulating proportional relations algebraically
- identify variables and express relations between variables algebraically and graphically
- make and test conjectures about patterns and relationships; look for proofs or counter-examples
- begin to reason deductively in geometry, number and algebra, including using geometrical constructions

- interpret when the structure of a numerical problem requires additive, multiplicative or proportional reasoning
- explore what can and cannot be inferred in statistical and probabilistic settings, and begin to express their arguments formally.

Solve problems

- develop their mathematical knowledge, in part through solving problems and evaluating the outcomes, including multi-step problems
- develop their use of formal mathematical knowledge to interpret and solve problems, including in financial mathematics
- begin to model situations mathematically and express the results using a range of formal mathematical representations
- select appropriate concepts, methods and techniques to apply to unfamiliar and non-routine problems.

Subject content

Number

Pupils should be taught to:

- understand and use place value for decimals, measures and integers of any size
- order positive and negative integers, decimals and fractions; use the number line as a model for ordering of the real numbers; use the symbols =, ≠, <, >, ≤, ≥
- use the concepts and vocabulary of prime numbers, factors (or divisors), multiples, common factors, common multiples, highest common factor, lowest common multiple, prime factorisation, including using product notation and the unique factorisation property
- use the four operations, including formal written methods, applied to integers, decimals, proper and improper fractions, and mixed numbers, all both positive and negative
- use conventional notation for the priority of operations, including brackets, powers, roots and reciprocals
- recognise and use relationships between operations including inverse operations
- use integer powers and associated real roots (square, cube and higher), recognise powers of 2, 3, 4, 5 and distinguish between exact representations of roots and their decimal approximations
- interpret and compare numbers in standard form $A \times 10^n$ $1 \le A < 10$, where n is a positive or negative integer or zero
- work interchangeably with terminating decimals and their corresponding fractions (such as 3.5 and $\frac{7}{2}$ or 0.375 and $\frac{3}{8}$)
- define percentage as 'number of parts per hundred', interpret percentages and percentage changes as a fraction or a decimal, interpret these multiplicatively, express one quantity as a percentage of another, compare two quantities using percentages, and work with percentages greater than 100%
- interpret fractions and percentages as operators
- use standard units of mass, length, time, money and other measures, including with decimal quantities
- round numbers and measures to an appropriate degree of accuracy [for example, to a number of decimal places or significant figures]
- use approximation through rounding to estimate answers and calculate possible resulting errors expressed using inequality notation $a < x \le b$
- use a calculator and other technologies to calculate results accurately and then interpret them appropriately
- appreciate the infinite nature of the sets of integers, real and rational numbers.

Algebra

Pupils should be taught to:

- use and interpret algebraic notation, including:

  - ab in place of $a \times b$
  - $3y$ in place of $y + y + y$ and $3 \times y$
  - a^2 in place of $a \times a$, a^3 in place of $a \times a \times a$; a^2b in place of $a \times a \times b$
  - $\frac{a}{b}$ in place of $a \div b$
  - coefficients written as fractions rather than as decimals
  - brackets

- substitute numerical values into formulae and expressions, including scientific formulae
- understand and use the concepts and vocabulary of expressions, equations, inequalities, terms and factors
- simplify and manipulate algebraic expressions to maintain equivalence by:

  - collecting like terms
  - multiplying a single term over a bracket
  - taking out common factors
  - expanding products of two or more binomials

- understand and use standard mathematical formulae; rearrange formulae to change the subject
- model situations or procedures by translating them into algebraic expressions or formulae and by using graphs
- use algebraic methods to solve linear equations in one variable (including all forms that require rearrangement)
- work with coordinates in all four quadrants
- recognise, sketch and produce graphs of linear and quadratic functions of one variable with appropriate scaling, using equations in x and y and the Cartesian plane
- interpret mathematical relationships both algebraically and graphically
- reduce a given linear equation in two variables to the standard form $y = mx + c$; calculate and interpret gradients and intercepts of graphs of such linear equations numerically, graphically and algebraically
- use linear and quadratic graphs to estimate values of y for given values of x and vice versa and to find approximate solutions of simultaneous linear equations
- find approximate solutions to contextual problems from given graphs of a variety of functions, including piece-wise linear, exponential and reciprocal graphs
- generate terms of a sequence from either a term-to-term or a position-to-term rule
- recognise arithmetic sequences and find the nth term
- recognise geometric sequences and appreciate other sequences that arise.

Ratio, proportion and rates of change

Pupils should be taught to:

- change freely between related standard units [for example time, length, area, volume/capacity, mass]
- use scale factors, scale diagrams and maps
- express one quantity as a fraction of another, where the fraction is less than 1 and greater than 1
- use ratio notation, including reduction to simplest form
- divide a given quantity into two parts in a given part:part or part:whole ratio; express the division of a quantity into two parts as a ratio

- understand that a multiplicative relationship between two quantities can be expressed as a ratio or a fraction
- relate the language of ratios and the associated calculations to the arithmetic of fractions and to linear functions
- solve problems involving percentage change, including: percentage increase, decrease and original value problems and simple interest in financial mathematics
- solve problems involving direct and inverse proportion, including graphical and algebraic representations
- use compound units such as speed, unit pricing and density to solve problems.

Geometry and measures

Pupils should be taught to:

- derive and apply formulae to calculate and solve problems involving: perimeter and area of triangles, parallelograms, trapezia, volume of cuboids (including cubes) and other prisms (including cylinders)
- calculate and solve problems involving: perimeters of 2-D shapes (including circles), areas of circles and composite shapes
- draw and measure line segments and angles in geometric figures, including interpreting scale drawings
- derive and use the standard ruler and compass constructions (perpendicular bisector of a line segment, constructing a perpendicular to a given line from/at a given point, bisecting a given angle); recognise and use the perpendicular distance from a point to a line as the shortest distance to the line
- describe, sketch and draw using conventional terms and notations: points, lines, parallel lines, perpendicular lines, right angles, regular polygons, and other polygons that are reflectively and rotationally symmetric
- use the standard conventions for labelling the sides and angles of triangle ABC, and know and use the criteria for congruence of triangles
- derive and illustrate properties of triangles, quadrilaterals, circles, and other plane figures [for example, equal lengths and angles] using appropriate language and technologies
- identify properties of, and describe the results of, translations, rotations and reflections applied to given figures
- identify and construct congruent triangles, and construct similar shapes by enlargement, with and without coordinate grids
- apply the properties of angles at a point, angles at a point on a straight line, vertically opposite angles
- understand and use the relationship between parallel lines and alternate and corresponding angles
- derive and use the sum of angles in a triangle and use it to deduce the angle sum in any polygon, and to derive properties of regular polygons
- apply angle facts, triangle congruence, similarity and properties of quadrilaterals to derive results about angles and sides, including Pythagoras' Theorem, and use known results to obtain simple proofs
- use Pythagoras' Theorem and trigonometric ratios in similar triangles to solve problems involving right-angled triangles
- use the properties of faces, surfaces, edges and vertices of cubes, cuboids, prisms, cylinders, pyramids, cones and spheres to solve problems in 3-D
- interpret mathematical relationships both algebraically and geometrically.

Probability

Pupils should be taught to:

- record, describe and analyse the frequency of outcomes of simple probability experiments involving randomness, fairness, equally and unequally likely outcomes, using appropriate language and the 0–1 probability scale
- understand that the probabilities of all possible outcomes sum to 1
- enumerate sets and unions/intersections of sets systematically, using tables, grids and Venn diagrams
- generate theoretical sample spaces for single and combined events with equally likely, mutually exclusive outcomes and use these to calculate theoretical probabilities.

Statistics

Pupils should be taught to:

- describe, interpret and compare observed distributions of a single variable through: appropriate graphical representation involving discrete, continuous and grouped data; and appropriate measures of central tendency (mean, mode, median) and spread (range, consideration of outliers)
- construct and interpret appropriate tables, charts, and diagrams, including frequency tables, bar charts, pie charts, and pictograms for categorical data, and vertical line (or bar) charts for ungrouped and grouped numerical data
- describe simple mathematical relationships between two variables (bivariate data) in observational and experimental contexts and illustrate using scatter graphs.

Key Stage 4

Introduction

Mathematics is an interconnected subject in which pupils need to be able to move fluently between representations of mathematical ideas. The programme of study for key stage 4 is organised into apparently distinct domains, but pupils should develop and consolidate connections across mathematical ideas. They should build on learning from key stage 3 to further develop fluency, mathematical reasoning and competence in solving increasingly sophisticated problems. They should also apply their mathematical knowledge wherever relevant in other subjects and in financial contexts.

The expectation is that the majority of pupils will move through the programme of study at broadly the same pace. However, decisions about when to progress should always be based on the security of pupils' understanding and their readiness to progress. Pupils who grasp concepts rapidly should be challenged through being offered rich and sophisticated problems before any acceleration through new content. Those who are not sufficiently fluent with earlier material should consolidate their understanding, including through additional practice, before moving on.

This programme of study specifies:

- the mathematical content that should be taught to all pupils, in standard type; and
- additional mathematical content to be taught to more highly attaining pupils, in **bold** type and braces { }.

Together, the mathematical content set out in the key stage 3 and key stage 4 programmes of study covers the full range of material contained in the GCSE Mathematics qualification. Wherever it is appropriate, given pupils' security of understanding and readiness to progress, pupils should be taught the full content set out in this programme of study.

Working mathematically

Through the mathematics content, pupils should be taught to:

Develop fluency

- consolidate their numerical and mathematical capability from key stage 3 and extend their understanding of the number system to include powers, roots **{and fractional indices}**
- select and use appropriate calculation strategies to solve increasingly complex problems, including exact calculations involving multiples of π **{and surds}**, use of standard form and application and interpretation of limits of accuracy
- consolidate their algebraic capability from key stage 3 and extend their understanding of algebraic simplification and manipulation to include quadratic expressions, **{and expressions involving surds and algebraic fractions}**
- extend fluency with expressions and equations from key stage 3, to include quadratic equations, simultaneous equations and inequalities
- move freely between different numerical, algebraic, graphical and diagrammatic representations, including of linear, quadratic, reciprocal, **{exponential and trigonometric}** functions
- use mathematical language and properties precisely.

Reason mathematically

- extend and formalise their knowledge of ratio and proportion, including trigonometric ratios, in working with measures and geometry, and in working with proportional relations algebraically and graphically
- extend their ability to identify variables and express relations between variables algebraically and graphically
- make and test conjectures about the generalisations that underlie patterns and relationships; look for proofs or counter-examples; begin to use algebra to support and construct arguments **{and proofs}**
- reason deductively in geometry, number and algebra, including using geometrical constructions
- interpret when the structure of a numerical problem requires additive, multiplicative or proportional reasoning
- explore what can and cannot be inferred in statistical and probabilistic settings, and express their arguments formally
- assess the validity of an argument and the accuracy of a given way of presenting information.

Solve problems

- develop their mathematical knowledge, in part through solving problems and evaluating the outcomes, including multi-step problems
- develop their use of formal mathematical knowledge to interpret and solve problems, including in financial contexts
- make and use connections between different parts of mathematics to solve problems

- model situations mathematically and express the results using a range of formal mathematical representations, reflecting on how their solutions may have been affected by any modelling assumptions
- select appropriate concepts, methods and techniques to apply to unfamiliar and non-routine problems; interpret their solution in the context of the given problem.

Subject content

Number

In addition to consolidating subject content from key stage 3, pupils should be taught to:

- apply systematic listing strategies, {including use of the product rule for counting}
- {estimate powers and roots of any given positive number}
- calculate with roots, and with integer {and fractional} indices
- calculate exactly with fractions, {surds} and multiples of π; {simplify surd expressions involving squares [for example $\sqrt{12} = \sqrt{4 \times 3} = \sqrt{4} \times \sqrt{3} = 2\sqrt{3}$] and rationalise denominators}
- calculate with numbers in standard form $A \times 10^n$, where $1 \leq A < 10$ and n is an integer
- {change recurring decimals into their corresponding fractions and vice versa}
- identify and work with fractions in ratio problems
- apply and interpret limits of accuracy when rounding or truncating, {including upper and lower bounds}.

Algebra

In addition to consolidating subject content from key stage 3, pupils should be taught to:

- simplify and manipulate algebraic expressions (including those involving surds {and algebraic fractions}) by:
  - factorising quadratic expressions of the form $x^2 + bx + c$, including the difference of two squares; {factorising quadratic expressions of the form $ax^2 + bx + c$}
  - simplifying expressions involving sums, products and powers, including the laws of indices

- know the difference between an equation and an identity; argue mathematically to show algebraic expressions are equivalent, and use algebra to support and construct arguments {and proofs}
- where appropriate, interpret simple expressions as functions with inputs and outputs; {interpret the reverse process as the 'inverse function'; interpret the succession of two functions as a 'composite function'}
- use the form $y = mx + c$ to identify parallel {and perpendicular} lines; find the equation of the line through two given points, or through one point with a given gradient
- identify and interpret roots, intercepts and turning points of quadratic functions graphically; deduce roots algebraically {and turning points by completing the square}
- recognise, sketch and interpret graphs of linear functions, quadratic functions, simple cubic functions, the reciprocal function $y = \frac{1}{x}$ with $x \neq 0$, {the exponential function $y = k^x$ for positive values of k, and the trigonometric functions (with arguments in degrees) $y = \sin x$, $y = \cos x$ and $y = \tan x$ for angles of any size}
- {sketch translations and reflections of the graph of a given function}
- plot and interpret graphs (including reciprocal graphs {and exponential graphs}) and graphs of non-standard functions in real contexts, to find approximate solutions to problems such as simple kinematic problems involving distance, speed and acceleration

- **{calculate or estimate gradients of graphs and areas under graphs (including quadratic and other non-linear graphs), and interpret results in cases such as distance-time graphs, velocity-time graphs and graphs in financial contexts}**
- **{recognise and use the equation of a circle with centre at the origin; find the equation of a tangent to a circle at a given point}**
- solve quadratic equations **{including those that require rearrangement}** algebraically by factorising, **{by completing the square and by using the quadratic formula}**; find approximate solutions using a graph
- solve two simultaneous equations in two variables (linear/linear **{or linear/quadratic}**) algebraically; find approximate solutions using a graph
- **{find approximate solutions to equations numerically using iteration}**
- translate simple situations or procedures into algebraic expressions or formulae; derive an equation (or two simultaneous equations), solve the equation(s) and interpret the solution
- solve linear inequalities in one **{or two}** variable**{s}**, **{and quadratic inequalities in one variable}**; represent the solution set on a number line, **{using set notation and on a graph}**
- recognise and use sequences of triangular, square and cube numbers, simple arithmetic progressions, Fibonacci type sequences, quadratic sequences, and simple geometric progressions (r^n where n is an integer, and r is a positive rational number **{or a surd}**) **{and other sequences}**
- deduce expressions to calculate the nth term of linear **{and quadratic}** sequences.

Ratio, proportion and rates of change

In addition to consolidating subject content from key stage 3, pupils should be taught to:

- compare lengths, areas and volumes using ratio notation and/or scale factors; make links to similarity (including trigonometric ratios)
- convert between related compound units (speed, rates of pay, prices, density, pressure) in numerical and algebraic contexts
- understand that X is inversely proportional to Y is equivalent to X is proportional to $\frac{1}{Y}$; **{construct and}** interpret equations that describe direct and inverse proportion
- interpret the gradient of a straight line graph as a rate of change; recognise and interpret graphs that illustrate direct and inverse proportion
- **{interpret the gradient at a point on a curve as the instantaneous rate of change; apply the concepts of instantaneous and average rate of change (gradients of tangents and chords) in numerical, algebraic and graphical contexts}**
- set up, solve and interpret the answers in growth and decay problems, including compound interest **{and work with general iterative processes}**.

Geometry and measures

In addition to consolidating subject content from key stage 3, pupils should be taught to:

- interpret and use fractional **{and negative}** scale factors for enlargements
- **{describe the changes and invariance achieved by combinations of rotations, reflections and translations}**
- identify and apply circle definitions and properties, including: centre, radius, chord, diameter, circumference, tangent, arc, sector and segment
- **{apply and prove the standard circle theorems concerning angles, radii, tangents and chords, and use them to prove related results}**
- construct and interpret plans and elevations of 3D shapes
- interpret and use bearings

- calculate arc lengths, angles and areas of sectors of circles
- calculate surface areas and volumes of spheres, pyramids, cones and composite solids
- apply the concepts of congruence and similarity, including the relationships between lengths, {**areas and volumes**} in similar figures
- apply Pythagoras' Theorem and trigonometric ratios to find angles and lengths in right-angled triangles {**and, where possible, general triangles**} in two {**and three**} dimensional figures
- know the exact values of $\sin\theta$ and $\cos\theta$ for $\theta = 0°$, 30°, 45°, 60^0 and 90^0; know the exact value of $\tan\theta$ for $\theta = 0^0$, 30^0, 45° and 60^0
- {**know and apply the sine rule,** $\dfrac{a}{\sin A} = \dfrac{b}{\sin B} = \dfrac{c}{\sin C}$ **and cosine rule,** $a^2 = b^2 + c^2 - 2bc$ $\cos A$ **, to find unknown lengths and angles**}
- {**know and apply Area** $= \dfrac{1}{2} ab \sin C$ **to calculate the area, sides or angles of any triangle**}
- describe translations as 2D vectors
- apply addition and subtraction of vectors, multiplication of vectors by a scalar, and diagrammatic and column representations of vectors; {**use vectors to construct geometric arguments and proofs**}.

Probability

In addition to consolidating subject content from key stage 3, pupils should be taught to:

- apply the property that the probabilities of an exhaustive set of mutually exclusive events sum to one
- use a probability model to predict the outcomes of future experiments; understand that empirical unbiased samples tend towards theoretical probability distributions, with increasing sample size
- calculate the probability of independent and dependent combined events, including using tree diagrams and other representations, and know the underlying assumptions
- {**calculate and interpret conditional probabilities through representation using expected frequencies with two-way tables, tree diagrams and Venn diagrams**}.

Statistics

In addition to consolidating subject content from key stage 3, pupils should be taught to:

- infer properties of populations or distributions from a sample, whilst knowing the limitations of sampling
- interpret and construct tables and line graphs for time series data
- {**construct and interpret diagrams for grouped discrete data and continuous data, i.e. histograms with equal and unequal class intervals and cumulative frequency graphs, and know their appropriate use**}
- interpret, analyse and compare the distributions of data sets from univariate empirical distributions through:

  o appropriate graphical representation involving discrete, continuous and grouped data, {**including box plots**}
  o appropriate measures of central tendency (including modal class) and spread {**including quartiles and inter-quartile range**}

- apply statistics to describe a population
- use and interpret scatter graphs of bivariate data; recognise correlation and know that it does not indicate causation; draw estimated lines of best fit; make predictions; interpolate and extrapolate apparent trends whilst knowing the dangers of so doing.

SCIENCE

Purpose of study

A high-quality science education provides the foundations for understanding the world through the specific disciplines of biology, chemistry and physics. Science has changed our lives and is vital to the world's future prosperity, and all pupils should be taught essential aspects of the knowledge, methods, processes and uses of science. Through building up a body of key foundational knowledge and concepts, pupils should be encouraged to recognise the power of rational explanation and develop a sense of excitement and curiosity about natural phenomena. They should be encouraged to understand how science can be used to explain what is occurring, predict how things will behave, and analyse causes.

Aims

The national curriculum for science aims to ensure that all pupils:

- develop **scientific knowledge and conceptual understanding** through the specific disciplines of biology, chemistry and physics
- develop understanding of the **nature, processes and methods of science** through different types of science enquiries that help them to answer scientific questions about the world around them
- are equipped with the scientific knowledge required to understand the **uses and implications** of science, today and for the future.

Scientific knowledge and conceptual understanding

The programmes of study describe a sequence of knowledge and concepts. While it is important that pupils make progress, it is also vitally important that they develop secure understanding of each key block of knowledge and concepts in order to progress to the next stage. Insecure, superficial understanding will not allow genuine progression: pupils may struggle at key points of transition (such as between primary and secondary school), build up serious misconceptions, and/or have significant difficulties in understanding higher-order content.

Pupils should be able to describe associated processes and key characteristics in common language, but they should also be familiar with, and use, technical terminology accurately and precisely. They should build up an extended specialist vocabulary. They should also apply their mathematical knowledge to their understanding of science, including collecting, presenting and analysing data. The social and economic implications of science are important but, generally, they are taught most appropriately within the wider school curriculum: teachers will wish to use different contexts to maximise their pupils' engagement with and motivation to study science.

The nature, processes and methods of science

'Working scientifically' specifies the understanding of the nature, processes and methods of science for each year group. It should not be taught as a separate strand.

The notes and guidance give examples of how 'working scientifically' might be embedded within the content of biology, chemistry and physics, focusing on the key features of scientific enquiry, so that pupils learn to use a variety of approaches to answer relevant scientific questions. These types of scientific enquiry should include: observing over time; pattern seeking; identifying, classifying and grouping; comparative and fair testing (controlled investigations); and researching using secondary sources. Pupils should seek answers to questions through collecting, analysing and presenting data. 'Working scientifically' will be developed further at key stages 3 and 4, once pupils have built up sufficient understanding of science to engage meaningfully in more sophisticated discussion of experimental design and control.

Spoken language

The national curriculum for science reflects the importance of spoken language in pupils' development across the whole curriculum – cognitively, socially and linguistically. The quality and variety of language that pupils hear and speak are key factors in developing their scientific vocabulary and articulating scientific concepts clearly and precisely. They must be assisted in making their thinking clear, both to themselves and others, and teachers should ensure that pupils build secure foundations by using discussion to probe and remedy their misconceptions.

School curriculum

The programmes of study for science are set out year by year for key stages 1 and 2. Schools are, however, only required to teach the relevant programme of study by the end of the key stage. Within each key stage, schools therefore have the flexibility to introduce content earlier or later than set out in the programme of study. In addition, schools can introduce key stage content during an earlier key stage if appropriate. All schools are also required to set out their school curriculum for science on a year-by-year basis and make this information available online.

Attainment targets

By the end of each key stage, pupils are expected to know, apply and understand the matters, skills and processes specified in the relevant programme of study.

Schools are not required by law to teach the content indicated as being 'nonstatutory'.

Key stage 1

The principal focus of science teaching in key stage 1 is to enable pupils to experience and observe phenomena, looking more closely at the natural and humanly-constructed world around them. They should be encouraged to be curious and ask questions about what they notice. They should be helped to develop their understanding of scientific ideas by using different types of scientific enquiry to answer their own questions, including observing changes over a period of time, noticing patterns, grouping and classifying things, carrying out simple comparative tests, and finding things out using secondary sources of information. They should begin to use simple scientific language to talk about what they have found out and communicate their ideas to a range of audiences in a variety of ways. Most of the learning about science should be done through the use of first-hand practical experiences, but there should also be some use of appropriate secondary sources, such as books, photographs and videos.

'Working scientifically' is described separately in the programme of study, but must **always** be taught through and clearly related to the teaching of substantive science content in the programme of study. Throughout the notes and guidance, examples show how scientific methods and skills might be linked to specific elements of the content.

Pupils should read and spell scientific vocabulary at a level consistent with their increasing word reading and spelling knowledge at key stage 1.

Key stage 1 programme of study – years 1 and 2

Working scientifically

Statutory requirements

During years 1 and 2, pupils should be taught to use the following practical scientific methods, processes and skills through the teaching of the programme of study content:

- asking simple questions and recognising that they can be answered in different ways
- observing closely, using simple equipment
- performing simple tests
- identifying and classifying
- using their observations and ideas to suggest answers to questions
- gathering and recording data to help in answering questions.

Notes and guidance (non-statutory)

Pupils in years 1 and 2 should explore the world around them and raise their own questions. They should experience different types of scientific enquiries, including practical activities, and begin to recognise ways in which they might answer scientific questions. They should use simple features to compare objects, materials and living things and, with help, decide how to sort and group them, observe changes over time, and, with guidance, they should begin to notice patterns and relationships. They should ask people questions and use simple secondary sources to find answers. They should use simple measurements and equipment (for example, hand lenses, egg timers) to gather data, carry out simple tests, record simple data, and talk about what they have found out and how they found it out. With help, they should record and communicate their findings in a range of ways and begin to use simple scientific language.

These opportunities for working scientifically should be provided across years 1 and 2 so that the expectations in the programme of study can be met by the end of year 2. Pupils are not expected to cover each aspect for every area of study.

Year 1 programme of study

Plants

Statutory requirements

Pupils should be taught to:

- identify and name a variety of common wild and garden plants, including deciduous and evergreen trees
- identify and describe the basic structure of a variety of common flowering plants, including trees.

Notes and guidance (non-statutory)

Pupils should use the local environment throughout the year to explore and answer questions about plants growing in their habitat. Where possible, they should observe the growth of flowers and vegetables that they have planted.

They should become familiar with common names of flowers, examples of deciduous and evergreen trees, and plant structures (including leaves, flowers (blossom), petals, fruit, roots, bulb, seed, trunk, branches, stem).

Pupils might work scientifically by: observing closely, perhaps using magnifying glasses, and comparing and contrasting familiar plants; describing how they were able to identify and group them, and drawing diagrams showing the parts of different plants including trees. Pupils might keep records of how plants have changed over time, for example the leaves falling off trees and buds opening; and compare and contrast what they have found out about different plants.

Animals, including humans

Statutory requirements

Pupils should be taught to:

- identify and name a variety of common animals including fish, amphibians, reptiles, birds and mammals
- identify and name a variety of common animals that are carnivores, herbivores and omnivores
- describe and compare the structure of a variety of common animals (fish, amphibians, reptiles, birds and mammals, including pets)
- identify, name, draw and label the basic parts of the human body and say which part of the body is associated with each sense.

Notes and guidance (non-statutory)

Pupils should use the local environment throughout the year to explore and answer questions about animals in their habitat. They should understand how to take care of animals taken from their local environment and the need to return them safely after study. Pupils should become familiar with the common names of some fish, amphibians, reptiles, birds and mammals, including those that are kept as pets.

Pupils should have plenty of opportunities to learn the names of the main body parts (including head, neck, arms, elbows, legs, knees, face, ears, eyes, hair, mouth, teeth) through games, actions, songs and rhymes.

Pupils might work scientifically by: using their observations to compare and contrast animals at first hand or through videos and photographs, describing how they identify and group them; grouping animals according to what they eat; and using their senses to compare different textures, sounds and smells.

Everyday materials

Statutory requirements

Pupils should be taught to:

- distinguish between an object and the material from which it is made
- identify and name a variety of everyday materials, including wood, plastic, glass, metal, water, and rock
- describe the simple physical properties of a variety of everyday materials
- compare and group together a variety of everyday materials on the basis of their simple physical properties.

Notes and guidance (non-statutory)

Pupils should explore, name, discuss and raise and answer questions about everyday materials so that they become familiar with the names of materials and properties such as: hard/soft; stretchy/stiff; shiny/dull; rough/smooth; bendy/not bendy; waterproof/ not waterproof; absorbent/not absorbent; opaque/transparent. Pupils should explore and experiment with a wide variety of materials, not only those listed in the programme of study, but including for example: brick, paper, fabrics, elastic, foil.

Pupils might work scientifically by: performing simple tests to explore questions, for example: 'What is the best material for an umbrella?...for lining a dog basket?...for curtains?...for a bookshelf?...for a gymnast's leotard?'

Seasonal changes

Statutory requirements

Pupils should be taught to:

- observe changes across the four seasons
- observe and describe weather associated with the seasons and how day length varies.

Notes and guidance (non-statutory)

Pupils should observe and talk about changes in the weather and the seasons.

Note: Pupils should be warned that it is not safe to look directly at the Sun, even when wearing dark glasses.

Pupils might work scientifically by: making tables and charts about the weather; and making displays of what happens in the world around them, including day length, as the seasons change.

Year 2 programme of study

Living things and their habitats

Statutory requirements

Pupils should be taught to:

- explore and compare the differences between things that are living, dead, and things that have never been alive
- identify that most living things live in habitats to which they are suited and describe how different habitats provide for the basic needs of different kinds of animals and plants, and how they depend on each other
- identify and name a variety of plants and animals in their habitats, including micro-habitats
- describe how animals obtain their food from plants and other animals, using the idea of a simple food chain, and identify and name different sources of food.

Notes and guidance (non-statutory)

Pupils should be introduced to the idea that all living things have certain characteristics that are essential for keeping them alive and healthy. They should raise and answer questions that help them to become familiar with the life processes that are common to all living things. Pupils should be introduced to the terms 'habitat' (a natural environment or home of a variety of plants and animals) and 'micro-habitat' (a very small habitat, for example for woodlice under stones, logs or leaf litter). They should raise and answer questions about the local environment that help them to identify and study a variety of plants and animals within their habitat and observe how living things depend on each other, for example, plants serving as a source of food and shelter for animals. Pupils should compare animals in familiar habitats with animals found in less familiar habitats, for example, on the seashore, in woodland, in the ocean, in the rainforest.

Pupils might work scientifically by: sorting and classifying things according to whether they are living, dead or were never alive, and recording their findings using charts. They should describe how they decided where to place things, exploring questions for example: 'Is a flame alive? Is a deciduous tree dead in winter?' and talk about ways of answering their questions. They could construct a simple food chain that includes humans (e.g. grass, cow, human). They could describe the conditions in different habitats and micro-habitats (under log, on stony path, under bushes) and find out how the conditions affect the number and type(s) of plants and animals that live there.

Plants

Statutory requirements

Pupils should be taught to:

- observe and describe how seeds and bulbs grow into mature plants
- find out and describe how plants need water, light and a suitable temperature to grow and stay healthy.

Notes and guidance (non-statutory)

Pupils should use the local environment throughout the year to observe how different plants grow. Pupils should be introduced to the requirements of plants for germination, growth and survival, as well as to the processes of reproduction and growth in plants.

Note: Seeds and bulbs need water to grow but most do not need light; seeds and bulbs have a store of food inside them.

Pupils might work scientifically by: observing and recording, with some accuracy, the growth of a variety of plants as they change over time from a seed or bulb, or observing similar plants at different stages of growth; setting up a comparative test to show that plants need light and water to stay healthy.

Animals, including humans

Statutory requirements

Pupils should be taught to:

- notice that animals, including humans, have offspring which grow into adults
- find out about and describe the basic needs of animals, including humans, for survival (water, food and air)
- describe the importance for humans of exercise, eating the right amounts of different types of food, and hygiene.

Notes and guidance (non-statutory)

Pupils should be introduced to the basic needs of animals for survival, as well as the importance of exercise and nutrition for humans. They should also be introduced to the processes of reproduction and growth in animals. The focus at this stage should be on questions that help pupils to recognise growth; they should not be expected to understand how reproduction occurs.

The following examples might be used: egg, chick, chicken; egg, caterpillar, pupa, butterfly; spawn, tadpole, frog; lamb, sheep. Growing into adults can include reference to baby, toddler, child, teenager, adult.

Pupils might work scientifically by: observing, through video or first-hand observation and measurement, how different animals, including humans, grow; asking questions about what things animals need for survival and what humans need to stay healthy; and suggesting ways to find answers to their questions.

Uses of everyday materials

Statutory requirements

Pupils should be taught to:

- identify and compare the suitability of a variety of everyday materials, including wood, metal, plastic, glass, brick, rock, paper and cardboard for particular uses
- find out how the shapes of solid objects made from some materials can be changed by squashing, bending, twisting and stretching.

Notes and guidance (non-statutory)

Pupils should identify and discuss the uses of different everyday materials so that they become familiar with how some materials are used for more than one thing (metal can be used for coins, cans, cars and table legs; wood can be used for matches, floors, and telegraph poles) or different materials are used for the same thing (spoons can be made from plastic, wood, metal, but not normally from glass). They should think about the properties of materials that make them suitable or unsuitable for particular purposes and they should be encouraged to think about unusual and creative uses for everyday materials. Pupils might find out about people who have developed useful new materials, for example John Dunlop, Charles Macintosh or John McAdam.

Pupils might work scientifically by: comparing the uses of everyday materials in and around the school with materials found in other places (at home, the journey to school, on visits, and in stories, rhymes and songs); observing closely, identifying and classifying the uses of different materials, and recording their observations.

Lower key stage 2 – years 3 and 4

The principal focus of science teaching in lower key stage 2 is to enable pupils to broaden their scientific view of the world around them. They should do this through exploring, talking about, testing and developing ideas about everyday phenomena and the relationships between living things and familiar environments, and by beginning to develop their ideas about functions, relationships and interactions. They should ask their own questions about what they observe and make some decisions about which types of scientific enquiry are likely to be the best ways of answering them, including observing changes over time, noticing patterns, grouping and classifying things, carrying out simple comparative and fair tests and finding things out using secondary sources of information. They should draw simple conclusions and use some scientific language, first, to talk about and, later, to write about what they have found out.

'Working scientifically' is described separately at the beginning of the programme of study, but must **always** be taught through and clearly related to substantive science content in the programme of study. Throughout the notes and guidance, examples show how scientific methods and skills might be linked to specific elements of the content.

Pupils should read and spell scientific vocabulary correctly and with confidence, using their growing word reading and spelling knowledge.

Lower key stage 2 programme of study

Working scientifically

Statutory requirements

During years 3 and 4, pupils should be taught to use the following practical scientific methods, processes and skills through the teaching of the programme of study content:

- asking relevant questions and using different types of scientific enquiries to answer them
- setting up simple practical enquiries, comparative and fair tests
- making systematic and careful observations and, where appropriate, taking accurate measurements using standard units, using a range of equipment, including thermometers and data loggers
- gathering, recording, classifying and presenting data in a variety of ways to help in answering questions
- recording findings using simple scientific language, drawings, labelled diagrams, keys, bar charts, and tables
- reporting on findings from enquiries, including oral and written explanations, displays or presentations of results and conclusions
- using results to draw simple conclusions, make predictions for new values, suggest improvements and raise further questions
- identifying differences, similarities or changes related to simple scientific ideas and processes
- using straightforward scientific evidence to answer questions or to support their findings.

Notes and guidance (non-statutory)

Pupils in years 3 and 4 should be given a range of scientific experiences to enable them to raise their own questions about the world around them. They should start to make their own decisions about the most appropriate type of scientific enquiry they might use to answer questions; recognise when a simple fair test is necessary and help to decide how to set it up; talk about criteria for grouping, sorting and classifying; and use simple keys. They should begin to look for naturally occurring patterns and relationships and decide what data to collect to identify them. They should help to make decisions about what observations to make, how long to make them for and the type of simple equipment that might be used.

They should learn how to use new equipment, such as data loggers, appropriately. They should collect data from their own observations and measurements, using notes, simple tables and standard units, and help to make decisions about how to record and analyse this data. With help, pupils should look for changes, patterns, similarities and differences in their data in order to draw simple conclusions and answer questions. With support, they should identify new questions arising from the data, making predictions for new values within or beyond the data they have collected and finding ways of improving what they have already done. They should also recognise when and how secondary sources might help them to answer questions that cannot be answered through practical investigations. Pupils should use relevant scientific language to discuss their ideas and communicate their findings in ways that are appropriate for different audiences.

These opportunities for working scientifically should be provided across years 3 and 4 so that the expectations in the programme of study can be met by the end of year 4. Pupils are not expected to cover each aspect for every area of study.

Year 3 programme of study

Plants

Statutory requirements

Pupils should be taught to:

- identify and describe the functions of different parts of flowering plants: roots, stem/trunk, leaves and flowers
- explore the requirements of plants for life and growth (air, light, water, nutrients from soil, and room to grow) and how they vary from plant to plant
- investigate the way in which water is transported within plants
- explore the part that flowers play in the life cycle of flowering plants, including pollination, seed formation and seed dispersal.

Notes and guidance (non-statutory)

Pupils should be introduced to the relationship between structure and function: the idea that every part has a job to do. They should explore questions that focus on the role of the roots and stem in nutrition and support, leaves for nutrition and flowers for reproduction.

Note: Pupils can be introduced to the idea that plants can make their own food, but at this stage they do not need to understand how this happens.

Pupils might work scientifically by: comparing the effect of different factors on plant growth, for example, the amount of light, the amount of fertiliser; discovering how seeds are formed by observing the different stages of plant life cycles over a period of time; looking for patterns in the structure of fruits that relate to how the seeds are dispersed. They might observe how water is transported in plants, for example, by putting cut, white carnations into coloured water and observing how water travels up the stem to the flowers.

Animals, including humans

Statutory requirements

Pupils should be taught to:

- identify that animals, including humans, need the right types and amount of nutrition, and that they cannot make their own food; they get nutrition from what they eat
- identify that humans and some other animals have skeletons and muscles for support, protection and movement.

Notes and guidance (non-statutory)

Pupils should continue to learn about the importance of nutrition and should be introduced to the main body parts associated with the skeleton and muscles, finding out how different parts of the body have special functions.

Pupils might work scientifically by: identifying and grouping animals with and without skeletons and observing and comparing their movement; exploring ideas about what would happen if humans did not have skeletons. They might compare and contrast the diets of different animals (including their pets) and decide ways of grouping them according to what they eat. They might research different food groups and how they keep us healthy and design meals based on what they find out.

Rocks

Statutory requirements

Pupils should be taught to:

- compare and group together different kinds of rocks on the basis of their appearance and simple physical properties
- describe in simple terms how fossils are formed when things that have lived are trapped within rock
- recognise that soils are made from rocks and organic matter.

Notes and guidance (non-statutory)

Linked with work in geography, pupils should explore different kinds of rocks and soils, including those in the local environment.

Pupils might work scientifically by: observing rocks, including those used in buildings and gravestones, and exploring how and why they might have changed over time; using a hand lens or microscope to help them to identify and classify rocks according to whether they have grains or crystals, and whether they have fossils in them. Pupils might research and discuss the different kinds of living things whose fossils are found in sedimentary rock and explore how fossils are formed. Pupils could explore different soils and identify similarities and differences between them and investigate what happens when rocks are rubbed together or what changes occur when they are in water. They can raise and answer questions about the way soils are formed.

Light

Statutory requirements

Pupils should be taught to:

- recognise that they need light in order to see things and that dark is the absence of light
- notice that light is reflected from surfaces

- recognise that light from the sun can be dangerous and that there are ways to protect their eyes
- recognise that shadows are formed when the light from a light source is blocked by an opaque object
- find patterns in the way that the size of shadows change.

Notes and guidance (non-statutory)

Pupils should explore what happens when light reflects off a mirror or other reflective surfaces, including playing mirror games to help them to answer questions about how light behaves. They should think about why it is important to protect their eyes from bright lights. They should look for, and measure, shadows, and find out how they are formed and what might cause the shadows to change.

Note: Pupils should be warned that it is not safe to look directly at the Sun, even when wearing dark glasses.

Pupils might work scientifically by: looking for patterns in what happens to shadows when the light source moves or the distance between the light source and the object changes.

Forces and magnets

Statutory requirements

Pupils should be taught to:

- compare how things move on different surfaces
- notice that some forces need contact between two objects, but magnetic forces can act at a distance
- observe how magnets attract or repel each other and attract some materials and not others
- compare and group together a variety of everyday materials on the basis of whether they are attracted to a magnet, and identify some magnetic materials
- describe magnets as having two poles
- predict whether two magnets will attract or repel each other, depending on which poles are facing.

Notes and guidance (non-statutory)

Pupils should observe that magnetic forces can act without direct contact, unlike most forces, where direct contact is necessary (for example, opening a door, pushing a swing). They should explore the behaviour and everyday uses of different magnets (for example, bar, ring, button and horseshoe).

Pupils might work scientifically by: comparing how different things move and grouping them; raising questions and carrying out tests to find out how far things move on

(Continued)

(Continued)

different surfaces and gathering and recording data to find answers their questions; exploring the strengths of different magnets and finding a fair way to compare them; sorting materials into those that are magnetic and those that are not; looking for patterns in the way that magnets behave in relation to each other and what might affect this, for example, the strength of the magnet or which pole faces another; identifying how these properties make magnets useful in everyday items and suggesting creative uses for different magnets.

Year 4 programme of study

Living things and their habitats

Statutory requirements

Pupils should be taught to:

- recognise that living things can be grouped in a variety of ways
- explore and use classification keys to help group, identify and name a variety of living things in their local and wider environment
- recognise that environments can change and that this can sometimes pose dangers to living things.

Notes and guidance (non-statutory)

Pupils should use the local environment throughout the year to raise and answer questions that help them to identify and study plants and animals in their habitat. They should identify how the habitat changes throughout the year. Pupils should explore possible ways of grouping a wide selection of living things that include animals and flowering plants and non-flowering plants. Pupils could begin to put vertebrate animals into groups such as fish, amphibians, reptiles, birds, and mammals; and invertebrates into snails and slugs, worms, spiders, and insects.

Note: Plants can be grouped into categories such as flowering plants (including grasses) and non-flowering plants, such as ferns and mosses.

Pupils should explore examples of human impact (both positive and negative) on environments, for example, the positive effects of nature reserves, ecologically planned parks, or garden ponds, and the negative effects of population and development, litter or deforestation.

Pupils might work scientifically by: using and making simple guides or keys to explore and identify local plants and animals; making a guide to local living things; raising and answering questions based on their observations of animals and what they have found out about other animals that they have researched.

Animals, including humans

Statutory requirements

Pupils should be taught to:

- describe the simple functions of the basic parts of the digestive system in humans
- identify the different types of teeth in humans and their simple functions
- construct and interpret a variety of food chains, identifying producers, predators and prey.

Notes and guidance (non-statutory)

Pupils should be introduced to the main body parts associated with the digestive system, for example, mouth, tongue, teeth, oesophagus, stomach and small and large intestine and explore questions that help them to understand their special functions.

Pupils might work scientifically by: comparing the teeth of carnivores and herbivores, and suggesting reasons for differences; finding out what damages teeth and how to look after them. They might draw and discuss their ideas about the digestive system and compare them with models or images.

States of matter

Statutory requirements

Pupils should be taught to:

- compare and group materials together, according to whether they are solids, liquids or gases
- observe that some materials change state when they are heated or cooled, and measure or research the temperature at which this happens in degrees Celsius (°C)
- identify the part played by evaporation and condensation in the water cycle and associate the rate of evaporation with temperature.

Notes and guidance (non-statutory)

Pupils should explore a variety of everyday materials and develop simple descriptions of the states of matter (solids hold their shape; liquids form a pool not a pile; gases escape from an unsealed container). Pupils should observe water as a solid, a liquid and a gas and should note the changes to water when it is heated or cooled.

Note: Teachers should avoid using materials where heating is associated with chemical change, for example, through baking or burning.

(Continued)

(Continued)

Pupils might work scientifically by: grouping and classifying a variety of different materials; exploring the effect of temperature on substances such as chocolate, butter, cream (for example, to make food such as chocolate crispy cakes and ice-cream for a party). They could research the temperature at which materials change state, for example, when iron melts or when oxygen condenses into a liquid. They might observe and record evaporation over a period of time, for example, a puddle in the playground or washing on a line, and investigate the effect of temperature on washing drying or snowmen melting.

Sound

Statutory requirements

Pupils should be taught to:

- identify how sounds are made, associating some of them with something vibrating
- recognise that vibrations from sounds travel through a medium to the ear
- find patterns between the pitch of a sound and features of the object that produced it
- find patterns between the volume of a sound and the strength of the vibrations that produced it
- recognise that sounds get fainter as the distance from the sound source increases.

Notes and guidance (non-statutory)

Pupils should explore and identify the way sound is made through vibration in a range of different musical instruments from around the world; and find out how the pitch and volume of sounds can be changed in a variety of ways.

Pupils might work scientifically by: finding patterns in the sounds that are made by different objects such as saucepan lids of different sizes or elastic bands of different thicknesses. They might make earmuffs from a variety of different materials to investigate which provides the best insulation against sound. They could make and play their own instruments by using what they have found out about pitch and volume.

Electricity

Statutory requirements

Pupils should be taught to:

- identify common appliances that run on electricity
- construct a simple series electrical circuit, identifying and naming its basic parts, including cells, wires, bulbs, switches and buzzers
- identify whether or not a lamp will light in a simple series circuit, based on whether or not the lamp is part of a complete loop with a battery
- recognise that a switch opens and closes a circuit and associate this with whether or not a lamp lights in a simple series circuit
- recognise some common conductors and insulators, and associate metals with being good conductors.

Notes and guidance (non-statutory)

Pupils should construct simple series circuits, trying different components, for example, bulbs, buzzers and motors, and including switches, and use their circuits to create simple devices. Pupils should draw the circuit as a pictorial representation, not necessarily using conventional circuit symbols at this stage; these will be introduced in year 6.

Note: Pupils might use the terms current and voltage, but these should not be introduced or defined formally at this stage. Pupils should be taught about precautions for working safely with electricity.

Pupils might work scientifically by: observing patterns, for example, that bulbs get brighter if more cells are added, that metals tend to be conductors of electricity, and that some materials can and some cannot be used to connect across a gap in a circuit.

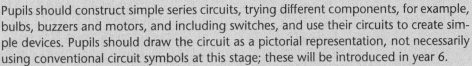

Upper key stage 2 – years 5 and 6

The principal focus of science teaching in upper key stage 2 is to enable pupils to develop a deeper understanding of a wide range of scientific ideas. They should do this through exploring and talking about their ideas; asking their own questions about scientific phenomena; and analysing functions, relationships and interactions more systematically. At upper key stage 2, they should encounter more abstract ideas and begin to recognise how these ideas help them to understand and predict how the world operates. They should also begin to recognise that scientific ideas change and develop over time. They should select the most appropriate ways to answer science questions using different types of scientific enquiry, including observing changes over different periods of time, noticing patterns, grouping and classifying things, carrying out comparative and fair tests and finding things out using a wide range of secondary sources of information. Pupils should draw conclusions based on their data and observations, use evidence to justify their ideas, and use their scientific knowledge and understanding to explain their findings.

'Working and thinking scientifically' is described separately at the beginning of the programme of study, but must **always** be taught through and clearly related to substantive science content in the programme of study. Throughout the notes and guidance, examples show how scientific methods and skills might be linked to specific elements of the content.

Pupils should read, spell and pronounce scientific vocabulary correctly.

Upper key stage 2 programme of study

Working scientifically

Statutory requirements

During years 5 and 6, pupils should be taught to use the following practical scientific methods, processes and skills through the teaching of the programme of study content:

* planning different types of scientific enquiries to answer questions, including recognising and controlling variables where necessary
* taking measurements, using a range of scientific equipment, with increasing accuracy and precision, taking repeat readings when appropriate

(Continued)

(Continued)

- recording data and results of increasing complexity using scientific diagrams and labels, classification keys, tables, scatter graphs, bar and line graphs
- using test results to make predictions to set up further comparative and fair tests
- reporting and presenting findings from enquiries, including conclusions, causal relationships and explanations of and degree of trust in results, in oral and written forms such as displays and other presentations
- identifying scientific evidence that has been used to support or refute ideas or arguments.

Notes and guidance (non-statutory)

Pupils in years 5 and 6 should use their science experiences to: explore ideas and raise different kinds of questions; select and plan the most appropriate type of scientific enquiry to use to answer scientific questions; recognise when and how to set up comparative and fair tests and explain which variables need to be controlled and why. They should use and develop keys and other information records to identify, classify and describe living things and materials, and identify patterns that might be found in the natural environment. They should make their own decisions about what observations to make, what measurements to use and how long to make them for, and whether to repeat them; choose the most appropriate equipment to make measurements and explain how to use it accurately. They should decide how to record data from a choice of familiar approaches; look for different causal relationships in their data and identify evidence that refutes or supports their ideas. They should use their results to identify when further tests and observations might be needed; recognise which secondary sources will be most useful to research their ideas and begin to separate opinion from fact. They should use relevant scientific language and illustrations to discuss, communicate and justify their scientific ideas and should talk about how scientific ideas have developed over time.

These opportunities for working scientifically should be provided across years 5 and 6 so that the expectations in the programme of study can be met by the end of year 6. Pupils are not expected to cover each aspect for every area of study.

Year 5 programme of study

Living things and their habitats

Statutory requirements

Pupils should be taught to:

- describe the differences in the life cycles of a mammal, an amphibian, an insect and a bird
- describe the life process of reproduction in some plants and animals.

Notes and guidance (non-statutory)

Pupils should study and raise questions about their local environment throughout the year. They should observe life-cycle changes in a variety of living things, for example, plants in the vegetable garden or flower border, and animals in the local environment. They should find out about the work of naturalists and animal behaviourists, for example, David Attenborough and Jane Goodall.

Pupils should find out about different types of reproduction, including sexual and asexual reproduction in plants, and sexual reproduction in animals.

Pupils might work scientifically by: observing and comparing the life cycles of plants and animals in their local environment with other plants and animals around the world (in the rainforest, in the oceans, in desert areas and in prehistoric times), asking pertinent questions and suggesting reasons for similarities and differences. They might try to grow new plants from different parts of the parent plant, for example, seeds, stem and root cuttings, tubers, bulbs. They might observe changes in an animal over a period of time (for example, by hatching and rearing chicks), comparing how different animals reproduce and grow.

Animals, including humans

Statutory requirements

Pupils should be taught to:

- describe the changes as humans develop to old age.

Notes and guidance (non-statutory)

Pupils should draw a timeline to indicate stages in the growth and development of humans. They should learn about the changes experienced in puberty.

Pupils could work scientifically by researching the gestation periods of other animals and comparing them with humans; by finding out and recording the length and mass of a baby as it grows.

Properties and changes of materials

Statutory requirements

Pupils should be taught to:

- compare and group together everyday materials on the basis of their properties, including their hardness, solubility, transparency, conductivity (electrical and thermal), and response to magnets
- know that some materials will dissolve in liquid to form a solution, and describe how to recover a substance from a solution

(Continued)

(Continued)

- use knowledge of solids, liquids and gases to decide how mixtures might be separated, including through filtering, sieving and evaporating
- give reasons, based on evidence from comparative and fair tests, for the particular uses of everyday materials, including metals, wood and plastic
- demonstrate that dissolving, mixing and changes of state are reversible changes
- explain that some changes result in the formation of new materials, and that this kind of change is not usually reversible, including changes associated with burning and the action of acid on bicarbonate of soda.

Notes and guidance (non-statutory)

Pupils should build a more systematic understanding of materials by exploring and comparing the properties of a broad range of materials, including relating these to what they learnt about magnetism in year 3 and about electricity in year 4. They should explore reversible changes, including, evaporating, filtering, sieving, melting and dissolving, recognising that melting and dissolving are different processes. Pupils should explore changes that are difficult to reverse, for example, burning, rusting and other reactions, for example, vinegar with bicarbonate of soda. They should find out about how chemists create new materials, for example, Spencer Silver, who invented the glue for sticky notes or Ruth Benerito, who invented wrinkle-free cotton.

Note: Pupils are not required to make quantitative measurements about conductivity and insulation at this stage. It is sufficient for them to observe that some conductors will produce a brighter bulb in a circuit than others and that some materials will feel hotter than others when a heat source is placed against them. Safety guidelines should be followed when burning materials.

Pupils might work scientifically by: carrying out tests to answer questions, for example, 'Which materials would be the most effective for making a warm jacket, for wrapping ice cream to stop it melting, or for making blackout curtains?' They might compare materials in order to make a switch in a circuit. They could observe and compare the changes that take place, for example, when burning different materials or baking bread or cakes. They might research and discuss how chemical changes have an impact on our lives, for example, cooking, and discuss the creative use of new materials such as polymers, super-sticky and super-thin materials.

Earth and space

Statutory requirements

Pupils should be taught to:

- describe the movement of the Earth, and other planets, relative to the Sun in the solar system
- describe the movement of the Moon relative to the Earth
- describe the Sun, Earth and Moon as approximately spherical bodies
- use the idea of the Earth's rotation to explain day and night and the apparent movement of the sun across the sky.

Pupils should be introduced to a model of the Sun and Earth that enables them to explain day and night. Pupils should learn that the Sun is a star at the centre of our solar system and that it has eight planets: Mercury, Venus, Earth, Mars, Jupiter, Saturn, Uranus and Neptune (Pluto was reclassified as a 'dwarf planet' in 2006). They should understand that a moon is a celestial body that orbits a planet (Earth has one moon; Jupiter has four large moons and numerous smaller ones).

Note: Pupils should be warned that it is not safe to look directly at the Sun, even when wearing dark glasses.

Pupils should find out about the way that ideas about the solar system have developed, understanding how the geocentric model of the solar system gave way to the heliocentric model by considering the work of scientists such as Ptolemy, Alhazen and Copernicus.

Pupils might work scientifically by: comparing the time of day at different places on the Earth through internet links and direct communication; creating simple models of the solar system; constructing simple shadow clocks and sundials, calibrated to show midday and the start and end of the school day; finding out why some people think that structures such as Stonehenge might have been used as astronomical clocks.

Forces

Statutory requirements

Pupils should be taught to:

- explain that unsupported objects fall towards the Earth because of the force of gravity acting between the Earth and the falling object
- identify the effects of air resistance, water resistance and friction, that act between moving surfaces
- recognise that some mechanisms, including levers, pulleys and gears, allow a smaller force to have a greater effect.

Notes and guidance (non-statutory)

Pupils should explore falling objects and raise questions about the effects of air resistance. They should explore the effects of air resistance by observing how different objects such as parachutes and sycamore seeds fall. They should experience forces that make things begin to move, get faster or slow down. Pupils should explore the effects of friction on movement and find out how it slows or stops moving objects, for example, by observing the effects of a brake on a bicycle wheel. Pupils should explore the effects of levers, pulleys and simple machines on movement. Pupils might find out how scientists, for example, Galileo Galilei and Isaac Newton helped to develop the theory of gravitation.

Pupils might work scientifically by: exploring falling paper cones or cup-cake cases, and designing and making a variety of parachutes and carrying out fair tests to determine which designs are the most effective. They might explore resistance in water by making and testing boats of different shapes. They might design and make products that use levers, pulleys, gears and/or springs and explore their effects.

Year 6 programme of study

Living things and their habitats

Statutory requirements

Pupils should be taught to:

- describe how living things are classified into broad groups according to common observable characteristics and based on similarities and differences, including micro-organisms, plants and animals
- give reasons for classifying plants and animals based on specific characteristics.

Notes and guidance (non-statutory)

Pupils should build on their learning about grouping living things in year 4 by looking at the classification system in more detail. They should be introduced to the idea that broad groupings, such as micro-organisms, plants and animals can be subdivided. Through direct observations where possible, they should classify animals into commonly found invertebrates (such as insects, spiders, snails, worms) and vertebrates (fish, amphibians, reptiles, birds and mammals). They should discuss reasons why living things are placed in one group and not another.

Pupils might find out about the significance of the work of scientists such as Carl Linnaeus, a pioneer of classification.

Pupils might work scientifically by: using classification systems and keys to identify some animals and plants in the immediate environment. They could research unfamiliar animals and plants from a broad range of other habitats and decide where they belong in the classification system.

Animals including humans

Statutory requirements

Pupils should be taught to:

- identify and name the main parts of the human circulatory system, and describe the functions of the heart, blood vessels and blood
- recognise the impact of diet, exercise, drugs and lifestyle on the way their bodies function
- describe the ways in which nutrients and water are transported within animals, including humans.

Notes and guidance (non-statutory)

Pupils should build on their learning from years 3 and 4 about the main body parts and internal organs (skeletal, muscular and digestive system) to explore and answer questions that help them to understand how the circulatory system enables the body to function.

Pupils should learn how to keep their bodies healthy and how their bodies might be damaged – including how some drugs and other substances can be harmful to the human body.

Pupils might work scientifically by: exploring the work of scientists and scientific research about the relationship between diet, exercise, drugs, lifestyle and health.

Evolution and inheritance

Statutory requirements

Pupils should be taught to:

- recognise that living things have changed over time and that fossils provide information about living things that inhabited the Earth millions of years ago
- recognise that living things produce offspring of the same kind, but normally offspring vary and are not identical to their parents
- identify how animals and plants are adapted to suit their environment in different ways and that adaptation may lead to evolution.

Notes and guidance (non-statutory)

Building on what they learned about fossils in the topic on rocks in year 3, pupils should find out more about how living things on Earth have changed over time. They should be introduced to the idea that characteristics are passed from parents to their offspring, for instance by considering different breeds of dogs, and what happens when, for example, labradors are crossed with poodles. They should also appreciate that variation in offspring over time can make animals more or less able to survive in particular environments, for example, by exploring how giraffes' necks got longer, or the development of insulating fur on the arctic fox. Pupils might find out about the work of palaeontologists such as Mary Anning and about how Charles Darwin and Alfred Wallace developed their ideas on evolution.

Note: At this stage, pupils are not expected to understand how genes and chromosomes work.

Pupils might work scientifically by: observing and raising questions about local animals and how they are adapted to their environment; comparing how some living things are adapted to survive in extreme conditions, for example, cactuses, penguins and camels. They might analyse the advantages and disadvantages of specific adaptations, such as being on two feet rather than four, having a long or a short beak, having gills or lungs, tendrils on climbing plants, brightly coloured and scented flowers.

Light

Statutory requirements

Pupils should be taught to:

- recognise that light appears to travel in straight lines
- use the idea that light travels in straight lines to explain that objects are seen because they give out or reflect light into the eye

(Continued)

(Continued)

- explain that we see things because light travels from light sources to our eyes or from light sources to objects and then to our eyes
- use the idea that light travels in straight lines to explain why shadows have the same shape as the objects that cast them.

Notes and guidance (non-statutory)

Pupils should build on the work on light in year 3, exploring the way that light behaves, including light sources, reflection and shadows. They should talk about what happens and make predictions.

Pupils might work scientifically by: deciding where to place rear-view mirrors on cars; designing and making a periscope and using the idea that light appears to travel in straight lines to explain how it works. They might investigate the relationship between light sources, objects and shadows by using shadow puppets. They could extend their experience of light by looking a range of phenomena including rainbows, colours on soap bubbles, objects looking bent in water and coloured filters (they do not need to explain why these phenomena occur).

Electricity

Statutory requirements

Pupils should be taught to:

- associate the brightness of a lamp or the volume of a buzzer with the number and voltage of cells used in the circuit
- compare and give reasons for variations in how components function, including the brightness of bulbs, the loudness of buzzers and the on/off position of switches
- use recognised symbols when representing a simple circuit in a diagram.

Notes and guidance (non-statutory)

Building on their work in year 4, pupils should construct simple series circuits, to help them to answer questions about what happens when they try different components, for example, switches, bulbs, buzzers and motors. They should learn how to represent a simple circuit in a diagram using recognised symbols.

Note: Pupils are expected to learn only about series circuits, not parallel circuits. Pupils should be taught to take the necessary precautions for working safely with electricity.

Pupils might work scientifically by: systematically identifying the effect of changing one component at a time in a circuit; designing and making a set of traffic lights, a burglar alarm or some other useful circuit.

Key stage 3

The principal focus of science teaching in key stage 3 is to develop a deeper understanding of a range of scientific ideas in the subject disciplines of biology, chemistry and physics. Pupils should begin to see the connections between these subject areas and become aware of some of the big ideas underpinning scientific knowledge and understanding. Examples of these big ideas are the links between structure and function in living organisms, the particulate model as the key to understanding the properties and interactions of matter in all its forms, and the resources and means of transfer of energy as key determinants of all of these interactions. They should be encouraged to relate scientific explanations to phenomena in the world around them and start to use modelling and abstract ideas to develop and evaluate explanations.

Pupils should understand that science is about working objectively, modifying explanations to take account of new evidence and ideas and subjecting results to peer review. Pupils should decide on the appropriate type of scientific enquiry to undertake to answer their own questions and develop a deeper understanding of factors to be taken into account when collecting, recording and processing data. They should evaluate their results and identify further questions arising from them.

'Working scientifically' is described separately at the beginning of the programme of study, but must always be taught through and clearly related to substantive science content in the programme of study. Teachers should feel free to choose examples that serve a variety of purposes, from showing how scientific ideas have developed historically to reflecting modern developments in science.

Pupils should develop their use of scientific vocabulary, including the use of scientific nomenclature and units and mathematical representations.

Working scientifically

Through the content across all three disciplines, pupils should be taught to:

Scientific attitudes

- pay attention to objectivity and concern for accuracy, precision, repeatability and reproducibility
- understand that scientific methods and theories develop as earlier explanations are modified to take account of new evidence and ideas, together with the importance of publishing results and peer review
- evaluate risks.

Experimental skills and investigations

- ask questions and develop a line of enquiry based on observations of the real world, alongside prior knowledge and experience
- make predictions using scientific knowledge and understanding
- select, plan and carry out the most appropriate types of scientific enquiries to test predictions, including identifying independent, dependent and control variables, where appropriate
- use appropriate techniques, apparatus, and materials during fieldwork and laboratory work, paying attention to health and safety
- make and record observations and measurements using a range of methods for different investigations; and evaluate the reliability of methods and suggest possible improvements
- apply sampling techniques.

Analysis and evaluation

- apply mathematical concepts and calculate results
- present observations and data using appropriate methods, including tables and graphs
- interpret observations and data, including identifying patterns and using observations, measurements and data to draw conclusions
- present reasoned explanations, including explaining data in relation to predictions and hypotheses
- evaluate data, showing awareness of potential sources of random and systematic error
- identify further questions arising from their results.

Measurement

- understand and use SI units and IUPAC (International Union of Pure and Applied Chemistry) chemical nomenclature
- use and derive simple equations and carry out appropriate calculations
- undertake basic data analysis including simple statistical techniques

Subject content – Biology

Pupils should be taught about:

Structure and function of living organisms

Cells and organisation

- cells as the fundamental unit of living organisms, including how to observe, interpret and record cell structure using a light microscope
- the functions of the cell wall, cell membrane, cytoplasm, nucleus, vacuole, mitochondria and chloroplasts
- the similarities and differences between plant and animal cells
- the role of diffusion in the movement of materials in and between cells
- the structural adaptations of some unicellular organisms
- the hierarchical organisation of multicellular organisms: from cells to tissues to organs to systems to organisms.

The skeletal and muscular systems

- the structure and functions of the human skeleton, to include support, protection, movement and making blood cells
- biomechanics – the interaction between skeleton and muscles, including the measurement of force exerted by different muscles
- the function of muscles and examples of antagonistic muscles.

Nutrition and digestion

- content of a healthy human diet: carbohydrates, lipids (fats and oils), proteins, vitamins, minerals, dietary fibre and water, and why each is needed
- calculations of energy requirements in a healthy daily diet
- the consequences of imbalances in the diet, including obesity, starvation and deficiency diseases

- the tissues and organs of the human digestive system, including adaptations to function and how the digestive system digests food (enzymes simply as biological catalysts)
- the importance of bacteria in the human digestive system
- plants making carbohydrates in their leaves by photosynthesis and gaining mineral nutrients and water from the soil via their roots.

Gas exchange systems

- the structure and functions of the gas exchange system in humans, including adaptations to function
- the mechanism of breathing to move air in and out of the lungs, using a pressure model to explain the movement of gases, including simple measurements of lung volume
- the impact of exercise, asthma and smoking on the human gas exchange system
- the role of leaf stomata in gas exchange in plants.

Reproduction

- reproduction in humans (as an example of a mammal), including the structure and function of the male and female reproductive systems, menstrual cycle (without details of hormones), gametes, fertilisation, gestation and birth, to include the effect of maternal lifestyle on the foetus through the placenta
- reproduction in plants, including flower structure, wind and insect pollination, fertilisation, seed and fruit formation and dispersal, including quantitative investigation of some dispersal mechanisms.

Health

- the effects of recreational drugs (including substance misuse) on behaviour, health and life processes.

Material cycles and energy

Photosynthesis

- the reactants in, and products of, photosynthesis, and a word summary for photosynthesis
- the dependence of almost all life on Earth on the ability of photosynthetic organisms, such as plants and algae, to use sunlight in photosynthesis to build organic molecules that are an essential energy store and to maintain levels of oxygen and carbon dioxide in the atmosphere
- the adaptations of leaves for photosynthesis.

Cellular respiration

- aerobic and anaerobic respiration in living organisms, including the breakdown of organic molecules to enable all the other chemical processes necessary for life
- a word summary for aerobic respiration
- the process of anaerobic respiration in humans and micro-organisms, including fermentation, and a word summary for anaerobic respiration
- the differences between aerobic and anaerobic respiration in terms of the reactants, the products formed and the implications for the organism.

Interactions and interdependencies

Relationships in an ecosystem

- the interdependence of organisms in an ecosystem, including food webs and insect pollinated crops
- the importance of plant reproduction through insect pollination in human food security
- how organisms affect, and are affected by, their environment, including the accumulation of toxic materials.

Genetics and evolution

Inheritance, chromosomes, DNA and genes

- heredity as the process by which genetic information is transmitted from one generation to the next
- a simple model of chromosomes, genes and DNA in heredity, including the part played by Watson, Crick, Wilkins and Franklin in the development of the DNA model
- differences between species
- the variation between individuals within a species being continuous or discontinuous, to include measurement and graphical representation of variation
- the variation between species and between individuals of the same species means some organisms compete more successfully, which can drive natural selection
- changes in the environment may leave individuals within a species, and some entire species, less well adapted to compete successfully and reproduce, which in turn may lead to extinction
- the importance of maintaining biodiversity and the use of gene banks to preserve hereditary material.

Subject content – Chemistry

Pupils should be taught about:

The particulate nature of matter

- the properties of the different states of matter (solid, liquid and gas) in terms of the particle model, including gas pressure
- changes of state in terms of the particle model.

Atoms, elements and compounds

- a simple (Dalton) atomic model
- differences between atoms, elements and compounds
- chemical symbols and formulae for elements and compounds
- conservation of mass changes of state and chemical reactions.

Pure and impure substances

- the concept of a pure substance
- mixtures, including dissolving

- diffusion in terms of the particle model
- simple techniques for separating mixtures: filtration, evaporation, distillation and chromatography
- the identification of pure substances.

Chemical reactions

- chemical reactions as the rearrangement of atoms
- representing chemical reactions using formulae and using equations
- combustion, thermal decomposition, oxidation and displacement reactions
- defining acids and alkalis in terms of neutralisation reactions
- the pH scale for measuring acidity/alkalinity; and indicators
- reactions of acids with metals to produce a salt plus hydrogen
- reactions of acids with alkalis to produce a salt plus water
- what catalysts do.

Energetics

- energy changes on changes of state (qualitative)
- exothermic and endothermic chemical reactions (qualitative).

The Periodic Table

- the varying physical and chemical properties of different elements
- the principles underpinning the Mendeleev Periodic Table
- the Periodic Table: periods and groups; metals and non-metals
- how patterns in reactions can be predicted with reference to the Periodic Table
- the properties of metals and non-metals
- the chemical properties of metal and non-metal oxides with respect to acidity.

Materials

- the order of metals and carbon in the reactivity series
- the use of carbon in obtaining metals from metal oxides
- properties of ceramics, polymers and composites (qualitative).

Earth and atmosphere

- the composition of the Earth
- the structure of the Earth
- the rock cycle and the formation of igneous, sedimentary and metamorphic rocks
- Earth as a source of limited resources and the efficacy of recycling
- the carbon cycle
- the composition of the atmosphere
- the production of carbon dioxide by human activity and the impact on climate.

Subject content – Physics

Pupils should be taught about:

Energy

Calculation of fuel uses and costs in the domestic context

- comparing energy values of different foods (from labels) (kJ)
- comparing power ratings of appliances in watts (W, kW)
- comparing amounts of energy transferred (J, kJ, kW hour)
- domestic fuel bills, fuel use and costs
- fuels and energy resources.

Energy changes and transfers

- simple machines give bigger force but at the expense of smaller movement (and vice versa): product of force and displacement unchanged
- heating and thermal equilibrium: temperature difference between two objects leading to energy transfer from the hotter to the cooler one, through contact (conduction) or radiation; such transfers tending to reduce the temperature difference: use of insulators
- other processes that involve energy transfer: changing motion, dropping an object, completing an electrical circuit, stretching a spring, metabolism of food, burning fuels.

Changes in systems

- energy as a quantity that can be quantified and calculated; the total energy has the same value before and after a change
- comparing the starting with the final conditions of a system and describing increases and decreases in the amounts of energy associated with movements, temperatures, changes in positions in a field, in elastic distortions and in chemical compositions
- using physical processes and mechanisms, rather than energy, to explain the intermediate steps that bring about such changes.

Motion and forces

Describing motion

- speed and the quantitative relationship between average speed, distance and time (speed = distance ÷ time)
- the representation of a journey on a distance-time graph
- relative motion: trains and cars passing one another.

Forces

- forces as pushes or pulls, arising from the interaction between two objects
- using force arrows in diagrams, adding forces in one dimension, balanced and unbalanced forces
- moment as the turning effect of a force
- forces: associated with deforming objects; stretching and squashing – springs; with rubbing and friction between surfaces, with pushing things out of the way; resistance to motion of air and water
- forces measured in newtons, measurements of stretch or compression as force is changed
- force-extension linear relation; Hooke's Law as a special case
- work done and energy changes on deformation
- non-contact forces: gravity forces acting at a distance on Earth and in space, forces between magnets and forces due to static electricity.

Pressure in fluids

- atmospheric pressure, decreases with increase of height as weight of air above decreases with height
- pressure in liquids, increasing with depth; upthrust effects, floating and sinking
- pressure measured by ratio of force over area – acting normal to any surface.

Balanced forces

- opposing forces and equilibrium: weight held by stretched spring or supported on a compressed surface.

Forces and motion

- forces being needed to cause objects to stop or start moving, or to change their speed or direction of motion (qualitative only)
- change depending on direction of force and its size.

Waves

Observed waves

- waves on water as undulations which travel through water with transverse motion; these waves can be reflected, and add or cancel – superposition.

Sound waves

- frequencies of sound waves, measured in hertz (Hz); echoes, reflection and absorption of sound
- sound needs a medium to travel, the speed of sound in air, in water, in solids
- sound produced by vibrations of objects, in loud speakers, detected by their effects on microphone diaphragm and the ear drum; sound waves are longitudinal
- auditory range of humans and animals.

Energy and waves

- pressure waves transferring energy; use for cleaning and physiotherapy by ultra-sound; waves transferring information for conversion to electrical signals by microphone.

Light waves

- the similarities and differences between light waves and waves in matter
- light waves travelling through a vacuum; speed of light
- the transmission of light through materials: absorption, diffuse scattering and specular reflection at a surface
- use of ray model to explain imaging in mirrors, the pinhole camera, the refraction of light and action of convex lens in focusing (qualitative); the human eye
- light transferring energy from source to absorber leading to chemical and electrical effects; photo-sensitive material in the retina and in cameras
- colours and the different frequencies of light, white light and prisms (qualitative only); differential colour effects in absorption and diffuse reflection.

Electricity and electromagnetism Current electricity

- electric current, measured in amperes, in circuits, series and parallel circuits, currents add where branches meet and current as flow of charge
- potential difference, measured in volts, battery and bulb ratings; resistance, measured in ohms, as the ratio of potential difference (p.d.) to current
- differences in resistance between conducting and insulating components (quantitative).

Static electricity

- separation of positive or negative charges when objects are rubbed together: transfer of electrons, forces between charged objects
- the idea of electric field, forces acting across the space between objects not in contact.

Magnetism

- magnetic poles, attraction and repulsion
- magnetic fields by plotting with compass, representation by field lines
- Earth's magnetism, compass and navigation
- the magnetic effect of a current, electromagnets, D.C. motors (principles only).

Matter

Physical changes

- conservation of material and of mass, and reversibility, in melting, freezing, evaporation, sublimation, condensation, dissolving
- similarities and differences, including density differences, between solids, liquids and gases
- Brownian motion in gases
- diffusion in liquids and gases driven by differences in concentration
- the difference between chemical and physical changes.

Particle model

- the differences in arrangements, in motion and in closeness of particles explaining changes of state, shape and density, the anomaly of ice-water transition
- atoms and molecules as particles.

Energy in matter

- changes with temperature in motion and spacing of particles
- internal energy stored in materials.

Space physics

- gravity force, weight = mass x gravitational field strength (g), on Earth g=10 N/kg, different on other planets and stars; gravity forces between Earth and Moon, and between Earth and Sun (qualitative only)
- our Sun as a star, other stars in our galaxy, other galaxies
- the seasons and the Earth's tilt, day length at different times of year, in different hemispheres
- the light year as a unit of astronomical distance.

Teaching in the sciences in key stage 4 continues with the process of building upon and deepening scientific knowledge and the understanding of ideas developed in earlier key stages in the subject disciplines of biology, chemistry and physics.

For some students, studying the sciences in key stage 4 provides the platform for more advanced studies, establishing the basis for a wide range of careers. For others, it will be their last formal study of subjects that provide the foundations for understanding the natural world and will enhance their lives in an increasingly technological society.

Science is changing our lives and is vital to the world's future prosperity, and all students should be taught essential aspects of the knowledge, methods, processes and uses of science. They should be helped to appreciate the achievements of science in showing how the complex and diverse phenomena of the natural world can be described in terms of a number of key ideas relating to the sciences which are inter-linked, and which are of universal application. These key ideas include:

- the use of conceptual models and theories to make sense of the observed diversity of natural phenomena
- the assumption that every effect has one or more cause
- that change is driven by interactions between different objects and systems
- that many such interactions occur over a distance and over time
- that science progresses through a cycle of hypothesis, practical experimentation, observation, theory development and review
- that quantitative analysis is a central element both of many theories and of scientific methods of inquiry.

The sciences should be taught in ways that ensure students have the knowledge to enable them to develop curiosity about the natural world, insight into working scientifically, and appreciation of the relevance of science to their everyday lives, so that students:

- develop scientific knowledge and conceptual understanding through the specific disciplines of biology, chemistry and physics;
- develop understanding of the nature, processes and methods of science, through different types of scientific enquiry that help them to answer scientific questions about the world around them;
- develop and learn to apply observational, practical, modelling, enquiry, problem-solving skills and mathematical skills, both in the laboratory, in the field and in other environments;
- develop their ability to evaluate claims based on science through critical analysis of the methodology, evidence and conclusions, both qualitatively and quantitatively.

Curricula at key stage 4 should comprise approximately equal proportions of biology, chemistry and physics. The relevant mathematical skills required are covered in the programme of study for mathematics and should be embedded in the science context.

'Working scientifically' is described separately at the beginning of the programme of study, but must always be taught through and clearly related to substantive science content in the programme of study. Teachers should feel free to choose examples that serve a variety of purposes, from showing how scientific ideas have developed historically to reflecting modern developments in science and informing students of the role of science in understanding the causes of and solutions to some of the challenges facing society.

The scope and nature of their study should be broad, coherent, practical and rigorous, so that students are inspired and challenged by the subject and its achievements.

Working scientifically

Through the content across all three disciplines, students should be taught so that they develop understanding and first-hand experience of:

The development of scientific thinking

- the ways in which scientific methods and theories develop over time
- using a variety of concepts and models to develop scientific explanations and understanding
- appreciating the power and limitations of science and considering ethical issues which may arise
- explaining everyday and technological applications of science; evaluating associated personal, social, economic and environmental implications; and making decisions based on the evaluation of evidence and arguments
- evaluating risks both in practical science and the wider societal context, including perception of risk
- recognising the importance of peer review of results and of communication of results to a range of audiences.

Experimental skills and strategies

- using scientific theories and explanations to develop hypotheses
- planning experiments to make observations, test hypotheses or explore phenomena
- applying a knowledge of a range of techniques, apparatus, and materials to select those appropriate both for fieldwork and for experiments
- carrying out experiments appropriately, having due regard to the correct manipulation of apparatus, the accuracy of measurements and health and safety considerations
- recognising when to apply a knowledge of sampling techniques to ensure any samples collected are representative
- making and recording observations and measurements using a range of apparatus and methods
- evaluating methods and suggesting possible improvements and further investigations.

Analysis and evaluation

- applying the cycle of collecting, presenting and analysing data, including:
- presenting observations and other data using appropriate methods
- translating data from one form to another
- carrying out and representing mathematical and statistical analysis
- representing distributions of results and making estimations of uncertainty
- interpreting observations and other data, including identifying patterns and trends, making inferences and drawing conclusions
- presenting reasoned explanations, including relating data to hypotheses
- being objective, evaluating data in terms of accuracy, precision, repeatability and reproducibility and identifying potential sources of random and systematic error
- communicating the scientific rationale for investigations, including the methods used, the findings and reasoned conclusions, using paper-based and electronic reports and presentations.

Vocabulary, units, symbols and nomenclature

- developing their use of scientific vocabulary and nomenclature
- recognising the importance of scientific quantities and understanding how they are determined
- using SI units and IUPAC chemical nomenclature unless inappropriate
- using prefixes and powers of ten for orders of magnitude (e.g. tera, giga, mega, kilo, centi, milli, micro and nano)
- interconverting units
- using an appropriate number of significant figures in calculations.

Subject content – Biology

Biology is the science of living organisms (including animals, plants, fungi and microorganisms) and their interactions with each other and the environment. The study of biology involves collecting and interpreting information about the natural world to identify patterns and relate possible cause and effect. Biology is used to help humans improve their own lives and to understand the world around them.

Students should be helped to understand how, through the ideas of biology, the complex and diverse phenomena of the natural world can be described in terms of a number of key ideas which are of universal application, and which can be illustrated in the separate topics set out below. These ideas include:

- life processes depend on molecules whose structure is related to their function
- the fundamental units of living organisms are cells, which may be part of highly adapted structures including tissues, organs and organ systems, enabling life processes to be performed more effectively
- living organisms may form populations of single species, communities of many species and ecosystems, interacting with each other, with the environment and with humans in many different ways
- living organisms are interdependent and show adaptations to their environment
- life on Earth is dependent on photosynthesis in which green plants and algae trap light from the Sun to fix carbon dioxide and combine it with hydrogen from water to make organic compounds and oxygen
- organic compounds are used as fuels in cellular respiration to allow the other chemical reactions necessary for life
- the chemicals in ecosystems are continually cycling through the natural world
- the characteristics of a living organism are influenced by its genome and its interaction with the environment
- evolution occurs by the process of natural selection and accounts both for biodiversity and how organisms are all related to varying degrees.

Students should be taught about:

Cell biology

- cells as the basic structural unit of all organisms; adaptations of cells related to their functions; the main sub-cellular structures of eukaryotic and prokaryotic cells
- stem cells in animals and meristems in plants
- enzymes

- factors affecting the rate of enzymatic reactions
- the importance of cellular respiration; the processes of aerobic and anaerobic respiration
- carbohydrates, proteins, nucleic acids and lipids as key biological molecules.

Transport systems

- the need for transport systems in multicellular organisms, including plants
- the relationship between the structure and functions of the human circulatory system.

Health, disease and the development of medicines

- the relationship between health and disease
- communicable diseases including sexually transmitted infections in humans (including HIV/AIDs)
- non-communicable diseases
- bacteria, viruses and fungi as pathogens in animals and plants
- body defences against pathogens and the role of the immune system against disease
- reducing and preventing the spread of infectious diseases in animals and plants
- the process of discovery and development of new medicines
- the impact of lifestyle factors on the incidence of non-communicable diseases.

Coordination and control

- principles of nervous co-ordination and control in humans
- the relationship between the structure and function of the human nervous system
- the relationship between structure and function in a reflex arc
- principles of hormonal coordination and control in humans
- hormones in human reproduction, hormonal and non-hormonal methods of contraception
- homeostasis.

Photosynthesis

- photosynthesis as the key process for food production and therefore biomass for life
- the process of photosynthesis
- factors affecting the rate of photosynthesis.

Ecosystems

- levels of organisation within an ecosystem
- some abiotic and biotic factors which affect communities; the importance of interactions between organisms in a community
- how materials cycle through abiotic and biotic components of ecosystems
- the role of micro-organisms (decomposers) in the cycling of materials through an ecosystem
- organisms are interdependent and are adapted to their environment
- the importance of biodiversity
- methods of identifying species and measuring distribution, frequency and abundance of species within a habitat
- positive and negative human interactions with ecosystems.

Evolution, inheritance and variation

- the genome as the entire genetic material of an organism
- how the genome, and its interaction with the environment, influence the development of the phenotype of an organism
- the potential impact of genomics on medicine
- most phenotypic features being the result of multiple, rather than single, genes
- single gene inheritance and single gene crosses with dominant and recessive phenotypes
- sex determination in humans
- genetic variation in populations of a species
- the process of natural selection leading to evolution
- the evidence for evolution
- developments in biology affecting classification
- the importance of selective breeding of plants and animals in agriculture
- the uses of modern biotechnology including gene technology; some of the practical and ethical considerations of modern biotechnology.

Subject content – Chemistry

Chemistry is the science of the composition, structure, properties and reactions of matter, understood in terms of atoms, atomic particles and the way they are arranged and link together. It is concerned with the synthesis, formulation, analysis and characteristic properties of substances and materials of all kinds.

Students should be helped to appreciate the achievements of chemistry in showing how the complex and diverse phenomena of both the natural and man-made worlds can be described in terms of a number of key ideas which are of universal application, and which can be illustrated in the separate topics set out below. These ideas include:

- matter is composed of tiny particles called atoms and there are about 100 different naturally-occurring types of atoms called elements
- elements show periodic relationships in their chemical and physical properties
- these periodic properties can be explained in terms of the atomic structure of the elements
- atoms bond either by transferring electrons from one atom to another or by sharing electrons
- the shapes of molecules (groups of atoms bonded together) and the way giant structures are arranged is of great importance in terms of the way they behave
- reactions can occur when molecules collide and do so at different rates due to differences in molecular collisions
- chemical reactions take place in only three different ways:

  o proton transfer
  o electron transfer
  o electron sharing

- energy is conserved in chemical reactions so can therefore be neither created nor destroyed.

Students should be taught about:

Atomic structure and the Periodic Table

- a simple model of the atom consisting of the nucleus and electrons, relative atomic mass, electronic charge and isotopes
- the number of particles in a given mass of a substance

- the modern Periodic Table, showing elements arranged in order of atomic number
- position of elements in the Periodic Table in relation to their atomic structure and arrangement of outer electrons
- properties and trends in properties of elements in the same group
- characteristic properties of metals and non-metals
- chemical reactivity of elements in relation to their position in the Periodic Table.

Structure, bonding and the properties of matter

- changes of state of matter in terms of particle kinetics, energy transfers and the relative strength of chemical bonds and intermolecular forces
- types of chemical bonding: ionic, covalent, and metallic
- bulk properties of materials related to bonding and intermolecular forces
- bonding of carbon leading to the vast array of natural and synthetic organic compounds that occur due to the ability of carbon to form families of similar compounds, chains and rings
- structures, bonding and properties of diamond, graphite, fullerenes and graphene.

Chemical changes

- determination of empirical formulae from the ratio of atoms of different kinds
- balanced chemical equations, ionic equations and state symbols
- identification of common gases
- the chemistry of acids; reactions with some metals and carbonates
- pH as a measure of hydrogen ion concentration and its numerical scale
- electrolysis of molten ionic liquids and aqueous ionic solutions
- reduction and oxidation in terms of loss or gain of oxygen.

Energy changes in chemistry

- Measurement of energy changes in chemical reactions (qualitative)
- Bond breaking, bond making, activation energy and reaction profiles (qualitative).

Rate and extent of chemical change

- factors that influence the rate of reaction: varying temperature or concentration, changing the surface area of a solid reactant or by adding a catalyst
- factors affecting reversible reactions.

Chemical analysis

- distinguishing between pure and impure substances
- separation techniques for mixtures of substances: filtration, crystallisation, chromatography, simple and fractional distillation
- quantitative interpretation of balanced equations
- concentrations of solutions in relation to mass of solute and volume of solvent.

Chemical and allied industries

- life-cycle assessment and recycling to assess environmental impacts associated with all the stages of a product's life
- the viability of recycling of certain materials

- carbon compounds, both as fuels and feedstock, and the competing demands for limited resources
- fractional distillation of crude oil and cracking to make more useful materials
- extraction and purification of metals related to the position of carbon in a reactivity series.

Earth and atmospheric science

- evidence for composition and evolution of the Earth's atmosphere since its formation
- evidence, and uncertainties in evidence, for additional anthropogenic causes of climate change
- potential effects of, and mitigation of, increased levels of carbon dioxide and methane on the Earth's climate
- common atmospheric pollutants: sulphur dioxide, oxides of nitrogen, particulates and their sources
- the Earth's water resources and obtaining potable water.

Subject content – Physics

Physics is the science of the fundamental concepts of field, force, radiation and particle structures, which are inter-linked to form unified models of the behaviour of the material universe. From such models, a wide range of ideas, from the broadest issue of the development of the universe over time to the numerous and detailed ways in which new technologies may be invented, have emerged. These have enriched both our basic understanding of, and our many adaptations to, our material environment.

Students should be helped to understand how, through the ideas of physics, the complex and diverse phenomena of the natural world can be described in terms of a number of key ideas which are of universal application and which can be illustrated in the separate topics set out below. These ideas include:

- the use of models, as in the particle model of matter or the wave models of light and of sound
- the concept of cause and effect in explaining such links as those between force and acceleration, or between changes in atomic nuclei and radioactive emissions
- the phenomena of 'action at a distance' and the related concept of the field as the key to analysing electrical, magnetic and gravitational effects
- that differences, for example between pressures or temperatures or electrical potentials, are the drivers of change
- that proportionality, for example between weight and mass of an object or between force and extension in a spring, is an important aspect of many models in science.

Students should be taught about:

Energy

- energy changes in a system involving heating, doing work using forces, or doing work using an electric current; calculating the stored energies and energy changes involved
- power as the rate of transfer of energy
- conservation of energy in a closed system; dissipation
- calculating energy efficiency for any energy transfers
- renewable and non-renewable energy sources used on Earth; changes in how these are used.

Forces

- forces and fields: electrostatic, magnetic, gravity
- forces as vectors
- calculating work done as force x distance; elastic and inelastic stretching
- pressure in fluids acts in all directions: variation in Earth's atmosphere with height, with depth for liquids, up-thrust force (qualitative).

Forces and motion

- speed of sound; estimating speeds and accelerations in everyday contexts
- interpreting quantitatively graphs of distance, time, and speed
- acceleration caused by forces; Newton's First Law
- weight and gravitational field strength
- decelerations and braking distances involved on roads.

Wave motion

- amplitude, wavelength and frequency; relating velocity to frequency and wavelength
- transverse and longitudinal waves
- electromagnetic waves and their velocity in vacuum; waves transferring energy; wavelengths and frequencies from radio to gamma-rays
- velocities differing between media: absorption, reflection, refraction effects
- production and detection, by electrical circuits, or by changes in atoms and nuclei
- uses in the radio, microwave, infra-red, visible, ultra-violet, X-ray and gamma-ray regions, hazardous effects on bodily tissues.

Electricity

- measuring resistance using p.d. and current measurements
- exploring current, resistance and voltage relationships for different circuit elements, including their graphical representations
- quantity of charge flowing as the product of current and time
- drawing circuit diagrams; exploring equivalent resistance for resistors in series
- the domestic a.c. supply; live, neutral and earth mains wires; safety measures
- power transfer related to p.d. and current, or current and resistance.

Magnetism and electromagnetism

- exploring the magnetic fields of permanent and induced magnets, and the Earth's magnetic field, using a compass
- magnetic effects of currents; how solenoids enhance the effect
- how transformers are used in the national grid and the reasons for their use.

The structure of matter

- relating models of arrangements and motions of the molecules in solid, liquid and gas phases to their densities
- melting, evaporation, and sublimation as reversible changes

- calculating energy changes involved on heating, using specific heat capacity; and those involved in changes of state, using specific latent heat
- links between pressure and temperature of a gas at constant volume, related to the motion of its particles (qualitative).

Atomic structure

- the nuclear model and its development in the light of changing evidence
- masses and sizes of nuclei, atoms and small molecules
- differences in numbers of protons and neutrons related to masses and identities of nuclei; isotope characteristics and equations to represent changes
- ionisation; absorption or emission of radiation related to changes in electron orbits
- radioactive nuclei; emission of alpha or beta particles, neutrons, or gamma-rays, related to changes in the nuclear mass and/or charge
- radioactive materials, half-life, irradiation, contamination and their associated hazardous effects; waste disposal
- nuclear fission, nuclear fusion and our Sun's energy

Space physics

- the main features of the solar system.

ART AND DESIGN

Purpose of study

Art, craft and design embody some of the highest forms of human creativity. A high-quality art and design education should engage, inspire and challenge pupils, equipping them with the knowledge and skills to experiment, invent and create their own works of art, craft and design. As pupils progress, they should be able to think critically and develop a more rigorous understanding of art and design. They should also know how art and design both reflect and shape our history, and contribute to the culture, creativity and wealth of our nation.

Aims

The national curriculum for art and design aims to ensure that all pupils:

- produce creative work, exploring their ideas and recording their experiences
- become proficient in drawing, painting, sculpture and other art, craft and design techniques
- evaluate and analyse creative works using the language of art, craft and design
- know about great artists, craft makers and designers, and understand the historical and cultural development of their art forms.

Attainment targets

By the end of each key stage, pupils are expected to know, apply and understand the matters, skills and processes specified in the relevant programme of study.

Schools are not required by law to teach the example content in [square brackets].

Subject content

Key stage 1

Pupils should be taught:

- to use a range of materials creatively to design and make products
- to use drawing, painting and sculpture to develop and share their ideas, experiences and imagination
- to develop a wide range of art and design techniques in using colour, pattern, texture, line, shape, form and space
- about the work of a range of artists, craft makers and designers, describing the differences and similarities between different practices and disciplines, and making links to their own work.

Key stage 2

Pupils should be taught to develop their techniques, including their control and their use of materials, with creativity, experimentation and an increasing awareness of different kinds of art, craft and design.

Pupils should be taught:

- to create sketch books to record their observations and use them to review and revisit ideas
- to improve their mastery of art and design techniques, including drawing, painting and sculpture with a range of materials [for example, pencil, charcoal, paint, clay]
- about great artists, architects and designers in history.

Key stage 3

Pupils should be taught to develop their creativity and ideas, and increase proficiency in their execution. They should develop a critical understanding of artists, architects and designers, expressing reasoned judgements that can inform their own work.

Pupils should be taught:

- to use a range of techniques to record their observations in sketchbooks, journals and other media as a basis for exploring their ideas
- to use a range of techniques and media, including painting
- to increase their proficiency in the handling of different materials
- to analyse and evaluate their own work, and that of others, in order to strengthen the visual impact or applications of their work
- about the history of art, craft, design and architecture, including periods, styles and major movements from ancient times up to the present day.

CITIZENSHIP

Purpose of study

A high-quality citizenship education helps to provide pupils with knowledge, skills and understanding to prepare them to play a full and active part in society. In particular, citizenship education should foster pupils' keen awareness and understanding of democracy, government and how laws are made and upheld. Teaching should equip pupils with the skills and knowledge to explore political and social issues critically, to weigh evidence, debate and make reasoned arguments. It should also prepare pupils to take their place in society as responsible citizens, manage their money well and make sound financial decisions.

Aims

The national curriculum for citizenship aims to ensure that all pupils:

- acquire a sound knowledge and understanding of how the United Kingdom is governed, its political system and how citizens participate actively in its democratic systems of government
- develop a sound knowledge and understanding of the role of law and the justice system in our society and how laws are shaped and enforced
- develop an interest in, and commitment to, participation in volunteering as well as other forms of responsible activity, that they will take with them into adulthood
- are equipped with the skills to think critically and debate political questions, to enable them to manage their money on a day-to-day basis, and plan for future financial needs.

Attainment targets

By the end of each key stage, pupils are expected to know, apply and understand the matters, skills and processes specified in the relevant programme of study.

Subject content

Key stage 3

Teaching should develop pupils' understanding of democracy, government and the rights and responsibilities of citizens. Pupils should use and apply their knowledge and understanding whilst developing skills to research and interrogate evidence, debate and evaluate viewpoints, present reasoned arguments and take informed action.

Pupils should be taught about:

- the development of the political system of democratic government in the United Kingdom, including the roles of citizens, Parliament and the monarch
- the operation of Parliament, including voting and elections, and the role of political parties
- the precious liberties enjoyed by the citizens of the United Kingdom
- the nature of rules and laws and the justice system, including the role of the police and the operation of courts and tribunals
- the roles played by public institutions and voluntary groups in society, and the ways in which citizens work together to improve their communities, including opportunities to participate in school-based activities
- the functions and uses of money, the importance and practice of budgeting, and managing risk.

Key stage 4

Teaching should build on the key stage 3 programme of study to deepen pupils' understanding of democracy, government and the rights and responsibilities of citizens. Pupils should develop their skills to be able to use a range of research strategies, weigh up evidence, make persuasive arguments and substantiate their conclusions. They should experience and evaluate different ways that citizens can act together to solve problems and contribute to society.

Pupils should be taught about:

- parliamentary democracy and the key elements of the constitution of the United Kingdom, including the power of government, the role of citizens and Parliament in holding those in power to account, and the different roles of the executive, legislature and judiciary and a free press
- the different electoral systems used in and beyond the United Kingdom and actions citizens can take in democratic and electoral processes to influence decisions locally, nationally and beyond
- other systems and forms of government, both democratic and non-democratic, beyond the United Kingdom
- local, regional and international governance and the United Kingdom's relations with the rest of Europe, the Commonwealth, the United Nations and the wider world
- human rights and international law
- the legal system in the UK, different sources of law and how the law helps society deal with complex problems
- diverse national, regional, religious and ethnic identities in the United Kingdom and the need for mutual respect and understanding
- the different ways in which a citizen can contribute to the improvement of his or her community, to include the opportunity to participate actively in community volunteering, as well as other forms of responsible activity
- income and expenditure, credit and debt, insurance, savings and pensions, financial products and services, and how public money is raised and spent.

COMPUTING

Purpose of study

A high-quality computing education equips pupils to use computational thinking and creativity to understand and change the world. Computing has deep links with mathematics, science, and design and technology, and provides insights into both natural and artificial systems. The core of computing is computer science, in which pupils are taught the principles of information and computation, how digital systems work, and how to put this knowledge to use through programming. Building on this knowledge and understanding, pupils are equipped to use information technology to create programs, systems and a range of content. Computing also ensures that pupils become digitally literate – able to use, and express themselves and develop their ideas through, information and communication technology – at a level suitable for the future workplace and as active participants in a digital world.

Aims

The national curriculum for computing aims to ensure that all pupils:

- can understand and apply the fundamental principles and concepts of computer science, including abstraction, logic, algorithms and data representation
- can analyse problems in computational terms, and have repeated practical experience of writing computer programs in order to solve such problems
- can evaluate and apply information technology, including new or unfamiliar technologies, analytically to solve problems
- are responsible, competent, confident and creative users of information and communication technology.

Attainment targets

By the end of each key stage, pupils are expected to know, apply and understand the matters, skills and processes specified in the relevant programme of study.

Schools are not required by law to teach the example content in [square brackets].

Subject content

Key stage 1

Pupils should be taught to:

- understand what algorithms are; how they are implemented as programs on digital devices; and that programs execute by following precise and unambiguous instructions
- create and debug simple programs
- use logical reasoning to predict the behaviour of simple programs

- use technology purposefully to create, organise, store, manipulate and retrieve digital content
- recognise common uses of information technology beyond school
- use technology safely and respectfully, keeping personal information private; identify where to go for help and support when they have concerns about content or contact on the internet or other online technologies.

Key stage 2

Pupils should be taught to:

- design, write and debug programs that accomplish specific goals, including controlling or simulating physical systems; solve problems by decomposing them into smaller parts
- use sequence, selection, and repetition in programs; work with variables and various forms of input and output
- use logical reasoning to explain how some simple algorithms work and to detect and correct errors in algorithms and programs
- understand computer networks including the internet; how they can provide multiple services, such as the world wide web; and the opportunities they offer for communication and collaboration
- use search technologies effectively, appreciate how results are selected and ranked, and be discerning in evaluating digital content
- select, use and combine a variety of software (including internet services) on a range of digital devices to design and create a range of programs, systems and content that accomplish given goals, including collecting, analysing, evaluating and presenting data and information
- use technology safely, respectfully and responsibly; recognise acceptable/unacceptable behaviour; identify a range of ways to report concerns about content and contact.

Key stage 3

Pupils should be taught to:

- design, use and evaluate computational abstractions that model the state and behaviour of real-world problems and physical systems
- understand several key algorithms that reflect computational thinking [for example, ones for sorting and searching]; use logical reasoning to compare the utility of alternative algorithms for the same problem
- use two or more programming languages, at least one of which is textual, to solve a variety of computational problems; make appropriate use of data structures [for example, lists, tables or arrays]; design and develop modular programs that use procedures or functions
- understand simple Boolean logic [for example, AND, OR and NOT] and some of its uses in circuits and programming; understand how numbers can be represented in binary, and be able to carry out simple operations on binary numbers [for example, binary addition, and conversion between binary and decimal]
- understand the hardware and software components that make up computer systems, and how they communicate with one another and with other systems
- understand how instructions are stored and executed within a computer system; understand how data of various types (including text, sounds and pictures) can be represented and manipulated digitally, in the form of binary digits
- undertake creative projects that involve selecting, using, and combining multiple applications, preferably across a range of devices, to achieve challenging goals, including collecting and analysing data and meeting the needs of known users
- create, re-use, revise and re-purpose digital artefacts for a given audience, with attention to trustworthiness, design and usability
- understand a range of ways to use technology safely, respectfully, responsibly and securely, including protecting their online identity and privacy; recognise inappropriate content, contact and conduct and know how to report concerns.

Key stage 4

All pupils must have the opportunity to study aspects of information technology and computer science at sufficient depth to allow them to progress to higher levels of study or to a professional career.

All pupils should be taught to:

- develop their capability, creativity and knowledge in computer science, digital media and information technology
- develop and apply their analytic, problem-solving, design, and computational thinking skills
- understand how changes in technology affect safety, including new ways to protect their online privacy and identity, and how to identify and report a range of concerns.

DESIGN AND TECHNOLOGY

Purpose of study

Design and technology is an inspiring, rigorous and practical subject. Using creativity and imagination, pupils design and make products that solve real and relevant problems within a variety of contexts, considering their own and others' needs, wants and values. They acquire a broad range of subject knowledge and draw on disciplines such as mathematics, science, engineering, computing and art. Pupils learn how to take risks, becoming resourceful, innovative, enterprising and capable citizens. Through the evaluation of past and present design and technology, they develop a critical understanding of its impact on daily life and the wider world. High-quality design and technology education makes an essential contribution to the creativity, culture, wealth and well-being of the nation.

Aims

The national curriculum for design and technology aims to ensure that all pupils:

- develop the creative, technical and practical expertise needed to perform everyday tasks confidently and to participate successfully in an increasingly technological world
- build and apply a repertoire of knowledge, understanding and skills in order to design and make high-quality prototypes and products for a wide range of users
- critique, evaluate and test their ideas and products and the work of others
- understand and apply the principles of nutrition and learn how to cook.

Attainment targets

By the end of each key stage, pupils are expected to know, apply and understand the matters, skills and processes specified in the relevant programme of study.

Schools are not required by law to teach the example content in [square brackets].

Subject content

Key stage 1

Through a variety of creative and practical activities, pupils should be taught the knowledge, understanding and skills needed to engage in an iterative process of designing and making. They should work in a range of relevant contexts [for example, the home and school, gardens and playgrounds, the local community, industry and the wider environment].

When designing and making, pupils should be taught to:

Design

- design purposeful, functional, appealing products for themselves and other users based on design criteria
- generate, develop, model and communicate their ideas through talking, drawing, templates, mock-ups and, where appropriate, information and communication technology

Make

- select from and use a range of tools and equipment to perform practical tasks [for example, cutting, shaping, joining and finishing]
- select from and use a wide range of materials and components, including construction materials, textiles and ingredients, according to their characteristics

Evaluate

- explore and evaluate a range of existing products
- evaluate their ideas and products against design criteria

Technical knowledge

- build structures, exploring how they can be made stronger, stiffer and more stable
- explore and use mechanisms [for example, levers, sliders, wheels and axles], in their products.

Key stage 2

Through a variety of creative and practical activities, pupils should be taught the knowledge, understanding and skills needed to engage in an iterative process of designing and making. They should work in a range of relevant contexts [for example, the home, school, leisure, culture, enterprise, industry and the wider environment].

When designing and making, pupils should be taught to:

Design

- use research and develop design criteria to inform the design of innovative, functional, appealing products that are fit for purpose, aimed at particular individuals or groups
- generate, develop, model and communicate their ideas through discussion, annotated sketches, cross-sectional and exploded diagrams, prototypes, pattern pieces and computer-aided design

Make

- select from and use a wider range of tools and equipment to perform practical tasks [for example, cutting, shaping, joining and finishing], accurately
- select from and use a wider range of materials and components, including construction materials, textiles and ingredients, according to their functional properties and aesthetic qualities

Evaluate

- investigate and analyse a range of existing products
- evaluate their ideas and products against their own design criteria and consider the views of others to improve their work
- understand how key events and individuals in design and technology have helped shape the world

Technical knowledge

- apply their understanding of how to strengthen, stiffen and reinforce more complex structures
- understand and use mechanical systems in their products [for example, gears, pulleys, cams, levers and linkages]
- understand and use electrical systems in their products [for example, series circuits incorporating switches, bulbs, buzzers and motors]
- apply their understanding of computing to program, monitor and control their products.

Key stage 3

Through a variety of creative and practical activities, pupils should be taught the knowledge, understanding and skills needed to engage in an iterative process of designing and making. They should work in a range of domestic and local contexts [for example, the home, health, leisure and culture], and industrial contexts [for example, engineering, manufacturing, construction, food, energy, agriculture (including horticulture) and fashion].

When designing and making, pupils should be taught to:

Design

- use research and exploration, such as the study of different cultures, to identify and understand user needs
- identify and solve their own design problems and understand how to reformulate problems given to them
- develop specifications to inform the design of innovative, functional, appealing products that respond to needs in a variety of situations
- use a variety of approaches [for example, biomimicry and user-centred design], to generate creative ideas and avoid stereotypical responses
- develop and communicate design ideas using annotated sketches, detailed plans, 3-D and mathematical modelling, oral and digital presentations and computer-based tools

Make

- select from and use specialist tools, techniques, processes, equipment and machinery precisely, including computer-aided manufacture
- select from and use a wider, more complex range of materials, components and ingredients, taking into account their properties

Evaluate

- analyse the work of past and present professionals and others to develop and broaden their understanding
- investigate new and emerging technologies
- test, evaluate and refine their ideas and products against a specification, taking into account the views of intended users and other interested groups
- understand developments in design and technology, its impact on individuals, society and the environment, and the responsibilities of designers, engineers and technologists

Technical knowledge

- understand and use the properties of materials and the performance of structural elements to achieve functioning solutions
- understand how more advanced mechanical systems used in their products enable changes in movement and force
- understand how more advanced electrical and electronic systems can be powered and used in their products [for example, circuits with heat, light, sound and movement as inputs and outputs]
- apply computing and use electronics to embed intelligence in products that respond to inputs [for example, sensors], and control outputs [for example, actuators], using programmable components [for example, microcontrollers].

Cooking and nutrition

As part of their work with food, pupils should be taught how to cook and apply the principles of nutrition and healthy eating. Instilling a love of cooking in pupils will also open a door to one of the great expressions of human creativity. Learning how to cook is a crucial life skill that enables pupils to feed themselves and others affordably and well, now and in later life.

Pupils should be taught to:

Key stage 1

- use the basic principles of a healthy and varied diet to prepare dishes
- understand where food comes from.

Key stage 2

- understand and apply the principles of a healthy and varied diet
- prepare and cook a variety of predominantly savoury dishes using a range of cooking techniques
- understand seasonality, and know where and how a variety of ingredients are grown, reared, caught and processed.

Key stage 3

- understand and apply the principles of nutrition and health
- cook a repertoire of predominantly savoury dishes so that they are able to feed themselves and others a healthy and varied diet
- become competent in a range of cooking techniques [for example, selecting and preparing ingredients; using utensils and electrical equipment; applying heat in different ways; using awareness of taste, texture and smell to decide how to season dishes and combine ingredients; adapting and using their own recipes]
- understand the source, seasonality and characteristics of a broad range of ingredients.

 # GEOGRAPHY

Purpose of study

A high-quality geography education should inspire in pupils a curiosity and fascination about the world and its people that will remain with them for the rest of their lives. Teaching should equip pupils with knowledge about diverse places, people, resources and natural and human environments, together with a deep understanding of the Earth's key physical and human processes. As pupils progress, their growing knowledge about the world should help them to deepen their understanding of the interaction between physical and human processes, and of the formation and use of landscapes and environments. Geographical knowledge, understanding and skills provide the frameworks and approaches that explain how the Earth's features at different scales are shaped, interconnected and change over time.

Aims

The national curriculum for geography aims to ensure that all pupils:

- develop contextual knowledge of the location of globally significant places – both terrestrial and marine – including their defining physical and human characteristics and how these provide a geographical context for understanding the actions of processes
- understand the processes that give rise to key physical and human geographical features of the world, how these are interdependent and how they bring about spatial variation and change over time
- are competent in the geographical skills needed to:

  o collect, analyse and communicate with a range of data gathered through experiences of fieldwork that deepen their understanding of geographical processes
  o interpret a range of sources of geographical information, including maps, diagrams, globes, aerial photographs and Geographical Information Systems (GIS)
  o communicate geographical information in a variety of ways, including through maps, numerical and quantitative skills and writing at length.

Attainment targets

By the end of each key stage, pupils are expected to know, apply and understand the matters, skills and processes specified in the relevant programme of study.

Schools are not required by law to teach the example content in [square brackets].

Subject content

Key stage 1

Pupils should develop knowledge about the world, the United Kingdom and their locality. They should understand basic subject-specific vocabulary relating to human and physical geography and begin to use geographical skills, including first-hand observation, to enhance their locational awareness.

Pupils should be taught to:

Locational knowledge

- name and locate the world's seven continents and five oceans
- name, locate and identify characteristics of the four countries and capital cities of the United Kingdom and its surrounding seas

Place knowledge

- understand geographical similarities and differences through studying the human and physical geography of a small area of the United Kingdom, and of a small area in a contrasting non-European country

Human and physical geography

- identify seasonal and daily weather patterns in the United Kingdom and the location of hot and cold areas of the world in relation to the Equator and the North and South Poles
- use basic geographical vocabulary to refer to:
  o key physical features, including: beach, cliff, coast, forest, hill, mountain, sea, ocean, river, soil, valley, vegetation, season and weather
  o key human features, including: city, town, village, factory, farm, house, office, port, harbour and shop

Geographical skills and fieldwork

- use world maps, atlases and globes to identify the United Kingdom and its countries, as well as the countries, continents and oceans studied at this key stage
- use simple compass directions (North, South, East and West) and locational and directional language [for example, near and far; left and right], to describe the location of features and routes on a map
- use aerial photographs and plan perspectives to recognise landmarks and basic human and physical features; devise a simple map; and use and construct basic symbols in a key
- use simple fieldwork and observational skills to study the geography of their school and its grounds and the key human and physical features of its surrounding environment.

Key stage 2

Pupils should extend their knowledge and understanding beyond the local area to include the United Kingdom and Europe, North and South America. This will include the location and characteristics of a range of the world's most significant human and physical features. They should develop their use of geographical knowledge, understanding and skills to enhance their locational and place knowledge.

Pupils should be taught to:

Locational knowledge

- locate the world's countries, using maps to focus on Europe (including the location of Russia) and North and South America, concentrating on their environmental regions, key physical and human characteristics, countries, and major cities
- name and locate counties and cities of the United Kingdom, geographical regions and their identifying human and physical characteristics, key topographical features (including hills, mountains, coasts and rivers), and land-use patterns; and understand how some of these aspects have changed over time
- identify the position and significance of latitude, longitude, Equator, Northern Hemisphere, Southern Hemisphere, the Tropics of Cancer and Capricorn, Arctic and Antarctic Circles, the Prime/Greenwich Meridian and time zones (including day and night)

Place knowledge

- understand geographical similarities and differences through the study of human and physical geography of a region of the United Kingdom, a region in a European country, and a region within North or South America

Human and physical geography

- describe and understand key aspects of:
  - o physical geography, including: climate zones, biomes and vegetation belts, rivers, mountains, volcanoes and earthquakes, and the water cycle
  - o human geography, including: types of settlement and land use, economic activity including trade links, and the distribution of natural resources including energy, food, minerals and water

Geographical skills and fieldwork

- use maps, atlases, globes and digital/computer mapping to locate countries and describe features studied
- use the eight points of a compass, four- and six-figure grid references, symbols and key (including the use of Ordnance Survey maps) to build their knowledge of the United Kingdom and the wider world
- use fieldwork to observe, measure, record and present the human and physical features in the local area using a range of methods, including sketch maps, plans and graphs, and digital technologies.

Key stage 3

Pupils should consolidate and extend their knowledge of the world's major countries and their physical and human features. They should understand how geographical processes interact to create distinctive human and physical landscapes that change over time. In doing so, they should become aware of increasingly complex geographical systems in the world around them. They should develop greater competence in using geographical knowledge, approaches and concepts [such as models and theories] and geographical skills in analysing and interpreting different data sources. In this way pupils will continue to enrich their locational knowledge and spatial and environmental understanding.

Pupils should be taught to:

Locational knowledge

- extend their locational knowledge and deepen their spatial awareness of the world's countries using maps of the world to focus on Africa, Russia, Asia (including China and India), and the Middle East, focusing on their environmental regions, including polar and hot deserts, key physical and human characteristics, countries and major cities

Place knowledge

- understand geographical similarities, differences and links between places through the study of human and physical geography of a region within Africa, and of a region within Asia

Human and physical geography

- understand, through the use of detailed place-based exemplars at a variety of scales, the key processes in:

  o physical geography relating to: geological timescales and plate tectonics; rocks, weathering and soils; weather and climate, including the change in climate from the Ice Age to the present; and glaciation, hydrology and coasts
  o human geography relating to: population and urbanisation; international development; economic activity in the primary, secondary, tertiary and quaternary sectors; and the use of natural resources

- understand how human and physical processes interact to influence, and change landscapes, environments and the climate; and how human activity relies on effective functioning of natural systems

Geographical skills and fieldwork

- build on their knowledge of globes, maps and atlases and apply and develop this knowledge routinely in the classroom and in the field
- interpret Ordnance Survey maps in the classroom and the field, including using grid references and scale, topographical and other thematic mapping, and aerial and satellite photographs
- use Geographical Information Systems (GIS) to view, analyse and interpret places and data
- use fieldwork in contrasting locations to collect, analyse and draw conclusions from geographical data, using multiple sources of increasingly complex information.

 **HISTORY**

Purpose of study

A high-quality history education will help pupils gain a coherent knowledge and understanding of Britain's past and that of the wider world. It should inspire pupils' curiosity to know more about the past. Teaching should equip pupils to ask perceptive questions, think critically, weigh evidence, sift arguments, and develop perspective and judgement. History helps pupils to understand the complexity of people's lives, the process of change, the diversity of societies and relationships between different groups, as well as their own identity and the challenges of their time.

Aims

The national curriculum for history aims to ensure that all pupils:

- know and understand the history of these islands as a coherent, chronological narrative, from the earliest times to the present day: how people's lives have shaped this nation and how Britain has influenced and been influenced by the wider world
- know and understand significant aspects of the history of the wider world: the nature of ancient civilisations; the expansion and dissolution of empires; characteristic features of past non-European societies; achievements and follies of mankind
- gain and deploy a historically grounded understanding of abstract terms such as 'empire', 'civilisation', 'parliament' and 'peasantry'
- understand historical concepts such as continuity and change, cause and consequence, similarity, difference and significance, and use them to make connections, draw contrasts, analyse trends, frame historically-valid questions and create their own structured accounts, including written narratives and analyses
- understand the methods of historical enquiry, including how evidence is used rigorously to make historical claims, and discern how and why contrasting arguments and interpretations of the past have been constructed
- gain historical perspective by placing their growing knowledge into different contexts, understanding the connections between local, regional, national and international history; between cultural, economic, military, political, religious and social history; and between short- and long-term timescales.

Attainment targets

By the end of each key stage, pupils are expected to know, apply and understand the matters, skills and processes specified in the relevant programme of study.

Schools are not required by law to teach the example content in [square brackets] or the content indicated as being 'non-statutory'.

Subject content

Key stage 1

Pupils should develop an awareness of the past, using common words and phrases relating to the passing of time. They should know where the people and events they study fit within a chronological framework and identify similarities and differences between ways of life in different periods. They should use a wide vocabulary of everyday historical terms. They should ask and answer questions, choosing and using parts of stories and other sources to show that they know and understand key features of events. They should understand some of the ways in which we find out about the past and identify different ways in which it is represented.

In planning to ensure the progression described above through teaching about the people, events and changes outlined below, teachers are often introducing pupils to historical periods that they will study more fully at key stages 2 and 3.

Pupils should be taught about:

- changes within living memory. Where appropriate, these should be used to reveal aspects of change in national life
- events beyond living memory that are significant nationally or globally [for example, the Great Fire of London, the first aeroplane flight or events commemorated through festivals or anniversaries]
- the lives of significant individuals in the past who have contributed to national and international achievements. Some should be used to compare aspects of life in different periods [for example, Elizabeth I and Queen Victoria, Christopher Columbus and Neil Armstrong, William Caxton and Tim Berners-Lee, Pieter Bruegel the Elder and LS Lowry, Rosa Parks and Emily Davison, Mary Seacole and/or Florence Nightingale and Edith Cavell]
- significant historical events, people and places in their own locality.

Key stage 2

Pupils should continue to develop a chronologically secure knowledge and understanding of British, local and world history, establishing clear narratives within and across the periods they study. They should note connections, contrasts and trends over time and develop the appropriate use of historical terms. They should regularly address and sometimes devise historically valid questions about change, cause, similarity and difference, and significance. They should construct informed responses that involve thoughtful selection and organisation of relevant historical information. They should understand how our knowledge of the past is constructed from a range of sources.

In planning to ensure the progression described above through teaching the British, local and world history outlined below, teachers should combine overview and depth studies to help pupils understand both the long arc of development and the complexity of specific aspects of the content.

Pupils should be taught about:

- changes in Britain from the Stone Age to the Iron Age

Examples (non-statutory)

This could include:

- late Neolithic hunter-gatherers and early farmers, for example, Skara Brae
- Bronze Age religion, technology and travel, for example, Stonehenge
- Iron Age hill forts: tribal kingdoms, farming, art and culture

- the Roman Empire and its impact on Britain

Examples (non-statutory)

This could include:

- Julius Caesar's attempted invasion in 55–54 BC
- the Roman Empire by AD 42 and the power of its army
- successful invasion by Claudius and conquest, including Hadrian's Wall
- British resistance, for example, Boudica
- 'Romanisation' of Britain: sites such as Caerwent and the impact of technology, culture and beliefs, including early Christianity

- Britain's settlement by Anglo-Saxons and Scots

Examples (non-statutory)

This could include:

- Roman withdrawal from Britain in *c.* AD 410 and the fall of the western Roman Empire
- Scots invasions from Ireland to north Britain (now Scotland)
- Anglo-Saxon invasions, settlements and kingdoms: place names and village life
- Anglo-Saxon art and culture
- Christian conversion – Canterbury, Iona and Lindisfarne

- the Viking and Anglo-Saxon struggle for the Kingdom of England to the time of Edward the Confessor

Examples (non-statutory)

This could include:

- Viking raids and invasion
- resistance by Alfred the Great and Athelstan, first king of England
- further Viking invasions and Danegeld

- Anglo-Saxon laws and justice
- Edward the Confessor and his death in 1066

- a local history study

Examples (non-statutory)

- a depth study linked to one of the British areas of study listed above
- a study over time tracing how several aspects of national history are reflected in the locality (this can go beyond 1066)
- a study of an aspect of history or a site dating from a period beyond 1066 that is significant in the locality.

- a study of an aspect or theme in British history that extends pupils' chronological knowledge beyond 1066

Examples (non-statutory)

- the changing power of monarchs using case studies such as John, Anne and Victoria
- changes in an aspect of social history, such as crime and punishment from the Anglo-Saxons to the present or leisure and entertainment in the 20th Century
- the legacy of Greek or Roman culture (art, architecture or literature) on later periods in British history, including the present day
- a significant turning point in British history, for example, the first railways or the Battle of Britain

- the achievements of the earliest civilizations – an overview of where and when the first civilizations appeared and a depth study of one of the following: Ancient Sumer; The Indus Valley; Ancient Egypt; The Shang Dynasty of Ancient China
- Ancient Greece – a study of Greek life and achievements and their influence on the western world
- a non-European society that provides contrasts with British history – one study chosen from: early Islamic civilization, including a study of Baghdad *c*. AD 900; Mayan civilization *c*. AD 900; Benin (West Africa) *c*. AD 900–1300.

Key stage 3

Pupils should extend and deepen their chronologically secure knowledge and understanding of British, local and world history, so that it provides a well-informed context for wider learning. Pupils should identify significant events, make connections, draw contrasts, and analyse trends within periods and over long arcs of time. They should use historical terms and concepts in increasingly sophisticated ways. They should pursue historically valid enquiries including some they have framed themselves, and create relevant, structured and evidentially supported accounts in response. They should understand how different types of historical sources are used rigorously to make historical claims and discern how and why contrasting arguments and interpretations of the past have been constructed.

In planning to ensure the progression described above through teaching the British, local and world history outlined below, teachers should combine overview and depth studies to help pupils understand both the long arc of development and the complexity of specific aspects of the content.

Pupils should be taught about:

- the development of Church, state and society in Medieval Britain 1066–1509

Examples (non-statutory)

This could include:

- the Norman Conquest
- Christendom, the importance of religion and the Crusades
- the struggle between Church and crown
- Magna Carta and the emergence of Parliament
- the English campaigns to conquer Wales and Scotland up to 1314
- society, economy and culture: for example, feudalism, religion in daily life (parishes, monasteries, abbeys), farming, trade and towns (especially the wool trade), art, architecture and literature
- the Black Death and its social and economic impact
- the Peasants' Revolt
- the Hundred Years War
- the Wars of the Roses; Henry VII and attempts to restore stability

- the development of Church, state and society in Britain 1509–1745

Examples (non-statutory)

This could include:

- Renaissance and Reformation in Europe
- the English Reformation and Counter Reformation (Henry VIII to Mary I)
- the Elizabethan religious settlement and conflict with Catholics (including Scotland, Spain and Ireland)
- the first colony in America and first contact with India
- the causes and events of the civil wars throughout Britain
- the Interregnum (including Cromwell in Ireland)
- the Restoration, 'Glorious Revolution' and power of Parliament
- the Act of Union of 1707, the Hanoverian succession and the Jacobite rebellions of 1715 and 1745
- society, economy and culture across the period: for example, work and leisure in town and country, religion and superstition in daily life, theatre, art, music and literature

- ideas, political power, industry and empire: Britain, 1745–1901

Examples (non-statutory)

This could include:

- the Enlightenment in Europe and Britain, with links back to 17th-Century thinkers and scientists and the founding of the Royal Society
- Britain's transatlantic slave trade: its effects and its eventual abolition
- the Seven Years War and The American War of Independence
- the French Revolutionary wars
- Britain as the first industrial nation – the impact on society
- party politics, extension of the franchise and social reform
- the development of the British Empire with a depth study (for example, of India)
- Ireland and Home Rule
- Darwin's 'On The Origin of Species'

- challenges for Britain, Europe and the wider world 1901 to the present day

In addition to studying the Holocaust, this could include:

Examples (non-statutory)

- women's suffrage
- the First World War and the Peace Settlement
- the inter-war years: the Great Depression and the rise of dictators
- the Second World War and the wartime leadership of Winston Churchill
- the creation of the Welfare State
- Indian independence and end of Empire
- social, cultural and technological change in post-war British society
- Britain's place in the world since 1945

- a local history study

Examples (non-statutory)

- a depth study linked to one of the British areas of study listed above
- a study over time, testing how far sites in their locality reflect aspects of national history (some sites may predate 1066)
- a study of an aspect or site in local history dating from a period before 1066

- the study of an aspect or theme in British history that consolidates and extends pupils' chronological knowledge from before 1066

Examples (non-statutory)

- the changing nature of political power in Britain, traced through selective case studies from the Iron Age to the present
- Britain's changing landscape from the Iron Age to the present
- a study of an aspect of social history, such as the impact through time of the migration of people to, from and within the British Isles
- a study in depth into a significant turning point: for example, the Neolithic Revolution

- at least one study of a significant society or issue in world history and its interconnections with other world developments [for example, Mughal India 1526–1857; China's Qing dynasty 1644–1911; Changing Russian empires c.1800–1989; USA in the 20th Century].

 **LANGUAGES**

Purpose of study

Learning a foreign language is a liberation from insularity and provides an opening to other cultures. A high-quality languages education should foster pupils' curiosity and deepen their understanding of the world. The teaching should enable pupils to express their ideas and thoughts in another language and to understand and respond to its speakers, both in speech and in writing. It should also provide opportunities for them to communicate for practical purposes, learn new ways of thinking and read great literature in the original language. Language teaching should provide the foundation for learning further languages, equipping pupils to study and work in other countries.

Aims

The national curriculum for languages aims to ensure that all pupils:

- understand and respond to spoken and written language from a variety of authentic sources
- speak with increasing confidence, fluency and spontaneity, finding ways of communicating what they want to say, including through discussion and asking questions, and continually improving the accuracy of their pronunciation and intonation
- can write at varying length, for different purposes and audiences, using the variety of grammatical structures that they have learnt
- discover and develop an appreciation of a range of writing in the language studied.

Attainment targets

By the end of each key stage, pupils are expected to know, apply and understand the matters, skills and processes specified in the relevant programme of study.

Schools are not required by law to teach the example content in [square brackets].

Subject content

Key stage 2: Foreign language

Teaching may be of any modern or ancient foreign language and should focus on enabling pupils to make substantial progress in one language. The teaching should provide an appropriate balance of spoken and written language and should lay the foundations for further foreign language teaching at key stage 3. It should enable pupils to understand and communicate ideas, facts and feelings in speech and writing, focused on familiar and routine matters, using their knowledge of phonology, grammatical structures and vocabulary.

The focus of study in modern languages will be on practical communication. If an ancient language is chosen, the focus will be to provide a linguistic foundation for reading comprehension and an appreciation of classical civilisation. Pupils studying ancient languages may take part in simple oral exchanges, while discussion of what they read will be conducted in English. A linguistic foundation in ancient languages may support the study of modern languages at key stage 3.

Pupils should be taught to:

- listen attentively to spoken language and show understanding by joining in and responding
- explore the patterns and sounds of language through songs and rhymes and link the spelling, sound and meaning of words
- engage in conversations; ask and answer questions; express opinions and respond to those of others; seek clarification and help*
- speak in sentences, using familiar vocabulary, phrases and basic language structures
- develop accurate pronunciation and intonation so that others understand when they are reading aloud or using familiar words and phrases*
- present ideas and information orally to a range of audiences*
- read carefully and show understanding of words, phrases and simple writing
- appreciate stories, songs, poems and rhymes in the language
- broaden their vocabulary and develop their ability to understand new words that are introduced into familiar written material, including through using a dictionary
- write phrases from memory, and adapt these to create new sentences, to express ideas clearly
- describe people, places, things and actions orally* and in writing
- understand basic grammar appropriate to the language being studied, including (where relevant): feminine, masculine and neuter forms and the conjugation of high-frequency verbs; key features and patterns of the language; how to apply these, for instance, to build sentences; and how these differ from or are similar to English.

The starred (*) content above will not be applicable to ancient languages.

Key stage 3: Modern foreign language

Teaching may be of any modern foreign language and should build on the foundations of language learning laid at key stage 2, whether pupils continue with the same language or take up a new one. Teaching should focus on developing the breadth and depth of pupils' competence in listening, speaking, reading and writing, based on a sound foundation of core grammar and vocabulary. It should enable pupils to understand and communicate personal and factual information that goes beyond their immediate needs and interests, developing and justifying points of view in speech and writing, with increased spontaneity, independence and accuracy. It should provide suitable preparation for further study.

Pupils should be taught to:

Grammar and vocabulary

- identify and use tenses or other structures which convey the present, past, and future as appropriate to the language being studied
- use and manipulate a variety of key grammatical structures and patterns, including voices and moods, as appropriate
- develop and use a wide-ranging and deepening vocabulary that goes beyond their immediate needs and interests, allowing them to give and justify opinions and take part in discussion about wider issues
- use accurate grammar, spelling and punctuation.

Linguistic competence

- listen to a variety of forms of spoken language to obtain information and respond appropriately
- transcribe words and short sentences that they hear with increasing accuracy
- initiate and develop conversations, coping with unfamiliar language and unexpected responses, making use of important social conventions such as formal modes of address
- express and develop ideas clearly and with increasing accuracy, both orally and in writing
- speak coherently and confidently, with increasingly accurate pronunciation and intonation
- read and show comprehension of original and adapted materials from a range of different sources, understanding the purpose, important ideas and details, and provide an accurate English translation of short, suitable material
- read literary texts in the language [such as stories, songs, poems and letters], to stimulate ideas, develop creative expression and expand understanding of the language and culture
- write prose using an increasingly wide range of grammar and vocabulary, write creatively to express their own ideas and opinions, and translate short written text accurately into the foreign language.

MUSIC

Purpose of study

Music is a universal language that embodies one of the highest forms of creativity. A high-quality music education should engage and inspire pupils to develop a love of music and their talent as musicians, and so increase their self-confidence, creativity and sense of achievement. As pupils progress, they should develop a critical engagement with music, allowing them to compose, and to listen with discrimination to the best in the musical canon.

Aims

The national curriculum for music aims to ensure that all pupils:

- perform, listen to, review and evaluate music across a range of historical periods, genres, styles and traditions, including the works of the great composers and musicians
- learn to sing and to use their voices, to create and compose music on their own and with others, have the opportunity to learn a musical instrument, use technology appropriately and have the opportunity to progress to the next level of musical excellence
- understand and explore how music is created, produced and communicated, including through the inter-related dimensions: pitch, duration, dynamics, tempo, timbre, texture, structure and appropriate musical notations.

Attainment targets

By the end of each key stage, pupils are expected to know, apply and understand the matters, skills and processes specified in the relevant programme of study.

Subject content

Key stage 1

Pupils should be taught to:

- use their voices expressively and creatively by singing songs and speaking chants and rhymes
- play tuned and untuned instruments musically
- listen with concentration and understanding to a range of high-quality live and recorded music
- experiment with, create, select and combine sounds using the inter-related dimensions of music.

Key stage 2

Pupils should be taught to sing and play musically with increasing confidence and control. They should develop an understanding of musical composition, organising and manipulating ideas within musical structures and reproducing sounds from aural memory.

Pupils should be taught to:

- play and perform in solo and ensemble contexts, using their voices and playing musical instruments with increasing accuracy, fluency, control and expression
- improvise and compose music for a range of purposes using the inter-related dimensions of music
- listen with attention to detail and recall sounds with increasing aural memory
- use and understand staff and other musical notations
- appreciate and understand a wide range of high-quality live and recorded music drawn from different traditions and from great composers and musicians
- develop an understanding of the history of music.

Key stage 3

Pupils should build on their previous knowledge and skills through performing, composing and listening. They should develop their vocal and/or instrumental fluency, accuracy and expressiveness; and understand musical structures, styles, genres and traditions, identifying the expressive use of musical dimensions. They should listen with increasing discrimination and awareness to inform their practice as musicians. They should use technologies appropriately and appreciate and understand a wide range of musical contexts and styles.

Pupils should be taught to:

- play and perform confidently in a range of solo and ensemble contexts using their voice, playing instruments musically, fluently and with accuracy and expression
- improvise and compose; and extend and develop musical ideas by drawing on a range of musical structures, styles, genres and traditions
- use staff and other relevant notations appropriately and accurately in a range of musical styles, genres and traditions
- identify and use the inter-related dimensions of music expressively and with increasing sophistication, including use of tonalities, different types of scales and other musical devices
- listen with increasing discrimination to a wide range of music from great composers and musicians
- develop a deepening understanding of the music that they perform and to which they listen, and its history.

PHYSICAL EDUCATION

Purpose of study

A high-quality physical education curriculum inspires all pupils to succeed and excel in competitive sport and other physically-demanding activities. It should provide opportunities for pupils to become physically confident in a way which supports their health and fitness. Opportunities to compete in sport and other activities build character and help to embed values such as fairness and respect.

Aims

The national curriculum for physical education aims to ensure that all pupils:

- develop competence to excel in a broad range of physical activities
- are physically active for sustained periods of time
- engage in competitive sports and activities
- lead healthy, active lives.

Attainment targets

By the end of each key stage, pupils are expected to know, apply and understand the matters, skills and processes specified in the relevant programme of study.

Schools are not required by law to teach the example content in [square brackets].

Subject content

Key stage 1

Pupils should develop fundamental movement skills, become increasingly competent and confident and access a broad range of opportunities to extend their agility, balance and coordination, individually and with others. They should be able to engage in competitive (both against self and against others) and co-operative physical activities, in a range of increasingly challenging situations.

Pupils should be taught to:

- master basic movements including running, jumping, throwing and catching, as well as developing balance, agility and co-ordination, and begin to apply these in a range of activities
- participate in team games, developing simple tactics for attacking and defending
- perform dances using simple movement patterns.

Key stage 2

Pupils should continue to apply and develop a broader range of skills, learning how to use them in different ways and to link them to make actions and sequences of movement. They should enjoy communicating, collaborating and competing with each other. They should develop an understanding of how to improve in different physical activities and sports and learn how to evaluate and recognise their own success.

Pupils should be taught to:

- use running, jumping, throwing and catching in isolation and in combination
- play competitive games, modified where appropriate [for example, badminton, basketball, cricket, football, hockey, netball, rounders and tennis], and apply basic principles suitable for attacking and defending
- develop flexibility, strength, technique, control and balance [for example, through athletics and gymnastics]
- perform dances using a range of movement patterns
- take part in outdoor and adventurous activity challenges both individually and within a team
- compare their performances with previous ones and demonstrate improvement to achieve their personal best.

Swimming and water safety

All schools must provide swimming instruction either in key stage 1 or key stage 2.

In particular, pupils should be taught to:

- swim competently, confidently and proficiently over a distance of at least 25 metres
- use a range of strokes effectively [for example, front crawl, backstroke and breaststroke]
- perform safe self-rescue in different water-based situations.

Key stage 3

Pupils should build on and embed the physical development and skills learned in key stages 1 and 2, become more competent, confident and expert in their techniques, and apply them across different sports and physical activities. They should understand what makes a performance effective and how to apply these principles to their own and others' work. They should develop the confidence and interest to get involved in exercise, sports and activities out of school and in later life, and understand and apply the long-term health benefits of physical activity.

Pupils should be taught to:

- use a range of tactics and strategies to overcome opponents in direct competition through team and individual games [for example, badminton, basketball, cricket, football, hockey, netball, rounders, rugby and tennis]
- develop their technique and improve their performance in other competitive sports [for example, athletics and gymnastics]
- perform dances using advanced dance techniques within a range of dance styles and forms
- take part in outdoor and adventurous activities which present intellectual and physical challenges and be encouraged to work in a team, building on trust and developing skills to solve problems, either individually or as a group
- analyse their performances compared to previous ones and demonstrate improvement to achieve their personal best
- take part in competitive sports and activities outside school through community links or sports clubs.

Key stage 4

Pupils should tackle complex and demanding physical activities. They should get involved in a range of activities that develops personal fitness and promotes an active, healthy lifestyle.

Pupils should be taught to:

- use and develop a variety of tactics and strategies to overcome opponents in team and individual games [for example, badminton, basketball, cricket, football, hockey, netball, rounders, rugby and tennis]
- develop their technique and improve their performance in other competitive sports [for example, athletics and gymnastics], or other physical activities [for example, dance]
- take part in further outdoor and adventurous activities in a range of environments which present intellectual and physical challenges and which encourage pupils to work in a team, building on trust and developing skills to solve problems, either individually or as a group
- evaluate their performances compared to previous ones and demonstrate improvement across a range of physical activities to achieve their personal best
- continue to take part regularly in competitive sports and activities outside school through community links or sports clubs.

About this publication:

enquiries   www.education.gov.uk/contactus
download   www.gov.uk/dfe/nationalcurriculum

Reference: DFE-00177-2013

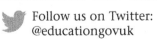 Follow us on Twitter:
@educationgovuk

 Like us on Facebook:
facebook.com/educationgovuk

SECTION 3

RELATIONSHIPS EDUCATION, RELATIONSHIPS AND SEX EDUCATION (RSE) AND HEALTH EDUCATION

What this guidance updates

This guidance replaces the Sex and Relationship Education guidance (2000). This guidance will be reviewed three years from first required teaching (September 2020) and every three years after that point.

The guidance should be read in conjunction with:

- Keeping Children Safe in Education (statutory guidance)
- Respectful School Communities: Self Review and Signposting Tool (a tool to support a whole school approach that promotes respect and discipline)
- Behaviour and Discipline in Schools (advice for schools, including advice for appropriate behaviour between pupils)
- Equality Act 2010 and schools
- SEND code of practice: 0 to 25 years (statutory guidance)
- Alternative Provision (statutory guidance)
- Mental Health and Behaviour in Schools (advice for schools)
- Preventing and Tackling Bullying (advice for schools, including advice on cyberbullying)
- Sexual violence and sexual harassment between children in schools (advice for schools)
- The Equality and Human Rights Commission Advice and Guidance (provides advice on avoiding discrimination in a variety of educational contexts)
- Promoting Fundamental British Values as part of SMSC in schools (guidance for maintained schools on promoting basic important British values as part of pupils' spiritual, moral, social and cultural (SMSC) development)
- SMSC requirements for independent schools (guidance for independent schools on how they should support pupils' spiritual, moral, social and cultural development)
- National Citizen Service guidance for schools

Introduction

1. To embrace the challenges of creating a happy and successful adult life, pupils need knowledge that will enable them to make informed decisions about their wellbeing, health and relationships and to build their self-efficacy. Pupils can also put this knowledge into practice as they develop the capacity to make sound decisions when facing risks, challenges and complex contexts. Everyone faces difficult situations in their lives. These subjects can support young people to develop resilience, to know how and when to ask for help, and to know where to access support.

2. High quality, evidence-based and age-appropriate teaching of these subjects can help prepare pupils for the opportunities, responsibilities and experiences of adult life. They can also enable schools to promote the spiritual, moral, social, cultural, mental and physical development of pupils, at school and in society. The duties on schools in this area are set out in legislation.[1]

---

[1]Maintained schools and academies are required to provide a curriculum, which is broad and balanced in accordance with Section 78 of the Education Act 2002. Part I of the Schedule to the Education (Independent School Standards) Regulations 2014 requires independent schools other than academies to make provision for PSHE (paragraph 2(2)(d)), and to prepare pupils for the opportunities, responsibilities and experiences of life in British society (paragraph 2(2)(i). Part 2 of the Schedule requires independent schools (including academies) to meet the standard relating to the Spiritual, Moral, Social and Cultural development of pupils.

3. The Relationships Education, Relationships and Sex Education and Health Education (England) Regulations 2019, made under sections 34 and 35 of the Children and Social Work Act 2017, make Relationships Education compulsory for all pupils receiving primary education and Relationships and Sex Education (RSE) compulsory for all pupils receiving secondary education.[2] They also make Health Education compulsory in all schools except independent schools. Personal, Social, Health and Economic Education (PSHE) continues to be compulsory in independent schools.

4. This guidance also sets out both the rights of parents/carers[3] to withdraw pupils from sex education (but not Relationships or Health Education) and the process that head teachers should follow in considering a request from a parent. Parents have the right to request that their child be withdrawn from some or all of sex education delivered as part of statutory RSE.

5. Schools are free to determine how to deliver the content set out in this guidance, in the context of a broad and balanced curriculum. Effective teaching in these subjects will ensure that core knowledge is broken down into units of manageable size and communicated clearly to pupils, in a carefully sequenced way, within a planned programme or lessons. Teaching will include sufficient well-chosen opportunities and contexts for pupils to embed new knowledge so that it can be used confidently in real life situations.

6. Many schools are choosing to deliver relationships or sex education as part of a timetabled PSHE programme, with good outcomes. Where that provision meets the requirements of this high level framework of core content they are free to continue with this model. Other schools may choose different curricular models for delivery.

7. The lead teacher will need to work closely with colleagues in related curriculum areas to ensure Relationships Education, RSE and Health Education programmes complement, and do not duplicate, content covered in national curriculum[4] subjects such as citizenship, science, computing and PE. It is important to check prior knowledge and build this into the planning process to ensure a smooth transition between primary and secondary. Further information on links to national curriculum subjects can be found on page 39.

8. Schools should be aware that for many young people the distinction between the online world and other aspects of life is less marked than for some adults. Young people often operate very freely in the online world and by secondary school age some are likely to be spending a substantial amount of time online. Where topics and issues outlined in this guidance are likely to be encountered by pupils online, schools should take this into account when planning how to support them in distinguishing between different types of online content and making well-founded decisions.

9. More broadly, the internet and social media have other important characteristics which young people should be aware of in order to help them use them discriminatingly. For example, social media users are sometimes prepared to say things in more extreme, unkind or exaggerated ways than they might in face to face situations, and some users present highly exaggerated or idealised profiles of themselves online. Some platforms attract large numbers of users with similar, sometimes extreme, views, who do not welcome dissent or debate. Young people should be aware that certain websites may share personal data

---

[2]For ease of reference, this guidance refers to primary schools and secondary schools, but the statutory requirements refer to pupils receiving primary/secondary education.

[3]Parents used henceforth to mean both parents and carers.

[4]The national curriculum does not apply to academies or independent schools.

about their users, and information collected on their internet use, for commercial purposes (i.e. to enable targeted advertising). In addition, criminals can operate online scams, for example using fake websites or emails to extort money or valuable personal information. This information can be used to the detriment of the person or wider society. Schools should take these factors into account when planning teaching of these subjects and consider the overlap with their wider curriculum to ensure pupils know how to keep themselves and their personal information safe.

10. In this guidance where topics occur equally on and offline they are accommodated in the core content under the most applicable theme with the assumption that teachers will deliver them in a way that reflects that pupils will be negotiating issues and opportunities in these areas in all contexts, including online. Where there are topics with exclusively online content or implications this is drawn out explicitly.

Summary of requirements

11. The subjects are part of the basic school curriculum (as previously for sex education in maintained secondary schools), which allows schools flexibility in developing their planned programme, integrated within a broad and balanced curriculum.

12. The guidance applies to:

Relationships Education	Relationships and Sex Education	Health Education
All schools providing primary education, including all-through schools and middle schools (includes schools as set out in the Summary section).	All schools providing secondary education, including all-through schools and middle schools (includes schools as set out in the Summary section).	All maintained schools including schools with a sixth form, academies, free schools, non-maintained special schools and alternative provision, including pupil referral units.
		The statutory requirement to provide Health Education does not apply to independent schools – PSHE is already compulsory as independent schools must meet the Independent School Standards as set out in the Education (Independent School Standards) Regulations 2014. Independent schools, however, may find the principles in the guidance on Health Education helpful in planning an age-appropriate curriculum.
The statutory requirements do not apply to sixth form colleges, 16–19 academies or Further Education (FE) colleges[5], although we would encourage them to support students by offering these subjects. These settings may find the principles helpful, especially in supporting pupils in the transition to FE.		

---

[5]Sixth form colleges and other 16–19 institutions that provide education for 14–16-year olds under an agreement with the Department for Education or its agencies are required by that agreement to follow guidance which covers a number of areas including the curriculum. The current guidance sets out the need to include the teaching of sex and relationship education in accordance with sections 403 and 405 of the Education Act. From September 2020, these institutions will need to teach the new subjects of Relationships and Sex Education and Health Education and to follow this guidance.

Developing a policy

13. All schools must have in place a written policy for Relationships Education and RSE. Schools must consult parents in developing and reviewing their policy. Schools should ensure that the policy meets the needs of pupils and parents and reflects the community they serve.

14. There are many excellent examples in which schools have established clear sex education policies in consultation with parents, governors and the wider community, and where they are already delivering effective programmes. Schools should build on that good work in adapting to these new requirements.

What is required?

15. All schools must have an up-to-date policy, which is made available to parents and others. Schools must provide a copy of the policy free of charge to anyone who asks for one and should publish the policy on the school website.[6]

16. The policy should:

Policies for mandatory subjects		Policy for non-mandatory subjects
For primary education[7]	**For secondary education**	**For primary schools that may choose to teach sex education**
Define Relationships Education	Define Relationships and Sex Education	Define any sex education they choose to teach other than that covered in the science curriculum.
Set out the subject content, how it is taught and who is responsible for teaching it.		
Describe how the subject is monitored and evaluated.		
Include information to clarify why parents do not have a right to withdraw their child.	Include information about a parent's right to request that their child be excused from sex education within RSE only.	Include information about a parent's right to request that their child be excused.
Confirm the date by which the policy will be reviewed.		
Typical policies are likely to include sections covering: • details of content/scheme of work and when each topic is taught, taking account of the age of pupils • who delivers either Relationships Education or RSE • how the policy has been produced, and how it will be kept under review, in both cases working with parents • how delivery of the content will be made accessible to all pupils, including those with SEND • explanation of the right to withdraw • requirements on schools in law e.g. the Equality Act (please see The Equality Act 2010 and schools: Departmental advice) • how often the policy is updated • who approves the policy		

---

[6]If a school does not have a website, they should ensure that the policy is available by other means.

[7]The regulations apply to the teaching of all primary and secondary pupils respectively. This includes all types of schools to which the regulations apply.

17. In secondary schools, RSE will often address aspects of relationships and sex education in an integrated way within a single topic. Schools should develop programmes of teaching which prioritise effective delivery of the content, and do not need artificially to separate sex education and Relationships Education.

18. The policy should also reflect the views of teachers and pupils. Listening and responding to the views of young people will strengthen the policy, ensuring that it meets the needs of all pupils.

Religion and belief, including teaching in schools with a religious character

19. A good understanding of pupils' faith backgrounds and positive relationships between the school and local faith communities help to create a constructive context for the teaching of these subjects.

20. In all schools, when teaching these subjects, the religious background of all pupils must be taken into account when planning teaching, so that the topics that are included in the core content in this guidance are appropriately handled. Schools must ensure they comply with the relevant provisions of the Equality Act 2010, under which religion or belief are amongst the protected characteristics.

21. All schools may teach about faith perspectives. In particular, schools with a religious character may teach the distinctive faith perspective on relationships, and balanced debate may take place about issues that are seen as contentious. For example, the school may wish to reflect on faith teachings about certain topics as well as how their faith institutions may support people in matters of relationships and sex.

22. In all schools, teaching should reflect the law (including the Equality Act 2010) as it applies to relationships, so that young people clearly understand what the law allows and does not allow, and the wider legal implications of decisions they may make.

Use of materials

23. There are a lot of excellent resources available, free-of-charge, which schools can draw on when delivering these subjects. Schools should assess each resource that they propose to use to ensure that it is appropriate for the age and maturity of pupils, and sensitive to their needs.

24. Schools should also ensure that, when they consult with parents, they provide examples of the resources that they plan to use as this can be reassuring for parents and enables them to continue the conversations started in class at home.

25. In addition, there are varieties of resources targeted at young people that can be helpful to use to complement teaching in the classroom. Public Health England, for example, have produced a website for young people which covers a broad range of health issues in a format which is accessible for young people, targeted at secondary-age pupils. This includes Rise Above resources for lessons linked from the PSHE Association website.

26. A list of some of the resources, which are available free-of-charge, can be found in Annex B.

Equality

27. Schools are required to comply with relevant requirements of the Equality Act 2010. Further guidance is available for schools in The Equality Act 2010 and schools advice. Schools[8] should pay particular attention to the Public sector equality duty (PSED) (s.149 of the Equality Act).

28. Under the provisions of the Equality Act, schools must not unlawfully discriminate against pupils because of their age, sex, race, disability, religion or belief, gender reassignment, pregnancy or maternity, marriage or civil partnership[9], or sexual orientation (collectively known as the protected characteristics). Schools must also make reasonable adjustments to alleviate disadvantage and be mindful of the SEND Code of Practice when planning for these subjects.

29. Provisions within the Equality Act allow schools to take positive action, where it can be shown that it is proportionate, to deal with particular disadvantages affecting one group because of a protected characteristic. This should be taken into consideration in designing and teaching these subjects. A school, could, for example, consider taking positive action to support girls if there was evidence that they were being disproportionately subjected to sexual violence or sexual harassment.

30. Schools should consider the makeup of their own student body, including the gender and age range of their pupils, and consider whether it is appropriate or necessary to put in place additional support for pupils with particular protected characteristics (which mean that they are potentially at greater risk). Schools should consider what they can do to foster healthy and respectful peer-to-peer communication and behaviour between boys and girls, and provide an environment, which challenges perceived limits on pupils based on their gender or any other characteristic, including through these subjects and as part of a whole-school approach.

31. Schools should be alive to issues such as everyday sexism, misogyny, homophobia and gender stereotypes and take positive action to build a culture where these are not tolerated, and any occurrences are identified and tackled. Staff have an important role to play in modelling positive behaviours. School pastoral and behaviour policies should support all pupils.

32. Schools should refer to the Department's advice, Sexual violence and sexual harassment between children in schools and colleges. The advice sets out what sexual violence and sexual harassment are, the current evidence on their preponderance in schools and colleges, how to minimise the risk of them occurring and what to do when they do occur or are alleged to have occurred. Schools should be aware of the importance of making clear that sexual violence and sexual harassment are not acceptable, will never be tolerated and are not an inevitable part of growing up. Any report of sexual violence or sexual harassment should be taken seriously; staff should be aware that statistically it is more likely that females will be the victims of sexual violence and sexual harassment than males, and that it is more likely that it will be perpetrated by males. However, males can also be the victims of sexual violence and

---

[8]Equality Act provisions in relation to schools are in Part 6, Chapter 1. Independent schools are not subject to the PSED.

[9]In the rest of this guidance, references to marriage should be read as marriage and civil partnership.

it can also happen in same-sex relationships. It is, however, essential that assumptions are not made about the behaviour of boys and young men and that they are not made to feel that this behaviour is an inevitable part of being male; most young men are respectful of young women and each other. An understanding for all pupils of healthy relationships, acceptable behaviour and the right of everyone to equal treatment will help ensure that pupils treat each other well and go on to be respectful and kind adults.

Pupils with special educational needs and disabilities (SEND)

33. Relationships Education, RSE and Health Education must be accessible for all pupils. This is particularly important when planning teaching for pupils with special educational needs and disabilities who represent a large minority of pupils. High quality teaching that is differentiated and personalised will be the starting point to ensure accessibility. Schools should also be mindful of the preparing for adulthood outcomes[10], as set out in the SEND code of practice, when teaching these subjects to those with SEND.

34. Schools should be aware that some pupils are more vulnerable to exploitation, bullying and other issues due to the nature of their SEND. Relationships Education and RSE can also be particularly important subjects for some pupils; for example those with Social, Emotional and Mental Health needs or learning disabilities. Such factors should be taken into consideration in designing and teaching these subjects.

35. In special schools and for some SEND pupils in mainstream schools there may be a need to tailor content and teaching to meet the specific needs of pupils at different developmental stages. As with all teaching for these subjects, schools should ensure that their teaching is sensitive, age-appropriate, developmentally appropriate and delivered with reference to the law.

Lesbian, Gay, Bisexual and Transgender (LGBT)

36. In teaching Relationships Education and RSE, schools should ensure that the needs of all pupils are appropriately met, and that all pupils understand the importance of equality and respect. Schools must ensure that they comply with the relevant provisions of the Equality Act 2010, (please see The Equality Act 2010 and schools: Departmental advice), under which sexual orientation and gender reassignment are amongst the protected characteristics.

37. Schools should ensure that all of their teaching is sensitive and age appropriate in approach and content. At the point at which schools consider it appropriate to teach their pupils about LGBT, they should ensure that this content is fully integrated into their programmes of study for this area of the curriculum rather than delivered as a stand-alone unit or lesson. Schools are free to determine how they do this, and we expect all pupils to have been taught LGBT content at a timely point as part of this area of the curriculum.

---

[10]"Preparing for adulthood" outcomes are set out at section 7.38 of the SEND code of practice: 0 to 25 years.

Governors

38. As well as fulfilling their legal obligations, the governing boards or management committee should also make sure that:
    - all pupils make progress in achieving the expected educational outcomes;
    - the subjects are well led, effectively managed and well planned;
    - the quality of provision is subject to regular and effective self-evaluation;
    - teaching is delivered in ways that are accessible to all pupils with SEND;
    - clear information is provided for parents on the subject content and the right to request that their child is withdrawn; and,
    - the subjects are resourced, staffed and timetabled in a way that ensures that the school can fulfil its legal obligations.

39. Foundation governors and trustees of faith academy trusts will also have wider responsibilities in relation to maintaining and developing the religious ethos of the schools.

Working with parents/carers and the wider community

40. The role of parents in the development of their children's understanding about relationships is vital. Parents are the first teachers of their children. They have the most significant influence in enabling their children to grow and mature and to form healthy relationships.

41. All schools should work closely with parents when planning and delivering these subjects. Schools should ensure that parents know what will be taught and when, and clearly communicate the fact that parents have the right to request that their child be withdrawn from some or all of sex education delivered as part of statutory RSE.

42. Parents should be given every opportunity to understand the purpose and content of Relationships Education and RSE. Good communication and opportunities for parents to understand and ask questions about the school's approach help increase confidence in the curriculum.

43. Many schools build a good relationship with parents on these subjects over time – for example by inviting parents into school to discuss what will be taught, address any concerns and help support parents in managing conversations with their children on these issues. This can be an important opportunity to talk about how these subjects contribute to wider support in terms of pupil wellbeing and keeping children safe. It is important through such processes to reach out to all parents, recognising that a range of approaches may be needed for doing so.

44. Many schools will have existing mechanisms in place to engage parents and should continue to draw on these as they respond to the new legal framework.

Right to be excused from sex education (commonly referred to as the right to withdraw)

45. Parents have the right to request that their child be withdrawn from some or all of sex education delivered as part of statutory RSE. Before granting any such request it would be good practice for the head teacher to discuss the request with parents and, as appropriate, with the child to ensure that their wishes are understood and to clarify the nature and purpose of the curriculum. Schools will want to document this process to ensure a record is kept.

46. Good practice is also likely to include the head teacher discussing with parents the benefits of receiving this important education and any detrimental effects that withdrawal might have on the child. This could include any social and emotional effects of being excluded, as well as the likelihood of the child hearing their peers' version of what was said in the classes, rather than what was directly said by the teacher (although the detrimental effects may be mitigated if the parents propose to deliver sex education to their child at home instead).

47. Once those discussions have taken place, except in exceptional circumstances, the school should respect the parents' request to withdraw the child, up to and until three terms before the child turns 16. After that point, if the child wishes to receive sex education rather than be withdrawn, the school should make arrangements to provide the child with sex education during one of those terms.

48. This process is the same for pupils with SEND. However there may be exceptional circumstances where the head teacher may want to take a pupil's specific needs arising from their SEND into account when making this decision. The approach outlined above should be reflected in the school's policy on RSE.

49. Head teachers will automatically grant a request to withdraw a pupil from any sex education delivered in primary schools, other than as part of the science curriculum.

50. If a pupil is excused from sex education, it is the school's responsibility to ensure that the pupil receives appropriate, purposeful education during the period of withdrawal. There is no right to withdraw from Relationships Education or Health Education.

Working with external agencies

51. Working with external organisations can enhance delivery of these subjects, bringing in specialist knowledge and different ways of engaging with young people.

52. As with any visitor, schools are responsible for ensuring that they check the visitor or visiting organisation's credentials. Schools should also ensure that the teaching delivered by the visitor fits with their planned programme and their published policy. It is important that schools discuss the detail of how the visitor will deliver their sessions and ensure that the content is age-appropriate and accessible for the pupils. Schools should ask to see the materials visitors will use as well as a lesson plan in advance, so that they can ensure it meets the full range of pupils' needs (e.g. special educational needs). It is important to agree how confidentiality will work in any lesson and that the visitor understands how safeguarding reports should be dealt with in line with school policy. Further information for teachers in handling potential safeguarding or child protection reports is on page 35.

53. Use of visitors should be to enhance teaching by an appropriate member of the teaching staff, rather than as a replacement for teaching by those staff.

Relationships Education (Primary)

54. The focus in primary school should be on teaching the fundamental building blocks and characteristics of positive relationships, with particular reference to friendships, family relationships, and relationships with other children and with adults.

55. This starts with pupils being taught about what a relationship is, what friendship is, what family means and who the people are who can support them. From the

beginning of primary school, building on early education, pupils should be taught how to take turns, how to treat each other with kindness, consideration and respect, the importance of honesty and truthfulness, permission seeking and giving, and the concept of personal privacy. Establishing personal space and boundaries, showing respect and understanding the differences between appropriate and inappropriate or unsafe physical, and other, contact – these are the forerunners of teaching about consent, which takes place at secondary.

56. Respect for others should be taught in an age-appropriate way, in terms of understanding one's own and others' boundaries in play, in negotiations about space, toys, books, resources and so on.

57. From the beginning, teachers should talk explicitly about the features of healthy friendships, family relationships and other relationships which young children are likely to encounter. Drawing attention to these in a range of contexts should enable pupils to form a strong early understanding of the features of relationships that are likely to lead to happiness and security. This will also help them to recognise any less positive relationships when they encounter them.

58. The principles of positive relationships also apply online especially as, by the end of primary school, many children will already be using the internet. When teaching relationships content, teachers should address online safety and appropriate behaviour in a way that is relevant to pupils' lives. Teachers should include content on how information and data is shared and used in all contexts, including online; for example, sharing pictures, understanding that many websites are businesses and how sites may use information provided by users in ways they might not expect.

59. Teaching about families requires sensitive and well-judged teaching based on knowledge of pupils and their circumstances. Families of many forms provide a nurturing environment for children. (Families can include for example, single parent families, LGBT parents, families headed by grandparents, adoptive parents, foster parents/carers amongst other structures.) Care needs to be taken to ensure that there is no stigmatisation of children based on their home circumstances and needs, to reflect sensitively that some children may have a different structure of support around them; e.g. looked after children or young carers.

60. A growing ability to form strong and positive relationships with others depends on the deliberate cultivation of character traits and positive personal attributes, (sometimes referred to as 'virtues') in the individual. In a school wide context which encourages the development and practice of resilience and other attributes, this includes character traits such as helping pupils to believe they can achieve, persevere with tasks, work towards long-term rewards and continue despite setbacks. Alongside understanding the importance of self-respect and self-worth, pupils should develop personal attributes including honesty, integrity, courage, humility, kindness, generosity, trustworthiness and a sense of justice. This can be achieved in a variety of ways including by providing planned opportunities for young people to undertake social action, active citizenship and voluntary service to others locally or more widely.

61. Relationships Education also creates an opportunity to enable pupils to be taught about positive emotional and mental wellbeing, including how friendships can support mental wellbeing.

62. Through Relationships Education (and RSE), schools should teach pupils the knowledge they need to recognise and to report abuse, including emotional, physical and sexual abuse. In primary schools, this can be delivered by focusing on boundaries and privacy, ensuring young people understand that they have

rights over their own bodies. This should also include understanding boundaries in friendships with peers and also in families and with others, in all contexts, including online. Pupils should know how to report concerns and seek advice when they suspect or know that something is wrong. At all stages it will be important to balance teaching children about making sensible decisions to stay safe (including online) whilst being clear it is never the fault of a child who is abused and why victim blaming is always wrong. These subjects complement Health Education and as part of a comprehensive programme and whole school approach, this knowledge can support safeguarding of children.

By the end of primary school:

Families and people who care for me	Pupils should know • that families are important for children growing up because they can give love, security and stability. • the characteristics of healthy family life, commitment to each other, including in times of difficulty, protection and care for children and other family members, the importance of spending time together and sharing each other's lives. • that others' families, either in school or in the wider world, sometimes look different from their family, but that they should respect those differences and know that other children's families are also characterised by love and care. • that stable, caring relationships, which may be of different types, are at the heart of happy families, and are important for children's security as they grow up. • that marriage[11] represents a formal and legally recognised commitment of two people to each other which is intended to be lifelong. • how to recognise if family relationships are making them feel unhappy or unsafe, and how to seek help or advice from others if needed.
Caring friendships	Pupils should know • how important friendships are in making us feel happy and secure, and how people choose and make friends. • the characteristics of friendships, including mutual respect, truthfulness, trustworthiness, loyalty, kindness, generosity, trust, sharing interests and experiences and support with problems and difficulties. • that healthy friendships are positive and welcoming towards others, and do not make others feel lonely or excluded. • that most friendships have ups and downs, and that these can often be worked through so that the friendship is repaired or even strengthened, and that resorting to violence is never right. • how to recognise who to trust and who not to trust, how to judge when a friendship is making them feel unhappy or uncomfortable, managing conflict, how to manage these situations and how to seek help or advice from others, if needed.

---

[11]Marriage in England and Wales is available to both opposite sex and same sex couples. The Marriage (Same Sex Couples) Act 2013 extended marriage to same sex couples in England and Wales. The ceremony through which a couple get married may be civil or religious.

Respectful relationships	Pupils should know
	<ul><li>the importance of respecting others, even when they are very different from them (for example, physically, in character, personality or backgrounds), or make different choices or have different preferences or beliefs.</li><li>practical steps they can take in a range of different contexts to improve or support respectful relationships.</li><li>the conventions of courtesy and manners.</li><li>the importance of self-respect and how this links to their own happiness.</li><li>that in school and in wider society they can expect to be treated with respect by others, and that in turn they should show due respect to others, including those in positions of authority.</li><li>about different types of bullying (including cyberbullying), the impact of bullying, responsibilities of bystanders (primarily reporting bullying to an adult) and how to get help.</li><li>what a stereotype is, and how stereotypes can be unfair, negative or destructive.</li><li>the importance of permission-seeking and giving in relationships with friends, peers and adults.</li></ul>
Online relationships	Pupils should know
	<ul><li>that people sometimes behave differently online, including by pretending to be someone they are not.</li><li>that the same principles apply to online relationships as to face-to-face relationships, including the importance of respect for others online including when we are anonymous.</li><li>the rules and principles for keeping safe online, how to recognise risks, harmful content and contact, and how to report them.</li><li>how to critically consider their online friendships and sources of information including awareness of the risks associated with people they have never met.</li><li>how information and data is shared and used online.</li></ul>
Being safe	Pupils should know
	<ul><li>what sorts of boundaries are appropriate in friendships with peers and others (including in a digital context).</li><li>about the concept of privacy and the implications of it for both children and adults; including that it is not always right to keep secrets if they relate to being safe.</li><li>that each person's body belongs to them, and the differences between appropriate and inappropriate or unsafe physical, and other, contact.</li><li>how to respond safely and appropriately to adults they may encounter (in all contexts, including online) whom they do not know.</li><li>how to recognise and report feelings of being unsafe or feeling bad about any adult.</li><li>how to ask for advice or help for themselves or others, and to keep trying until they are heard.</li><li>how to report concerns or abuse, and the vocabulary and confidence needed to do so.</li><li>where to get advice e.g. family, school and/or other sources.</li></ul>

Managing difficult questions

63. Primary-age pupils will often ask their teachers or other adults questions pertaining to sex or sexuality which go beyond what is set out for Relationships Education. The school's policy should cover how the school handles such questions. Given ease of access to the internet, children whose questions go unanswered may turn to inappropriate sources of information.

64. Meeting these objectives will require a graduated, age-appropriate programme of Relationships Education. Children of the same age may be developmentally at different stages, leading to differing types of questions or behaviours. Teaching methods should take account of these differences (including when they are due to specific special educational needs or disabilities) and the potential for discussion on a one-to-one basis or in small groups. Schools should consider what is appropriate and inappropriate in a whole-class setting, as teachers may require support and training in answering questions that are better not dealt with in front of a whole class.

Sex Education (Primary)

65. The Relationships Education, RSE, and Health Education (England) Regulations 2019 have made Relationships Education compulsory in all primary schools. Sex education is not compulsory in primary schools and the content set out in this guidance therefore focuses on Relationships Education.

66. The content set out in this guidance covers everything that primary schools should teach about relationships and health, including puberty. The national curriculum for science also includes subject content in related areas, such as the main external body parts, the human body as it grows from birth to old age (including puberty) and reproduction in some plants and animals. It will be for primary schools to determine whether they need to cover any additional content on sex education to meet the needs of their pupils. Many primary schools already choose to teach some aspects of sex education and will continue to do so, although it is not a requirement.

67. It is important that the transition phase before moving to secondary school supports pupils' ongoing emotional and physical development effectively. The Department continues to recommend therefore that all primary schools should have a sex education programme tailored to the age and the physical and emotional maturity of the pupils. It should ensure that both boys and girls are prepared for the changes that adolescence brings and – drawing on knowledge of the human life cycle set out in the national curriculum for science – how a baby is conceived and born. As well as consulting parents more generally about the school's overall policy, primary schools should consult parents before the final year of primary school about the detailed content of what will be taught. This process should include offering parents support in talking to their children about sex education and how to link this with what is being taught in school. Meeting these objectives will require a graduated, age-appropriate programme of sex education. Teaching needs to take account of the developmental differences of children.

68. Where a maintained primary school chooses to teach aspects of sex education (which go beyond the national curriculum for science), the school must set this out in their policy and all schools should consult with parents on what is to be covered.

Primary schools that choose to teach sex education must allow parents a right to withdraw their children. Unlike sex education in RSE at secondary, in primary schools, head teachers must comply with a parent's wish to withdraw their child from sex education beyond the national curriculum for science. Schools will want to draw on the good practice for conversations with parents around the right to withdraw as set out in paragraphs 45 and 46. Schools must also ensure that their teaching and materials are appropriate having regard to the age and religious backgrounds of their pupils. Schools will also want to recognise the significance of other factors, such as any special educational needs or disabilities of their pupils.

Relationships and Sex Education (RSE): Secondary

69. The aim of RSE is to give young people the information they need to help them develop healthy, nurturing relationships of all kinds, not just intimate relationships. It should enable them to know what a healthy relationship looks like and what makes a good friend, a good colleague and a successful marriage or other type of committed relationship. It should also cover contraception, developing intimate relationships and resisting pressure to have sex (and not applying pressure). It should teach what is acceptable and unacceptable behaviour in relationships. This will help pupils understand the positive effects that good relationships have on their mental wellbeing, identify when relationships are not right and understand how such situations can be managed.

70. Effective RSE does not encourage early sexual experimentation. It should teach young people to understand human sexuality and to respect themselves and others. It enables young people to mature, build their confidence and self-esteem and understand the reasons for delaying sexual activity. Effective RSE also supports people, throughout life, to develop safe, fulfilling and healthy sexual relationships, at the appropriate time.

71. Knowledge about safer sex and sexual health remains important to ensure that young people are equipped to make safe, informed and healthy choices as they progress through adult life. This should be delivered in a non-judgemental, factual way and allow scope for young people to ask questions in a safe environment. Many teachers use approaches such as distancing techniques, setting ground rules with the class to help manage sensitive discussion and using question boxes to allow pupils to raise issues anonymously.

72. RSE should provide clear progression from what is taught in primary school in Relationships Education. Teachers should build on the foundation of Relationships Education and, as pupils grow up, at the appropriate time extend teaching to include intimate relationships. Alongside being taught about intimate relationships, pupils should also be taught about family relationships, friendships and other kinds of relationships that are an equally important part of becoming a successful and happy adult. This teaching should enable pupils to distinguish between content and experiences that exemplify healthy relationships and those that are distorted or harmful.

73. Pupils should understand the benefits of healthy relationships to their mental wellbeing and self-respect. Through gaining the knowledge of what a healthy relationship is like, they can be empowered to identify when relationships are unhealthy. They should be taught that unhealthy relationships can have a lasting, negative impact on mental wellbeing.

74. As in primary, secondary Relationships Education can be underpinned by a wider, deliberate cultivation and practice of resilience and character in the individual. These should include character traits such as belief in achieving goals and persevering with tasks, as well as personal attributes such as honesty, integrity, courage, humility, kindness, generosity, trustworthiness and a sense of justice, underpinned by an understanding of the importance of self-respect and self-worth. There are many ways in which secondary schools should support the development of these attributes, for example by providing planned opportunities for young people to undertake social action, active citizenship and voluntary service to others locally or more widely.

75. Pupils should be taught the facts and the law about sex, sexuality, sexual health and gender identity in an age-appropriate and inclusive way. All pupils should feel that the content is relevant to them and their developing sexuality. Sexual orientation and gender identity should be explored at a timely point and in a clear, sensitive and respectful manner. When teaching about these topics, it must be recognised that young people may be discovering or understanding their sexual orientation or gender identity. There should be an equal opportunity to explore the features of stable and healthy same-sex relationships. This should be integrated appropriately into the RSE programme, rather than addressed separately or in only one lesson.

76. It is recognised that there will be a range of opinions regarding RSE. The starting principle when teaching each of these must be that the applicable law should be taught in a factual way so that pupils are clear on their rights and responsibilities as citizens.

77. Schools may choose to explore faith, or other perspectives, on some of these issues in other subjects such as Religious Education.

78. Pupils should be well informed about the full range of perspectives and, within the law, should be well equipped to make decisions for themselves about how to live their own lives, whilst respecting the right of others to make their own decisions and hold their own beliefs. Key aspects of the law relating to sex which should be taught include the age of consent, what consent is and is not, the definitions and recognition of rape, sexual assault and harassment, and choices permitted by the law around pregnancy.

79. Grooming, sexual exploitation and domestic abuse, including coercive and controlling behaviour, should also be addressed sensitively and clearly. Schools should address the physical and emotional damage caused by female genital mutilation (FGM). They should also be taught where to find support and that it is a criminal offence to perform or assist in the performance of FGM or fail to protect a person for whom you are responsible from FGM. As well as addressing this in the context of the law, pupils may also need support to recognise when relationships (including family relationships) are unhealthy or abusive (including the unacceptability of neglect, emotional, sexual and physical abuse and violence, including honour-based violence and forced marriage) and strategies to manage this or access support for oneself or others at risk. Schools should also be mindful that for pupils who are or have experienced unhealthy or unsafe relationships at home or socially, the school may have a particularly important role in being a place of consistency and safety where they can easily speak to trusted adults, report problems and find support.

80. Internet safety should also be addressed. Pupils should be taught the rules and principles for keeping safe online. This will include how to recognise risks,

harmful content and contact, and how and to whom to report issues. Pupils should have a strong understanding of how data is generated, collected, shared and used online, for example, how personal data is captured on social media or understanding the way that businesses may exploit the data available to them.

81. Some pupils are also exposed to harmful behaviours online, and via other forms of media, which may normalise violent sexual behaviours. A focus on healthy relationships and broader Relationships Education can help young people understand acceptable behaviours in relationships.

By the end of secondary school:

Schools should continue to develop knowledge on topics specified for primary as required <u>and in addition</u> cover the following content by the end of secondary:

Families	Pupils should know
	• that there are different types of committed, stable relationships.
	• how these relationships might contribute to human happiness and their importance for bringing up children.
	• what marriage is, including their legal status e.g. that marriage carries legal rights and protections not available to couples who are cohabiting or who have married, for example, in an unregistered religious ceremony.
	• why marriage is an important relationship choice for many couples and why it must be freely entered into.
	• the characteristics and legal status of other types of long-term relationships.
	• the roles and responsibilities of parents with respect to raising of children, including the characteristics of successful parenting.
	• how to: determine whether other children, adults or sources of information are trustworthy: judge when a family, friend, intimate or other relationship is unsafe (and to recognise this in others' relationships); and, how to seek help or advice, including reporting concerns about others, if needed.
Respectful relationships, including friendships	Pupils should know
	• the characteristics of positive and healthy friendships (in all contexts, including online) including: trust, respect, honesty, kindness, generosity, boundaries, privacy, consent and the management of conflict, reconciliation and ending relationships. This includes different (non-sexual) types of relationship.
	• practical steps they can take in a range of different contexts to improve or support respectful relationships.
	• how stereotypes, in particular stereotypes based on sex, gender, race, religion, sexual orientation or disability, can cause damage (e.g. how they might normalise non-consensual behaviour or encourage prejudice).
	• that in school and in wider society they can expect to be treated with respect by others, and that in turn they should show due respect to others, including people in positions of authority and due tolerance of other people's beliefs.

	• about different types of bullying (including cyberbullying), the impact of bullying, responsibilities of bystanders to report bullying and how and where to get help. • that some types of behaviour within relationships are criminal, including violent behaviour and coercive control. • what constitutes sexual harassment and sexual violence and why these are always unacceptable. • the legal rights and responsibilities regarding equality (particularly with reference to the protected characteristics as defined in the Equality Act 2010) and that everyone is unique and equal.
Online and media	Pupils should know • their rights, responsibilities and opportunities online, including that the same expectations of behaviour apply in all contexts, including online. • about online risks, including that any material someone provides to another has the potential to be shared online and the difficulty of removing potentially compromising material placed online. • not to provide material to others that they would not want shared further and not to share personal material which is sent to them. • what to do and where to get support to report material or manage issues online. • the impact of viewing harmful content. • that specifically sexually explicit material e.g. pornography presents a distorted picture of sexual behaviours, can damage the way people see themselves in relation to others and negatively affect how they behave towards sexual partners. • that sharing and viewing indecent images of children (including those created by children) is a criminal offence which carries severe penalties including jail. • how information and data is generated, collected, shared and used online.
Being safe	Pupils should know • the concepts of, and laws relating to, sexual consent, sexual exploitation, abuse, grooming, coercion, harassment, rape, domestic abuse, forced marriage, honour-based violence and FGM, and how these can affect current and future relationships. • how people can actively communicate and recognise consent from others, including sexual consent, and how and when consent can be withdrawn (in all contexts, including online).
Intimate and sexual relationships, including sexual health	Pupils should know • how to recognise the characteristics and positive aspects of healthy one-to-one intimate relationships, which include mutual respect, consent, loyalty, trust, shared interests and outlook, sex and friendship. • that all aspects of health can be affected by choices they make in sex and relationships, positively or negatively, e.g. physical, emotional, mental, sexual and reproductive health and wellbeing. • the facts about reproductive health, including fertility, and the potential impact of lifestyle on fertility for men and women and menopause.

- that there are a range of strategies for identifying and managing sexual pressure, including understanding peer pressure, resisting pressure and not pressurising others.
- that they have a choice to delay sex or to enjoy intimacy without sex.
- the facts about the full range of contraceptive choices, efficacy and options available.
- the facts around pregnancy including miscarriage.
- that there are choices in relation to pregnancy (with medically and legally accurate, impartial information on all options, including keeping the baby, adoption, abortion and where to get further help).
- how the different sexually transmitted infections (STIs), including HIV/AIDs, are transmitted, how risk can be reduced through safer sex (including through condom use) and the importance of and facts about testing.
- about the prevalence of some STIs, the impact they can have on those who contract them and key facts about treatment.
- how the use of alcohol and drugs can lead to risky sexual behaviour.
- how to get further advice, including how and where to access confidential sexual and reproductive health advice and treatment.

The Law

82. It is important to know what the law says about sex, relationships and young people, as well as broader safeguarding issues. This includes a range of important facts and the rules regarding sharing personal information, pictures, videos and other material using technology. This will help young people to know what is right and wrong in law, but it can also provide a good foundation of knowledge for deeper discussion about all types of relationships. There are also many different legal provisions whose purpose is to protect young people and which ensure young people take responsibility for their actions. Pupils should be made aware of the relevant legal provisions when relevant topics are being taught, including for example:

- marriage
- consent, including the age of consent
- violence against women and girls
- online behaviours including image and information sharing (including 'sexting', youth-produced sexual imagery, nudes, etc.)
- pornography
- abortion
- sexuality
- gender identity
- substance misuse
- violence and exploitation by gangs
- extremism/radicalisation
- criminal exploitation (for example, through gang involvement or 'county lines' drugs operations)
- hate crime
- female genital mutilation (FGM)

Physical health and mental wellbeing

83. The aim of teaching pupils about physical health and mental wellbeing is to give them the information that they need to make good decisions about their own health and wellbeing. It should enable them to recognise what is normal and what is an issue in themselves and others and, when issues arise, know how to seek support as early as possible from appropriate sources.
84. Physical health and mental wellbeing are interlinked, and it is important that pupils understand that good physical health contributes to good mental wellbeing, and vice versa.
85. It is important for schools to promote pupils' self-control and ability to self-regulate, and strategies for doing so. This will enable them to become confident in their ability to achieve well and persevere even when they encounter setbacks or when their goals are distant, and to respond calmly and rationally to setbacks and challenges. This integrated, whole-school approach to the teaching and promotion of health and wellbeing has a potential positive impact on behaviour and attainment.
86. Effective teaching should aim to reduce stigma attached to health issues, in particular those to do with mental wellbeing. Schools should engender an atmosphere that encourages openness. This will mean that pupils feel they can check their understanding and seek any necessary help and advice as they gain knowledge about how to promote good health and wellbeing.
87. Schools have flexibility to design and plan age-appropriate subject content, but this guidance sets out core areas for health and wellbeing that are appropriate for primary and secondary aged pupils.
88. Puberty including menstruation should be covered in Health Education and should, as far as possible, be addressed before onset. This should ensure male and female pupils are prepared for changes they and their peers will experience.

Menstruation

89. The onset of menstruation can be confusing or even alarming for girls if they are not prepared. Pupils should be taught key facts about the menstrual cycle including what is an average period, range of menstrual products and the implications for emotional and physical health. In addition to curriculum content, schools should also make adequate and sensitive arrangements to help girls prepare for and manage menstruation including with requests for menstrual products. Schools will need to consider the needs of their cohort of pupils in designing this content.

Physical health and mental wellbeing: Primary

90. The focus in primary school should be on teaching the characteristics of good physical health and mental wellbeing. Teachers should be clear that mental wellbeing is a normal part of daily life, in the same way as physical health.
91. This starts with pupils being taught about the benefits and importance of daily exercise, good nutrition and sufficient sleep, and giving pupils the language and knowledge to understand the normal range of emotions that everyone experiences. This should enable pupils to articulate how they are feeling,

develop the language to talk about their bodies, health and emotions and judge whether what they are feeling and how they are behaving is appropriate and proportionate for the situations that they experience.

92. Teachers should go on to talk about the steps pupils can take to protect and support their own and others' health and wellbeing, including simple self-care techniques, personal hygiene, prevention of health and wellbeing problems and basic first aid.

93. Emphasis should be given to the positive two-way relationship between good physical health and good mental wellbeing, and the benefits to mental wellbeing of physical exercise and time spent outdoors.

94. Pupils should also be taught the benefits of hobbies, interests and participation in their own communities. This teaching should make clear that people are social beings and that spending time with others, taking opportunities to consider the needs of others and practising service to others, including in organised and structured activities and groups (for example the scouts or girl guide movements), are beneficial for health and wellbeing.

95. Pupils should be taught about the benefits of rationing time spent online and the risks of excessive use of electronic devices. In later primary school, pupils should be taught why social media, computer games and online gaming have age restrictions and should be equipped to manage common difficulties encountered online.

96. A firm foundation in the benefits and characteristics of good health and wellbeing will enable teachers to talk about isolation, loneliness, unhappiness, bullying and the negative impact of poor health and wellbeing.

By the end of primary school:

Mental wellbeing	Pupils should know
	• that mental wellbeing is a normal part of daily life, in the same way as physical health.
	• that there is a normal range of emotions (e.g. happiness, sadness, anger, fear, surprise, nervousness) and scale of emotions that all humans experience in relation to different experiences and situations.
	• how to recognise and talk about their emotions, including having a varied vocabulary of words to use when talking about their own and others' feelings.
	• how to judge whether what they are feeling and how they are behaving is appropriate and proportionate.
	• the benefits of physical exercise, time outdoors, community participation, voluntary and service-based activity on mental wellbeing and happiness.
	• simple self-care techniques, including the importance of rest, time spent with friends and family and the benefits of hobbies and interests.
	• isolation and loneliness can affect children and that it is very important for children to discuss their feelings with an adult and seek support.
	• that bullying (including cyberbullying) has a negative and often lasting impact on mental wellbeing.

	<ul><li>where and how to seek support (including recognising the triggers for seeking support), including whom in school they should speak to if they are worried about their own or someone else's mental wellbeing or ability to control their emotions (including issues arising online).</li><li>it is common for people to experience mental ill health. For many people who do, the problems can be resolved if the right support is made available, especially if accessed early enough.</li></ul>
Internet safety and harms	Pupils should know <ul><li>that for most people the internet is an integral part of life and has many benefits.</li><li>about the benefits of rationing time spent online, the risks of excessive time spent on electronic devices and the impact of positive and negative content online on their own and others' mental and physical wellbeing.</li><li>how to consider the effect of their online actions on others and know how to recognise and display respectful behaviour online and the importance of keeping personal information private.</li><li>why social media, some computer games and online gaming, for example, are age restricted.</li><li>that the internet can also be a negative place where online abuse, trolling, bullying and harassment can take place, which can have a negative impact on mental health.</li><li>how to be a discerning consumer of information online including understanding that information, including that from search engines, is ranked, selected and targeted.</li><li>where and how to report concerns and get support with issues online.</li></ul>
Physical health and fitness	Pupils should know <ul><li>the characteristics and mental and physical benefits of an active lifestyle.</li><li>the importance of building regular exercise into daily and weekly routines and how to achieve this; for example walking or cycling to school, a daily active mile or other forms of regular, vigorous exercise.</li><li>the risks associated with an inactive lifestyle (including obesity).</li><li>how and when to seek support including which adults to speak to in school if they are worried about their health.</li></ul>
Healthy eating	Pupils should know <ul><li>what constitutes a healthy diet (including understanding calories and other nutritional content).</li><li>the principles of planning and preparing a range of healthy meals.</li><li>the characteristics of a poor diet and risks associated with unhealthy eating (including, for example, obesity and tooth decay) and other behaviours (e.g. the impact of alcohol on diet or health).</li></ul>
Drugs, alcohol and tobacco	Pupils should know <ul><li>the facts about legal and illegal harmful substances and associated risks, including smoking, alcohol use and drug-taking.</li></ul>

Health and prevention	Pupils should know
	• how to recognise early signs of physical illness, such as weight loss, or unexplained changes to the body.
	• about safe and unsafe exposure to the sun, and how to reduce the risk of sun damage, including skin cancer.
	• the importance of sufficient good quality sleep for good health and that a lack of sleep can affect weight, mood and ability to learn.
	• about dental health and the benefits of good oral hygiene and dental flossing, including regular check-ups at the dentist.
	• about personal hygiene and germs including bacteria, viruses, how they are spread and treated, and the importance of handwashing.
	• the facts and science relating to allergies, immunisation and vaccination.
Basic first aid	Pupils should know:
	• how to make a clear and efficient call to emergency services if necessary.
	• concepts of basic first-aid, for example dealing with common injuries, including head injuries.
Changing adolescent body	Pupils should know:
	• key facts about puberty and the changing adolescent body, particularly from age 9 through to age 11, including physical and emotional changes.
	• about menstrual wellbeing including the key facts about the menstrual cycle.

Physical health and mental wellbeing: Secondary

97. It is important that the starting point for health and wellbeing education should be a focus on enabling pupils to make well-informed, positive choices for themselves. In secondary school, teaching should build on primary content and should introduce new content to older pupils at appropriate points. This should enable pupils to understand how their bodies are changing, how they are feeling and why, to further develop the language that they use to talk about their bodies, health and emotions and to understand why terms associated with mental and physical health difficulties should not be used pejoratively. This knowledge should enable pupils to understand where normal variations in emotions and physical complaints end and health and wellbeing issues begin.

98. Teaching about the impact of puberty, which will have started in primary school, should continue in secondary school, so that pupils are able to understand the physical and emotional changes, which take place at this time and their impact on their wider health and wellbeing.

99. Emphasis should continue to be given to steps pupils can take to protect and support their own health and wellbeing. They should know that there is a relationship between good physical health and good mental wellbeing and that this can also influence their ability to learn. Teachers should cover self-care, the benefits of physical activity and time spent outdoors. This should be linked to information on the benefits of sufficient sleep, good nutrition and strategies for building resilience.

100. Pupils should know the contribution that hobbies, interests and participation in their own communities can make to overall wellbeing. They should understand that humans are social beings and that outward-facing activity, especially that with a service focus (for example, work, volunteering and participation in organisations such as the scouts or the girl guiding movements, the National Citizen Service or the Duke of Edinburgh Award) are beneficial for wellbeing. This can also contribute to the development of the attributes for a happy and successful adult life. Pupils should be supported to recognise what makes them feel lonely. Self-focused or isolating lifestyle choices can lead to unhappiness and being disconnected from society for those who have greater need for companionship and relationships.

101. Pupils should also be taught about problems and challenges. This should include factual information about the prevalence and characteristics of more serious mental and physical health conditions, drugs, alcohol and information about effective interventions. Schools may also choose to teach about issues such as eating disorders.[12]

102. Teachers should be aware of common 'adverse childhood experiences' (such as family breakdown, bereavement and exposure to domestic violence) and when and how these may be affecting any of their pupils and so may be influencing how they experience these subjects. The impact of time spent online, the positive aspects of online support and negotiating social media, including online forums and gaming, should also be included. Teachers should understand that pupils who have experienced problems at home may depend more on schools for support.

103. Pupils should be taught how to judge when they, or someone they know, needs support and where they can seek help if they have concerns. This should include details on which adults in school (e.g. school nurses), and externally can help.

Schools should continue to develop knowledge on topics specified for primary as required <u>and in addition</u> cover the following content by the end of secondary:

Mental wellbeing	Pupils should know
	<ul><li>how to talk about their emotions accurately and sensitively, using appropriate vocabulary.</li><li>that happiness is linked to being connected to others.</li><li>how to recognise the early signs of mental wellbeing concerns.</li><li>common types of mental ill health (e.g. anxiety and depression).</li><li>how to critically evaluate when something they do or are involved in has a positive or negative effect on their own or others' mental health.</li><li>the benefits and importance of physical exercise, time outdoors, community participation and voluntary and service-based activities on mental wellbeing and happiness.</li></ul>

---

[12]Eating disorders and extreme weight loss are a specialised area and schools should use qualified support or advice as needed. Schools may consider accessing support from the NHS or local specialist services who may be able to provide advice and CPD for teachers.

Internet safety and harms	Pupils should know • the similarities and differences between the online world and the physical world, including: the impact of unhealthy or obsessive comparison with others online (including through setting unrealistic expectations for body image), how people may curate a specific image of their life online, over-reliance on online relationships including social media, the risks related to online gambling including the accumulation of debt, how advertising and information is targeted at them and how to be a discerning consumer of information online. • how to identify harmful behaviours online (including bullying, abuse or harassment) and how to report, or find support, if they have been affected by those behaviours.
Physical health and fitness	Pupils should know • the positive associations between physical activity and promotion of mental wellbeing, including as an approach to combat stress. • the characteristics and evidence of what constitutes a healthy lifestyle, maintaining a healthy weight, including the links between an inactive lifestyle and ill health, including cancer and cardio-vascular ill-health. • about the science relating to blood, organ and stem cell donation.
Healthy eating	Pupils should know • how to maintain healthy eating and the links between a poor diet and health risks, including tooth decay and cancer.
Drugs, alcohol and tobacco	Pupils should know • the facts about legal and illegal drugs and their associated risks, including the link between drug use, and the associated risks, including the link to serious mental health conditions. • the law relating to the supply and possession of illegal substances. • the physical and psychological risks associated with alcohol consumption and what constitutes low risk alcohol consumption in adulthood. • the physical and psychological consequences of addiction, including alcohol dependency. • awareness of the dangers of drugs which are prescribed but still present serious health risks. • the facts about the harms from smoking tobacco (particularly the link to lung cancer), the benefits of quitting and how to access support to do so.
Health and prevention	Pupils should know • about personal hygiene, germs including bacteria, viruses, how they are spread, treatment and prevention of infection, and about antibiotics. • about dental health and the benefits of good oral hygiene and dental flossing, including healthy eating and regular check-ups at the dentist. • (late secondary) the benefits of regular self-examination and screening. • the facts and science relating to immunisation and vaccination. • the importance of sufficient good quality sleep for good health and how a lack of sleep can affect weight, mood and ability to learn.

Basic first aid	Pupils should know
	• basic treatment for common injuries. • life-saving skills, including how to administer CPR.[13] • the purpose of defibrillators and when one might be needed.
Changing adolescent body	Pupils should know
	• key facts about puberty, the changing adolescent body and menstrual wellbeing. • the main changes which take place in males and females, and the implications for emotional and physical health.

Delivery and teaching strategies

National curriculum subjects: citizenship, science, computing and PE

104. Relationships Education, RSE and Health Education complement several national curriculum subjects. Where schools are teaching the national curriculum, they should look for opportunities to draw links between the subjects and integrate teaching where appropriate. There continues to be no right of withdrawal from any part of the national curriculum.

105. The national curriculum for citizenship at key stages 3 and 4 aims to provide pupils with knowledge, skills and understanding to prepare them to play a full and active part in society. In particular, citizenship education should foster pupils' awareness and understanding of democracy, government and how laws are made and upheld. Teaching should equip pupils with the knowledge to explore political and social issues, to weigh evidence, debate and make reasoned arguments. It should also prepare pupils to take their place in society as responsible citizens, manage their money well and make sound financial decisions.

106. At key stages 1 and 2, the national curriculum for science includes teaching about the main external parts of the body and changes to the human body as it grows from birth to old age, including puberty. At key stage 3 and 4, it includes teaching about reproduction in humans; for example, the structure and function of the male and female reproductive systems, menstrual cycle, gametes, fertilisation, gestation, birth and HIV/AIDS.

107. The national curriculum for computing aims to ensure that all pupils can understand and apply the fundamental principles and concepts of computer science, including logic, algorithms and data representation. It also covers e-safety, with progression in the content to reflect the different and escalating risks that young people face as they get older. This includes how to use technology safely, responsibly, respectfully and securely, how to keep personal information private, and where to go for help and support.

108. The national curriculum for PE aims to ensure that pupils develop competence to excel in a broad range of physical activities, are physically active for sustained periods of time, engage in competitive sport and activities and lead healthy, active lives.

109. Schools need to consider how they can ensure that Relationships Education, RSE and Health Education complement existing national curriculum subjects

---

[13]Cardio Pulmonary Resuscitation is usually best taught after 12 years old.

and whole school approaches to wellbeing and health. For example, health education can complement what is taught through PE by developing core knowledge and broader understanding that enables people to lead healthy, active lives and citizenship can complement all of the new subjects in the coverage of law. Schools should tailor their curriculum to meet the needs of their pupils.

Pupil Referral Units/Alternative Provision

110. Pupil referral units (PRUs), alternative provision (AP) academies and free schools and independent schools that provide AP are required to make provision for Relationships Education, RSE and Health Education in the same way as mainstream schools; and they must have regard to this guidance in delivering their programme. In teaching these subjects in PRUs, AP academies and free schools, and independent[14] AP schools, specific thought should be given to the particular needs and vulnerabilities of the pupils.

Senior leadership and whole school approach

111. Schools which demonstrate effective practice often ensure clear responsibility for these subjects by a senior teacher in leadership position with dedicated time to lead specialist provision, e.g. a subject lead or co-ordinator.

112. All of these subjects should be set in the context of a wider whole-school approach to supporting pupils to be safe, happy and prepared for life beyond school. For example, the curriculum on relationships and on sex should complement, and be supported by, the school's wider policies on behaviour, inclusion, respect for equality and diversity, bullying and safeguarding (including handling of any reports pupils may make as a result of the subject content). The subjects will sit within the context of a school's broader ethos and approach to developing pupils socially, morally, spiritually and culturally; and its pastoral care system. This is also the case for teaching about mental health within health education. The curriculum on health education should similarly complement, and be supported by, the school's wider education on healthy lifestyles through physical education, food technology, science, sport, extra-curricular activity and school food.

113. Schools should consider how their teaching can help support the development of important attributes in pupils, such as honesty, kindness, tolerance, courtesy, resilience and self-efficacy, as well as how those attributes are also developed by other aspects of the school's provision. The curriculum should proactively address issues in a timely way in line with current evidence on children's physical, emotional and sexual development. This should be in line with pupil need, informed by pupil voice and participation in curriculum development and in response to issues as they arise in the school and wider community.

---

[14]Independent schools do not have to have regard to the guidance on Health Education, although they may find it helpful in planning.

Flexibility

114. Schools will retain freedom to determine an age-appropriate, developmental curriculum which meets the needs of young people, is developed in consultation with parents and the local community. Schools must also comply with the relevant provisions of the Equality Act as noted earlier. Where appropriate this may also require a differentiated curriculum. Schools have specific duties to increase the extent to which disabled pupils can participate in the curriculum.

115. Flexibility is important as it allows schools to respond to local public health and community issues, meet the needs of their community and adapt materials and programmes to meet the needs of pupils (for example in teaching about gangs or high local prevalence of specific sexually transmitted infections).

Safeguarding, reports of abuse and confidentiality

116. At the heart of these subjects there is a focus on keeping children safe, and schools can play an important role in preventative education. Keeping Children Safe in Education (KCSIE) sets out that all schools and colleges should ensure children are taught about safeguarding, including how to stay safe online, as part of providing a broad and balanced curriculum.

117. Good practice allows children an open forum to discuss potentially sensitive issues. Such discussions can lead to increased safeguarding reports. Children should be made aware of how to raise their concerns or make a report and how any report will be handled. This should include processes when they have a concern about a friend or peer.

118. KCSIE is clear that all staff should know what to do if a pupil tells them that they are being abused or neglected or are witnessing abuse. Staff should know how to manage the requirement to maintain an appropriate level of confidentiality. This means only involving those who need to be involved, such as the Designated Safeguarding Lead (or deputy) and children's social care. Staff should never promise a child that they will not tell anyone about a report of abuse, as this may ultimately not be in the best interests of the child.

119. Good practice would be to involve the Designated Safeguarding Lead (or a deputy) in anything that is safeguarding-related in the context of these subjects. They will potentially have knowledge of trusted, high quality local resources that could be engaged, links to the police and other agencies and the knowledge of any particular local issues which it may be appropriate to address in lessons.

120. Where a school invites external agencies in to support delivery of these subjects, they must agree in advance of the session how a safeguarding report should be dealt with by the external visitor. It is important that children understand how confidentiality will be handled in a lesson and what might happen if they choose to make a report.

121. There are some important points for teachers in terms of how they approach this content and how they consider their planning. When teaching the new subjects, schools should be aware that children may raise topics including self-harm and suicide. In talking about this content in the classroom, teachers must be aware of the risks of encouraging or making suicide seem a more

viable option for pupils and avoid material being instructive rather than preventative. To avoid this, they should take care to avoid giving instructions or methods of self-harm or suicide and avoid using emotive language, videos or images. *Teacher Guidance: preparing to teach about mental health and emotional wellbeing*[15] provides useful support for teachers in handling this material.

122. If teachers have concerns about a specific pupil in relation to self-harm or suicidal ideation or attempts, they must follow safeguarding procedures.

Assessment

123. Schools should have the same high expectations of the quality of pupils' work in these subjects as for other curriculum areas. A strong curriculum will build on the knowledge pupils have previously acquired, including in other subjects, with regular feedback provided on pupil progress.

124. Lessons should be planned to ensure that pupils of differing abilities, including the most able, are suitably challenged. Teaching should be assessed and assessments used to identify where pupils need extra support or intervention.

125. Whilst there is no formal examined assessment for these subjects, there are some areas to consider in strengthening quality of provision, and which demonstrate how teachers can assess outcomes. For example, tests, written assignments or self-evaluations, to capture progress.

Accountability

126. Key aspects of Relationships Education, RSE and Health Education are in scope for Ofsted inspection; for example, through inspectors' consideration of pupils' personal development, behaviour and welfare; and pupils' spiritual, moral, social and cultural development.

Annex A Regulations

Relationships Education, Relationships and Sex Education, and Health Education

The Relationships Education, Relationships and Sex Education, and Health Education (England) Regulations 2019 are made under sections 34 and 35 of the Children and Social Work Act 2017, and provide that pupils receiving primary education must be taught Relationships Education, pupils receiving secondary education must be taught RSE and that all primary and secondary pupils must be taught Health Education. The new subjects of Relationships Education and RSE must be taught in all maintained schools, academies and independent schools. This includes pupil referral units, maintained special schools, special academies, and non-maintained special schools. All schools, except independent schools, must make provision for Health Education.

To give effect to the duty in section 34 of the 2017 Act and the power in section 35 of that Act, the Relationships Education, Relationships and Sex Education and Health Education (England) Regulations 2019 amend existing provisions in the Education Act 1996 and the Education Act 2002 and insert new provisions

---

[15]Teacher Guidance: preparing to teach about mental health and wellbeing, PSHE association

into the Education (Pupil Referral Units) (Application of Enactments) (England) Regulations 2007, the Education (Independent School Standards) Regulations 2014 and the Non-Maintained Special Schools (England) Regulations 2015. The new provisions include a requirement for the Secretary of State to publish guidance on Relationships Education, RSE, and Health Education; require schools to have regard to that guidance; require schools to make a statement of policy on their provision of Relationships Education and RSE; and set out the circumstances in which a pupil is to be excused from RSE.

The regulations and guidance in relation to Health Education do not apply to independent schools – they will continue to make provision for the health education element of PSHE under the Education (Independent School Standards) Regulations 2014.

Annex B Suggested resources

Teaching resources

There are many excellent resources available, free of charge, which schools can draw on when delivering these subjects. Schools should assess each resource that they propose to use carefully to ensure it is appropriate for the age and maturity of pupils and sensitive to their needs, where relevant, schools should use resources that are medically accurate. Schools should also consider drawing on the expertise of the main subject associations who often quality assure third party resources. We also recognise that schools use resources from representative bodies (e.g. many Catholic and other schools draw on the model curricula provided by the Catholic Education Service.)

Schools should also ensure that, when they consult parents, they provide examples of the resources they plan to use, as this can be reassuring for parents, and enables them to continue the conversations started in class at home.

This is for illustrative purposes and is not an exhaustive list.

Relationships Education

Safeguarding: NSPCC PANTS rule with film.

Example of model primary curricula from Catholic Education.

Relationships and Sex Education

Sexual health and relationships: up to date information on all aspects of sexual and reproductive health available on Sexwise's website which teachers may find helpful for their knowledge.

Abuse in relationships: Disrespect NoBody from the Home Office and Government Equalities Office.

Consent: PSHE Association lesson plans from the PSHE association.

LGBT inclusivity: Stonewall lesson plans and materials for primary and secondary.

Resources covering all contexts, including online, and specifically relationships and bullying, alcohol, smoking, stress, body image from Public Health England website with videos made by young people and resources tested with teachers.

Example model secondary curricula from Catholic education.

Mental health

Mental health and emotional wellbeing lesson plans from PSHE Association.

MindEd educational resources on children and young people's mental health.

Online safety

Education for a Connected World is the UK Council for Internet safety (UKCCIS) framework of digital knowledge and skills for different ages and stages.

Sexting advice from UKCCIS for schools on preventative education and managing reports of sexting.

Thinkuknow is the education programme from National Crime Agency (NCA) and Child Exploitation Online Programme (CEOP), which protects children both online and offline. The site offers materials for parents, teachers and pupils on a wide range of online safety issues and facts about areas such as digital footprints, recognising fake websites and checking URLs.

PSHE

PSHE Association Programme of study for KS1-5

Drugs and alcohol

Planning effective drug and alcohol education from Mentor-ADEPIS research and briefing papers with ideas for lessons

Extremism and radicalisation

Practical advice and information from Educate Against Hate for teachers, teachers in leadership positions and parents on protecting children from extremism and radicalization.

Curriculum

Non-statutory framework for Citizenship KS 1 and 2 (Non-statutory programme of study). Schools may wish to draw on the Citizenship programme of study in their planning.

Data to understand the health and wellbeing needs of the local school-age population

Public Health England's Child and Maternal Health Intelligence Network brings together a range of publicly available data, information, reports, tools and resources on child and maternal health into one easily accessible hub.

It includes school-age health profiles and young people's health profiles.

The indicators allow areas to see how they perform against the national average and against other local areas. These tools, accompanied by local health intelligence, will be useful in supporting schools to identify and respond to the particular health and wellbeing needs of their local school-age population.

There are also early years health profiles.

Annex C Cross-government strategies

These subjects support many cross-government strategies of which schools will want to be aware. Whilst we have not referenced all strategies or supporting documents, we have included some of the key areas below.

- Transforming children and young people's mental health provision green paper. The green paper announced new support in and near schools and colleges to support children and young people with their mental health.
- The drug strategy 2017 sets out how the government and its partners, at local, national and international levels, will take new action to tackle drug misuse and the harms it causes.
- Internet Safety Strategy green paper sets out steps towards developing a coordinated strategic approach to online safety.
- The Children's Commissioner Digital 5 A Day provides a simple framework that reflects the concerns of parents as well as children's behaviours and needs.
- Government aims to significantly reduce England's rate of childhood obesity within the next ten years. The childhood obesity plan sets out the approach to reduce childhood obesity.
- Guidance from the Chief Medical Office (CMO) on how much physical activity people should be doing, along with supporting documents.
- Over the last 18 years, the teenage pregnancy rate has reduced by 60%. However, a continued focus is needed to maintain the downward trend and narrow inequalities in rates between and within local authorities. The Teenage Pregnancy prevention framework provides evidence based guidance for local authorities, including the important role of RSE and links to local sexual health services.
- Sustaining the downward trend and making further progress is one of the key objectives of the Department of Health and Social Care's Framework for Sexual Health Improvement in England. These subjects provide a key opportunity to strengthen support for young people to develop healthy relationships and prevent early unplanned pregnancy.
- Reproductive health – a public health issue. A consensus statement, data and women's experiences, covering reproductive health through the life course, from menstruation to menopause. (PHE. 2018)
- The cross-government loneliness strategy, which sets out the Government's vision for supporting individuals, businesses and communities to build and maintain strong relationships.

SECTION 4

INDEXES

National Curriculum by topic for KS1 and 2 – English

Grouped by topic to see progression

Spoken Language	
Y1 – 6	listen and respond appropriately to adults and their peers
	ask relevant questions to extend their understanding and knowledge
	use relevant strategies to build their vocabulary
	articulate and justify answers, arguments and opinions
	give well-structured descriptions, explanations and narratives for different purposes, including for expressing feelings
	maintain attention and participate actively in collaborative conversations, staying on topic and initiating and responding to comments
	use spoken language to develop understanding through speculating, hypothesising, imagining and exploring ideas
	speak audibly and fluently with an increasing command of Standard English
	participate in discussions, presentations, performances, role play, improvisations and debates
	gain, maintain and monitor the interest of the listener(s)
	consider and evaluate different viewpoints, attending to and building on the contributions of others
	select and use appropriate registers for effective communication.

Word Reading	
Y1	apply phonic knowledge and skills as the route to decode words
	respond speedily with the correct sound to graphemes (letters or groups of letters) for all 40+ phonemes, including, where applicable, alternative sounds for graphemes
	read accurately by blending sounds in unfamiliar words containing GPCs that have been taught
	read common exception words, noting unusual correspondences between spelling and sound and where these occur in the word
	read words containing taught GPCs and –s, –es, –ing, –ed, –er and –est endings
	read other words of more than one syllable that contain taught GPCs
	read words with contractions [for example, I'm, I'll, we'll], and understand that the apostrophe represents the omitted letter(s)
	read aloud accurately books that are consistent with their developing phonic knowledge and that do not require them to use other strategies to work out words
	re-read these books to build up their fluency and confidence in word reading.

Y2	continue to apply phonic knowledge and skills as the route to decode words until automatic decoding has become embedded and reading is fluent
	read accurately by blending the sounds in words that contain the graphemes taught so far, especially recognising alternative sounds for graphemes
	read accurately words of two or more syllables that contain the same graphemes as above
	read words containing common suffixes
	read further common exception words, noting unusual correspondences between spelling and sound and where these occur in the word
	read most words quickly and accurately, without overt sounding and blending, when they have been frequently encountered
	read aloud books closely matched to their improving phonic knowledge, sounding out unfamiliar words accurately, automatically and without undue hesitation
	re-read these books to build up their fluency and confidence in word reading.
Y3 & Y4	apply their growing knowledge of root words, prefixes and suffixes (etymology and morphology), in NC English Appendix 2 both to read aloud and to understand the meaning of new words they meet
	read further exception words, noting the unusual correspondences between spelling and sound, and where these occur in the word.
Y5 & Y6	use and understand the grammatical terminology in NC English Appendix 2 accurately and appropriately when discussing their writing and reading

Reading – Comprehension	
Y1	develop pleasure in reading, motivation to read, vocabulary and understanding by: • listening to and discussing a wide range of poems, stories and non-fiction at a level beyond that at which they can read independently • being encouraged to link what they read or hear read to their own experiences • becoming very familiar with key stories, fairy stories and traditional tales, retelling them and considering their particular characteristics • recognising and joining in with predictable phrases • learning to appreciate rhymes and poems, and to recite some by heart • discussing word meanings, linking new meanings to those already known
	understand both the books they can already read accurately and fluently and those they listen to by: • drawing on what they already know or on background information and vocabulary provided by the teacher • checking that the text makes sense to them as they read and correcting inaccurate reading • discussing the significance of the title and events • making inferences on the basis of what is being said and done • predicting what might happen on the basis of what has been read so far
	participate in discussion about what is read to them, taking turns and listening to what others say
	explain clearly their understanding of what is read to them.

Y2	develop pleasure in reading, motivation to read, vocabulary and understanding by:
	• listening to, discussing and expressing views about a wide range of contemporary and classic poetry, stories and non-fiction at a level beyond that at which they can read independently
	• discussing the sequence of events in books and how items of information are related
	• becoming increasingly familiar with and retelling a wider range of stories, fairy stories and traditional tales
	• being introduced to non-fiction books that are structured in different ways
	• recognising simple recurring literary language in stories and poetry
	• discussing and clarifying the meanings of words, linking new meanings to known vocabulary
	• discussing their favourite words and phrases
	• continuing to build up a repertoire of poems learnt by heart, appreciating these and reciting some, with appropriate intonation to make the meaning clear
	understand both the books that they can already read accurately and fluently and those that they listen to by:
	• drawing on what they already know or on background information and vocabulary provided by the teacher
	• checking that the text makes sense to them as they read and correcting inaccurate reading
	• making inferences on the basis of what is being said and done
	• answering and asking questions
	• predicting what might happen on the basis of what has been read so far
	participate in discussion about books, poems and other works that are read to them and those that they can read for themselves, taking turns and listening to what others say
	explain and discuss their understanding of books, poems and other material, both those that they listen to and those that they read for themselves.
Y3 & Y4	develop positive attitudes to reading and understanding of what they read by:
	• listening to and discussing a wide range of fiction, poetry, plays, non-fiction and reference books or textbooks
	• reading books that are structured in different ways and reading for a range of purposes
	• using dictionaries to check the meaning of words that they have read
	• increasing their familiarity with a wide range of books, including fairy stories, myths and legends, and retelling some of these orally
	• identifying themes and conventions in a wide range of books
Y5 & Y6	maintain positive attitudes to reading and understanding of what they read by:
	• continuing to read and discuss an increasingly wide range of fiction, poetry, plays, non-fiction and reference books or textbooks
	• reading books that are structured in different ways and reading for a range of purposes
	• increasing their familiarity with a wide range of books, including myths, legends and traditional stories, modern fiction, fiction from our literary heritage, and books from other cultures and traditions

Writing – Transcription	
Spelling	
Y1	spell: • words containing each of the 40+ phonemes already taught • common exception words • the days of the week
	name the letters of the alphabet: • naming the letters of the alphabet in order • using letter names to distinguish between alternative spellings of the same sound
	add prefixes and suffixes: • using the spelling rule for adding –s or –es as the plural marker for nouns and the third person singular marker for verbs • using the prefix un– • using –ing, –ed, –er and –est where no change is needed in the spelling of root words [for example, helping, helped, helper, eating, quicker, quickest]
	apply simple spelling rules and guidance, (listed in NC English Appendix 1)
	write from memory simple sentences dictated by the teacher that include words using the GPCs and common exception words taught so far.
Y2	spell by: • segmenting spoken words into phonemes and representing these by graphemes, spelling many correctly • learning new ways of spelling phonemes for which one or more spellings are already known, and learn some words with each spelling, including a few common homophones • learning to spell common exception words • learning to spell more words with contracted forms • learning the possessive apostrophe (singular) [for example, the girl's book] • distinguishing between homophones and near-homophones
	add suffixes to spell longer words, including –ment, –ness, –ful, –less, –ly
	apply spelling rules and guidance, (listed in NC English Appendix 1)
	write from memory simple sentences dictated by the teacher that include words using the GPCs, common exception words and punctuation taught so far.
Y3 & Y4	use further prefixes and suffixes and understand how to add them
	spell further homophones
	spell words that are often misspelt
	place the possessive apostrophe accurately in words with regular plurals [for example, girls', boys'] and in words with irregular plurals [for example, children's]
	use the first two or three letters of a word to check its spelling in a dictionary
	write from memory simple sentences, dictated by the teacher, that include words and punctuation taught so far.

Y5 & Y6	use further prefixes and suffixes and understand the guidance for adding them
	spell some words with 'silent' letters [for example, knight, psalm, solemn]
	continue to distinguish between homophones and other words which are often confused
	use knowledge of morphology and etymology in spelling and understand that the spelling of some words needs to be learnt specifically, as listed in English Appendix 1
	use dictionaries to check the spelling and meaning of words
	use the first three or four letters of a word to check spelling, meaning or both of these in a dictionary
	use a thesaurus.
Handwriting	
Y1	sit correctly at a table, holding a pencil comfortably and correctly
	begin to form lower-case letters in the correct direction, starting and finishing in the right place
	form capital letters
	form digits 0–9
	understand which letters belong to which handwriting 'families' (i.e. letters that are formed in similar ways) and to practise these.
Y2	form lower-case letters of the correct size relative to one another
	start using some of the diagonal and horizontal strokes needed to join letters and understand which letters, when adjacent to one another, are best left unjoined
	write capital letters and digits of the correct size, orientation and relationship to one another and to lower case letters
	use spacing between words that reflects the size of the letters
Y3 & Y4	use the diagonal and horizontal strokes that are needed to join letters and understand which letters, when adjacent to one another, are best left unjoined
	increase the legibility, consistency and quality of their handwriting [for example, by ensuring that the downstrokes of letters are parallel and equidistant; that lines of writing are spaced sufficiently so that the ascenders and descenders of letters do not touch].
Handwriting and presentation	
Y5 & Y6	write legibly, fluently and with increasing speed by: • choosing which shape of a letter to use when given choices and deciding whether or not to join specific letters • choosing the writing implement that is best suited for a task.

Writing – Composition	
Y1	write sentences by: • saying out loud what they are going to write about • composing a sentence orally before writing it • sequencing sentences to form short narratives • re-reading what they have written to check that it makes sense
	discuss what they have written with the teacher or other pupils
	read aloud their writing clearly enough to be heard by their peers and the teacher.
Y2	develop positive attitudes towards and stamina for writing by: • writing narratives about personal experiences and those of others (real and fictional) • writing about real events • writing poetry • writing for different purposes
	consider what they are going to write before beginning by: • planning or saying out loud what they are going to write about • writing down ideas and/or key words, including new vocabulary • encapsulating what they want to say, sentence by sentence
	make simple additions, revisions and corrections to their own writing by: • evaluating their writing with the teacher and other pupils • re-reading to check that their writing makes sense and that verbs to indicate time are used correctly and consistently, including verbs in the continuous form • proof-reading to check for errors in spelling, grammar and punctuation [for example, ends of sentences punctuated correctly]
	read aloud what they have written with appropriate intonation to make the meaning clear.
Y3 & Y4	plan their writing by: • discussing writing similar to that which they are planning to write in order to understand and learn from its structure, vocabulary and grammar • discussing and recording ideas
	draft and write by: • composing and rehearsing sentences orally (including dialogue), progressively building a varied and rich vocabulary and an increasing range of sentence structures • organising paragraphs around a theme • in narratives, creating settings, characters and plot • in non-narrative material, using simple organisational devices [for example, headings and sub-headings]
	evaluate and edit by: • assessing the effectiveness of their own and others' writing and suggesting improvements • proposing changes to grammar and vocabulary to improve consistency, including the accurate use of pronouns in sentences

	proof-read for spelling and punctuation errors
	read aloud their own writing, to a group or the whole class, using appropriate intonation and controlling the tone and volume so that the meaning is clear.
Y5 & Y6	plan their writing by: • identifying the audience for and purpose of the writing, selecting the appropriate form and using other similar writing as models for their own • noting and developing initial ideas, drawing on reading and research where necessary • in writing narratives, considering how authors have developed characters and settings in what pupils have read, listened to or seen performed
	draft and write by: • selecting appropriate grammar and vocabulary, understanding how such choices can change and enhance meaning • in narratives, describing settings, characters and atmosphere and integrating dialogue to convey character and advance the action • using a wide range of devices to build cohesion within and across paragraphs • using further organisational and presentational devices to structure text and to guide the reader [for example, headings, bullet points, underlining]
	evaluate and edit by: • assessing the effectiveness of their own and others' writing • proposing changes to vocabulary, grammar and punctuation to enhance effects and clarify meaning • ensuring the consistent and correct use of tense throughout a piece of writing • ensuring correct subject and verb agreement when using singular and plural, distinguishing between the language of speech and writing and choosing the appropriate register
	proof-read for spelling and punctuation errors
	perform their own compositions, using appropriate intonation, volume, and movement so that meaning is clear.

Writing – vocabulary, grammar and punctuation	
Y1	develop their understanding of the concepts set out in NC English Appendix 2 by: • leaving spaces between words • joining words and joining clauses using and • beginning to punctuate sentences using a capital letter and a full stop, question mark or exclamation mark • using a capital letter for names of people, places, the days of the week, and the personal pronoun 'I' • learning the grammar for year 1 in NC English Appendix 2
	use the grammatical terminology in discussing their writing

Y2	develop their understanding of the concepts set out in NC English Appendix 2 by: • learning how to use both familiar and new punctuation correctly, including full stops, capital letters, exclamation marks, question marks, commas for lists and apostrophes for contracted forms and the possessive (singular)
	learn how to use: • sentences with different forms: statement, question, exclamation, command • expanded noun phrases to describe and specify [for example, the blue butterfly] • the present and past tenses correctly and consistently including the progressive form • subordination (using when, if, that, or because) and co-ordination (using or, and, or but) • the grammar for year 2 • some features of written Standard English
	use and understand the grammatical terminology in NC English Appendix 2 in discussing their writing.
Y3 & Y4	develop their understanding of the concepts set out in NC English Appendix 2 by: • extending the range of sentences with more than one clause by using a wider range of conjunctions, including when, if, because, although • using the present perfect form of verbs in contrast to the past tense • choosing nouns or pronouns appropriately for clarity and cohesion and to avoid repetition • using conjunctions, adverbs and prepositions to express time and cause • using fronted adverbials • learning the grammar for years 3 and 4 in NC English Appendix 2
	indicate grammatical and other features by: • using commas after fronted adverbials • indicating possession by using the possessive apostrophe with plural nouns • using and punctuating direct speech
	use and understand the grammatical terminology in English Appendix 2 accurately and appropriately when discussing their writing and reading
Y5 & Y6	develop their understanding of the concepts set out in NC English Appendix 2 by: • recognising vocabulary and structures that are appropriate for formal speech and writing, including subjunctive forms • using passive verbs to affect the presentation of information in a sentence • using the perfect form of verbs to mark relationships of time and cause • using expanded noun phrases to convey complicated information concisely • using modal verbs or adverbs to indicate degrees of possibility • using relative clauses beginning with who, which, where, when, whose, that or with an implied (i.e. omitted) relative pronoun • learning the grammar for years 5 and 6 in NC English Appendix 2

indicate grammatical and other features by:

- using commas to clarify meaning or avoid ambiguity in writing
- using hyphens to avoid ambiguity
- using brackets, dashes or commas to indicate parenthesis
- using semi-colons, colons or dashes to mark boundaries between independent clauses
- using a colon to introduce a list
- punctuating bullet points consistently

use and understand the grammatical terminology in NC English Appendix 2 accurately and appropriately in discussing their writing and reading.

National Curriculum by topic for KS1 and 2 – Mathematics

Grouped by topic to see progression

Number – number and place value	
Y1	count to and across 100, forwards and backwards, beginning with 0 or 1, or from any given number
	count, read and write numbers to 100 in numerals; count in multiples of twos, fives and tens
	given a number, identify one more and one less
	identify and represent numbers using objects and pictorial representations including the number line, and use the language of: equal to, more than, less than (fewer), most, least
	read and write numbers from 1 to 20 in numerals and words.
Y2	count in steps of 2, 3, and 5 from 0, and in tens from any number, forward and backward
	recognise the place value of each digit in a two-digit number (tens, ones)
	identify, represent and estimate numbers using different representations, including the number line
	compare and order numbers from 0 up to 100; use <, > and = signs
	read and write numbers to at least 100 in numerals and in words
	use place value and number facts to solve problems.
Y3	count from 0 in multiples of 4, 8, 50 and 100; find 10 or 100 more or less than a given number
	recognise the place value of each digit in a three-digit number (hundreds, tens, ones)
	compare and order numbers up to 1000
	identify, represent and estimate numbers using different representations
	read and write numbers up to 1000 in numerals and in words
	solve number problems and practical problems involving these ideas
Y4	count in multiples of 6, 7, 9, 25 and 1000
	find 1000 more or less than a given number
	count backwards through zero to include negative numbers
	recognise the place value of each digit in a four-digit number (thousands, hundreds, tens, and ones)
	order and compare numbers beyond 1000
	identify, represent and estimate numbers using different representations
	round any number to the nearest 10, 100 or 1000
	solve number and practical problems that involve all of the above and with increasingly large positive numbers
	read Roman numerals to 100 (I to C) and know that over time, the numeral system changed to include the concept of zero and place value.

Y5	read, write, order and compare numbers to at least 1 000 000 and determine the value of each digit
	count forwards or backwards in steps of powers of 10 for any given number up to 1000000
	interpret negative numbers in context, count forwards and backwards with positive and negative whole numbers, including through zero
	round any number up to 1 000 000 to the nearest 10, 100, 1000, 10 000 and 100 000
	solve number problems and practical problems that involve all of the above
	read Roman numerals to 1000 (M) and recognise years written in Roman numerals.
Y6	read, write, order and compare numbers up to 10 000 000 and determine the value of each digit
	round any whole number to a required degree of accuracy
	use negative numbers in context, and calculate intervals across zero
	solve number and practical problems that involve all of the above

Number – addition and subtraction,	
Y1	read, write and interpret mathematical statements involving addition (+), subtraction (–) and equals (=) signs
	represent and use number bonds and related subtraction facts within 20
	add and subtract one-digit and two-digit numbers to 20, including zero
	solve one-step problems that involve addition and subtraction, using concrete objects and pictorial representations, and missing number problems such as $7 = - 9$.
Y2	solve problems with addition and subtraction: • using concrete objects and pictorial representations, including those involving numbers, quantities and measures • applying their increasing knowledge of mental and written methods
	recall and use addition and subtraction facts to 20 fluently, and derive and use related facts up to 100
	add and subtract numbers using concrete objects, pictorial representations, and mentally, including: • a two-digit number and ones • a two-digit number and tens • two two-digit numbers • adding three one-digit numbers
	show that addition of two numbers can be done in any order (commutative) and subtraction of one number from another cannot
	recognise and use the inverse relationship between addition and subtraction and use this to check calculations and solve missing number problems.

Y3	add and subtract numbers mentally, including: • a three-digit number and ones • a three-digit number and tens • a three-digit number and hundreds
	add and subtract numbers with up to three digits, using formal written methods of columnar addition and subtraction
	estimate the answer to a calculation and use inverse operations to check answers
	solve problems, including missing number problems, using number facts, place value, and more complex addition and subtraction
Y4	add and subtract numbers with up to 4 digits using the formal written methods of columnar addition and subtraction where appropriate
	estimate and use inverse operations to check answers to a calculation
	solve addition and subtraction two-step problems in contexts, deciding which operations and methods to use and why.
Y5	add and subtract whole numbers with more than 4 digits, including using formal written methods (columnar addition and subtraction)
	add and subtract numbers mentally with increasingly large numbers
	use rounding to check answers to calculations and determine, in the context of a problem, levels of accuracy
	solve addition and subtraction multi-step problems in contexts, deciding which operations and methods to use and why.
Y6	See multiplication and division

Number – multiplication and division

Y1	solve one-step problems involving multiplication and division, by calculating the answer using concrete objects, pictorial representations and arrays with the support of the teacher.
Y2	recall and use multiplication and division facts for the 2, 5 and 10 multiplication tables, including recognising odd and even numbers
	calculate mathematical statements for multiplication and division within the multiplication tables and write them using the multiplication ($\times$), division ($\div$) and equals ($=$) signs
	show that multiplication of two numbers can be done in any order (commutative) and division of one number by another cannot
	solve problems involving multiplication and division, using materials, arrays, repeated addition, mental methods, and multiplication and division facts, including problems in contexts.
Y3	recall and use multiplication and division facts for the 3, 4 and 8 multiplication tables
	write and calculate mathematical statements for multiplication and division using the multiplication tables that they know, including for two-digit numbers times one-digit numbers, using mental and progressing to formal written methods
	solve problems, including missing number problems, involving multiplication and division, including positive integer scaling problems and correspondence problems in which n objects are connected to m objects.

Y4	recall multiplication and division facts for multiplication tables up to 12×12
	use place value, known and derived facts to multiply and divide mentally, including: multiplying by 0 and 1; dividing by 1; multiplying together three numbers
	recognise and use factor pairs and commutativity in mental calculations
	multiply two-digit and three-digit numbers by a one-digit number using formal written layout
	solve problems involving multiplying and adding, including using the distributive law to multiply two digit numbers by one digit, integer scaling problems and harder correspondence problems such as n objects are connected to m objects.
Y5	identify multiples and factors, including finding all factor pairs of a number, and common factors of two numbers
	know and use the vocabulary of prime numbers, prime factors and composite (non-prime) numbers
	establish whether a number up to 100 is prime and recall prime numbers up to 19
	multiply numbers up to 4 digits by a one- or two-digit number using a formal written method, including long multiplication for two-digit numbers
	multiply and divide numbers mentally drawing upon known facts
	divide numbers up to 4 digits by a one-digit number using the formal written method of short division and interpret remainders appropriately for the context
	multiply and divide whole numbers and those involving decimals by 10, 100 and 1000
	recognise and use square numbers and cube numbers, and the notation for squared and cubed
	solve problems involving multiplication and division including using their knowledge of factors and multiples, squares and cubes
	solve problems involving addition, subtraction, multiplication and division and a combination of these, including understanding the meaning of the equals sign
	solve problems involving multiplication and division, including scaling by simple fractions and problems involving simple rates.
Y6	multiply multi-digit numbers up to 4 digits by a two-digit whole number using the formal written method of long multiplication
	divide numbers up to 4 digits by a two-digit whole number using the formal written method of long division, and interpret remainders as whole number remainders, fractions, or by rounding, as appropriate for the context
	divide numbers up to 4 digits by a two-digit number using the formal written method of short division where appropriate, interpreting remainders according to the context
	perform mental calculations, including with mixed operations and large numbers
	identify common factors, common multiples and prime numbers

	use their knowledge of the order of operations to carry out calculations involving the four operations
	solve addition and subtraction multi-step problems in contexts, deciding which operations and methods to use and why
	solve problems involving addition, subtraction, multiplication and division
	use estimation to check answers to calculations and determine, in the context of a problem, an appropriate degree of accuracy.

Number – Fractions	
Y1	recognise, find and name a half as one of two equal parts of an object, shape or quantity
	recognise, find and name a quarter as one of four equal parts of an object, shape or quantity
Y2	recognise, find, name and write fractions a third, a quarter, two quarters and three quarters of a length, shape, set of objects or quantity
	write simple fractions for example a half of 6 = 3 and recognise the equivalence of two quarters and a half
Y3	count up and down in tenths; recognise that tenths arise from dividing an object into 10 equal parts and in dividing one-digit numbers or quantities by 10
	recognise, find and write fractions of a discrete set of objects: unit fractions and non-unit fractions with small denominators
	recognise and use fractions as numbers: unit fractions and non-unit fractions with small denominators
	recognise and show, using diagrams, equivalent fractions with small denominators
	add and subtract fractions with the same denominator within one whole
	compare and order unit fractions, and fractions with the same denominators
	solve problems that involve all of the above.

Number – Fractions (including decimals)	
Y4	recognise and show, using diagrams, families of common equivalent fractions
	count up and down in hundredths; recognise that hundredths arise when dividing an object by one hundred and dividing tenths by ten
	solve problems involving increasingly harder fractions to calculate quantities, and fractions to divide quantities, including non-unit fractions where the answer is a whole number
	add and subtract fractions with the same denominator
	recognise and write decimal equivalents of any number of tenths or hundredths
	recognise and write decimal equivalents to a quarter, half and three quarters
	find the effect of dividing a one- or two-digit number by 10 and 100, identifying the value of the digits in the answer as ones, tenths and hundredths

	round decimals with one decimal place to the nearest whole number
	compare numbers with the same number of decimal places up to two decimal places
	solve simple measure and money problems involving fractions and decimals to two decimal places. *Used to be with a calculator*

Number – Fractions (including decimals and percentages)	
Y5	compare and order fractions whose denominators are all multiples of the same number
	identify, name and write equivalent fractions of a given fraction, represented visually, including tenths and hundredths
	recognise mixed numbers and improper fractions and convert from one form to the other and write mathematical statements > 1 as a mixed number
	add and subtract fractions with the same denominator and denominators that are multiples of the same number
	multiply proper fractions and mixed numbers by whole numbers, supported by materials and diagrams
	read and write decimal numbers as fractions
	recognise and use thousandths and relate them to tenths, hundredths and decimal equivalents
	round decimals with two decimal places to the nearest whole number and to one decimal place
	read, write, order and compare numbers with up to three decimal places
	solve problems involving number up to three decimal places
	recognise the per cent symbol (%) and understand that per cent relates to 'number of parts per hundred', and write percentages as a fraction with denominator 100, and as a decimal
	solve problems which require knowing percentage and decimal equivalents of and those fractions with a denominator of a multiple of 10 or 25.
Y6	use common factors to simplify fractions; use common multiples to express fractions in the same denomination
	compare and order fractions, including fractions > 1
	add and subtract fractions with different denominators and mixed numbers, using the concept of equivalent fractions
	multiply simple pairs of proper fractions, writing the answer in its simplest form
	divide proper fractions by whole numbers
	associate a fraction with division and calculate decimal fraction equivalents [for example, 0.375] for a simple fraction
	identify the value of each digit in numbers given to three decimal places and multiply and divide numbers by 10, 100 and 1000 giving answers up to three decimal places

	multiply one-digit numbers with up to two decimal places by whole numbers
	use written division methods in cases where the answer has up to two decimal places
	solve problems which require answers to be rounded to specified degrees of accuracy
	recall and use equivalences between simple fractions, decimals and percentages, including in different contexts.
Ratio and Proportion	
Y6	solve problems involving the relative sizes of two quantities where missing values can be found by using integer multiplication and division facts
	solve problems involving the calculation of percentages [for example, of measures, and such as 15% of 360] and the use of percentages for comparison
	solve problems involving similar shapes where the scale factor is known or can be found
	solve problems involving unequal sharing and grouping using knowledge of fractions and multiples.
Algebra	
Y6	use simple formulae
	generate and describe linear number sequences
	express missing number problems algebraically
	find pairs of numbers that satisfy an equation with two unknowns
	enumerate possibilities of combinations of two variables.
Measurement	
Y1	compare, describe and solve practical problems for: • lengths and heights [for example, long/short, longer/shorter, tall/short, double/half] • mass/weight [for example, heavy/light, heavier than, lighter than] • capacity and volume [for example, full/empty, more than, less than, half, half full, quarter] • time [for example, quicker, slower, earlier, later]
	measure and begin to record the following: • lengths and heights • mass/weight • capacity and volume • time (hours, minutes, seconds)
	recognise and know the value of different denominations of coins and notes
	sequence events in chronological order using language [for example, before and after, next, first, today, yesterday, tomorrow, morning, afternoon and evening]
	recognise and use language relating to dates, including days of the week, weeks, months and years
	tell the time to the hour and half past the hour and draw the hands on a clock face to show these times.

Y2	choose and use appropriate standard units to estimate and measure length/height in any direction (m/cm); mass (kg/g); temperature (°C); capacity (litres/ml) to the nearest appropriate unit, using rulers, scales, thermometers and measuring vessels
	compare and order lengths, mass, volume/capacity and record the results using >, < and =
	recognise and use symbols for pounds (£) and pence (p); combine amounts to make a particular value
	find different combinations of coins that equal the same amounts of money
	solve simple problems in a practical context involving addition and subtraction of money of the same unit, including giving change
	compare and sequence intervals of time
	tell and write the time to five minutes, including quarter past/to the hour and draw the hands on a clock face to show these times
	know the number of minutes in an hour and the number of hours in a day.
Y3	measure, compare, add and subtract: lengths (m/cm/mm); mass (kg/g); volume/capacity (l/ml)
	measure the perimeter of simple 2-D shapes
	add and subtract amounts of money to give change, using both £ and p in practical contexts
	tell and write the time from an analogue clock, including using Roman numerals from I to XII, and 12-hour and 24-hour clocks
	estimate and read time with increasing accuracy to the nearest minute; record and compare time in terms of seconds, minutes and hours; use vocabulary such as o'clock, a.m./p.m., morning, afternoon, noon and midnight
	know the number of seconds in a minute and the number of days in each month, year and leap year
	compare durations of events [for example to calculate the time taken by particular events or tasks].
Y4	convert between different units of measure [for example, kilometre to metre; hour to minute]
	measure and calculate the perimeter of a rectilinear figure (including squares) in centimetres and metres
	find the area of rectilinear shapes by counting squares
	estimate, compare and calculate different measures, including money in pounds and pence
Y5	convert between different units of metric measure (for example, kilometre and metre; centimetre and metre; centimetre and millimetre; gram and kilogram; litre and millilitre)
	understand and use approximate equivalences between metric units and common imperial units such as inches, pounds and pints

	measure and calculate the perimeter of composite rectilinear shapes in centimetres and metres (and representing algebraically)
	calculate and compare the area of rectangles (including squares), and including using standard units, square centimetres (cm²) and square metres (m²) and estimate the area of irregular shapes
	estimate volume [for example, using 1 cm³ blocks to build cuboids (including cubes)] and capacity [for example, using water]
	solve problems involving converting between units of time
	use all four operations to solve problems involving measure [for example, length, mass, volume, money] using decimal notation, including scaling.
Y6	solve problems involving the calculation and conversion of units of measure, using decimal notation up to three decimal places where appropriate
	use, read, write and convert between standard units, converting measurements of length, mass, volume and time from a smaller unit of measure to a larger unit, and vice versa, using decimal notation to up to three decimal places
	convert between miles and kilometres
	recognise that shapes with the same areas can have different perimeters and vice versa
	recognise when it is possible to use formulae for area and volume of shapes
	calculate the area of parallelograms and triangles
	calculate, estimate and compare volume of cubes and cuboids using standard units, including cubic centimetres (cm³) and cubic metres (m³), and extending to other units [for example, mm³ and km³].

Geometry – Properties of shapes

Y1	recognise and name common 2-D and 3-D shapes, including:
	2-D shapes [for example, rectangles (including squares), circles and triangles]
	3-D shapes [for example, cuboids (including cubes), pyramids and spheres].
Y2	identify and describe the properties of 2-D shapes, including the number of sides and line symmetry in a vertical line
	identify and describe the properties of 3-D shapes, including the number of edges, vertices and faces
	identify 2-D shapes on the surface of 3-D shapes, [for example, a circle on a cylinder and a triangle on a pyramid]
	compare and sort common 2-D and 3-D shapes and everyday objects.
Y3	draw 2-D shapes and make 3-D shapes using modelling materials; recognise 3-D shapes in different orientations and describe them
	recognise angles as a property of shape or a description of a turn
	identify right angles, recognise that two right angles make a half-turn, three make three quarters of a turn and four a complete turn; identify whether angles are greater than or less than a right angle
	identify horizontal and vertical lines and pairs of perpendicular and parallel lines

Y4	compare and classify geometric shapes, including quadrilaterals and triangles, based on their properties and sizes
	identify acute and obtuse angles and compare and order angles up to two right angles by size
	identify lines of symmetry in 2-D shapes presented in different orientations
	complete a simple symmetric figure with respect to a specific line of symmetry
Y5	identify 3-D shapes, including cubes and other cuboids, from 2-D representations
	know angles are measured in degrees: estimate and compare acute, obtuse and reflex angles
	draw given angles, and measure them in degrees
	identify: • angles at a point and one whole turn (total 360°) • angles at a point on a straight line and half a turn (total 180°) • other multiples of 90°
	use the properties of rectangles to deduce related facts and find missing lengths and angles
	distinguish between regular and irregular polygons based on reasoning about equal sides and angles.
Y6	draw 2-D shapes using given dimensions and angles
	recognise, describe and build simple 3-D shapes, including making nets
	compare and classify geometric shapes based on their properties and sizes and find unknown angles in any triangles, quadrilaterals, and regular polygons
	illustrate and name parts of circles, including radius, diameter and circumference and know that the diameter is twice the radius
	recognise angles where they meet at a point, are on a straight line, or are vertically opposite, and find missing angles.

Geometry – position and direction	
Y1	describe position, direction and movement, including whole, half, quarter and three-quarter turns.
Y2	order and arrange combinations of mathematical objects in patterns and sequences
	use mathematical vocabulary to describe position, direction and movement, including movement in a straight line and distinguishing between rotation as a turn and in terms of right angles for quarter, half and three-quarter turns (clockwise and anti-clockwise).
Y3	No content

Y4	describe positions on a 2-D grid as coordinates in the first quadrant
	describe movements between positions as translations of a given unit to the left/right and up/down
	plot specified points and draw sides to complete a given polygon
Y5	identify, describe and represent the position of a shape following a reflection or translation, using the appropriate language, and know that the shape has not changed.
Y6	describe positions on the full coordinate grid (all four quadrants)
	draw and translate simple shapes on the coordinate plane, and reflect them in the axes.

Statistics	
Y2	interpret and construct simple pictograms, tally charts, block diagrams and simple tables
	ask and answer simple questions by counting the number of objects in each category and sorting the categories by quantity
	ask and answer questions about totalling and comparing categorical data
Y3	interpret and present data using bar charts, pictograms and tables
	solve one-step and two-step questions [for example, 'How many more?' and 'How many fewer?'] using information presented in scaled bar charts and pictograms and tables.
Y4	interpret and present discrete and continuous data using appropriate graphical methods, including bar charts and time graphs.
	solve comparison, sum and difference problems using information presented in bar charts, pictograms, tables and other graphs.
Y5	solve comparison, sum and difference problems using information presented in a line graph
	complete, read and interpret information in tables, including timetables.
Y6	interpret and construct pie charts and line graphs and use these to solve problems
	calculate and interpret the mean as an average.

Book Index

Religious Education

Sex and relationship Education

School Curriculum

Science

PLANNING SURVIVAL TIP!

IDENTIFYING THE RESOURCES YOU WILL NEED FOR THE LESSON HELPS YOU TO BE PREPARED.

✓ Which resources will best support the intended learning? This may mean ordering resources from an outside source (e.g. visiting speaker, health education unit) or booking resources within the school (e.g. the laptops, the hall/gym).

✓ Which resources do you need to make or prepare?

✓ Where do you wish to hold the lesson? Would it work best outside the classroom and, if so, where? If you are working outside, particularly off-site, you will need to follow your school's risk assessment procedures and adhere to the recommended pupil : staff ratio.

✓ How will you organise the resources. Will they be accessible to children from the start or will they be given out or collected when required? How will this affect the extent to which children can be independent in their learning and how will it affect behaviour management in the classroom?

✓ Have you checked that all the resources you intend to use are safe for use within the classroom? Are there any children who may react negatively to some resources (e.g. some children hate puppets and others hate working outdoors)?

✓ Are there any resources which may exclude children, create barriers to learning or which promote or suggest stereotypes?

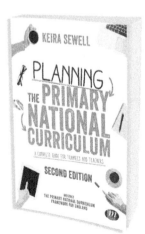

There are many other things you need to consider in addition to the content of the lesson such as seating arrangements and teaching strategies. **Planning the Primary National Curriculum** helps you to successfully plan and teach the national curriculum.

For each curriculum subject the programme of study is included, with notes to help you interpret it for your own class. This guide covers how the teaching of each subject can be organised, assessment opportunities, key and essential resources in each subject, and how ICT can best be used in each subject to enhance teaching. Also includes sequenced lesson examples! It's the one-stop for your curriculum planning and teaching.

Order at sagepub.co.uk

FREE LESSON PLANNING RESOURCES

Inspiration for your lesson planning from the Lessons in Teaching series

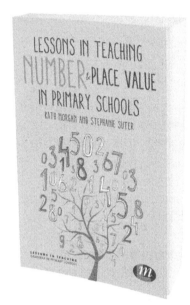

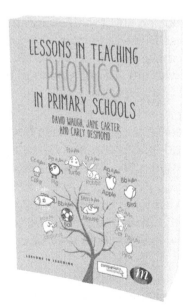

More free lesson planning support at

study.sagepub.com/lessonsinteaching

7 KEY PRINCIPLES FOR TEACHING GRAMMAR

Knowledge about grammar can make a significant difference to children's literacy development, but it is important to bear in mind seven key principles.

✓ Build up your own subject knowledge. To teach grammar you need explicit as well as implicit knowledge, so that you are confident about using the correct terms and explaining these. Don't just learn the next term you are teaching. It is important to be able to relate new learning to other features and the text as a whole.

✓ Give talk a high priority in your classroom. Children need to be able to select from a wardrobe of voices that includes Standard English.

✓ Remember the purpose of teaching grammar. Grammar is not simply the naming of parts of speech or for teaching the rules of English. It needs to be strongly embedded in classroom talk, reading and writing.

✓ Teach grammar in context. By introducing children to grammatical features and language in context, you will be helping them to internalise these principles. Try not to go for the ready-made solution by using a worksheet in a book. It will make very little difference to children's use of language and will be meaningless for those learners who are not yet able to think in abstract ways.

Sample chapter online

✓ Read aloud and discuss how authors use grammar. Children who read extensively and are read to will have a 'toolbox' of structures, patterns and rhythms to draw on.

✓ Be systematic. Make sure you know what the class you are working with have already learned and what they need to learn now. Link new learning with their prior knowledge.

✓ Make learning grammar fun. Teaching grammar can involve investigation, problem-solving and language play as part of developing children's awareness of and interest in how language works.

Excerpt from Ch 1, Waugh et al, Teaching Grammar, Punctuation and Spelling in Primary Schools 2e

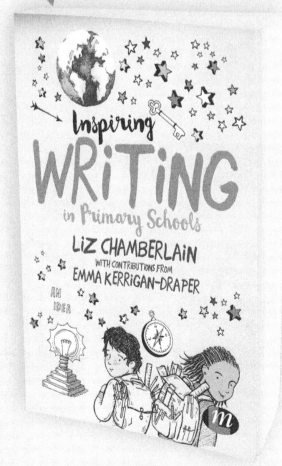

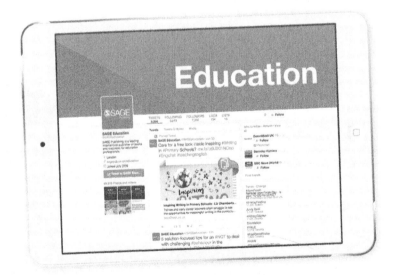